SAMS
Teach Yourself

AppleScript®

in 24 Hours

Jesse Feiler

SAMS   201 West 103rd St., Indianapolis, Indiana, 46290 USA

Sams Teach Yourself AppleScript® in 24 Hours

Copyright © 2003 by Sams Publishing

International Standard Book Number: 0-672-32518-7

Library of Congress Catalog Card Number: 2002115934

Printed in the United States of America

First Printing: May 2003

06   05   04   03   4   3   2   1

Trademarks

All terms mentioned in this book that are known to be trademarks or service marks have been appropriately capitalized. Sams Publishing cannot attest to the accuracy of this information. Use of a term in this book should not be regarded as affecting the validity of any trademark or service mark.

Warning and Disclaimer

Every effort has been made to make this book as complete and as accurate as possible, but no warranty or fitness is implied. The information provided is on an "as is" basis. The author and the publisher shall have neither liability nor responsibility to any person or entity with respect to any loss or damages arising from the information contained in this book.

Bulk Sales

Sams offers excellent discounts on this book when ordered in quantity for bulk purchases or special sales. For more information, please contact:

U.S. Corporate and Government Sales
1-800-382-3419
corpsales@pearsontechgroup.com

For sales outside of the U.S., please contact:

International Sales
+1-317-581-3793
international@pearsontechgroup.com

ACQUISITIONS EDITOR
Betsy Brown

DEVELOPMENT EDITOR
Damon Jordan

MANAGING EDITOR
Charlotte Clapp

PROJECT EDITOR
Matthew Purcell

COPY EDITOR
Margaret Berson

INDEXER
Ken Johnson

PROOFREADER
Katie Robinson

TECHNICAL EDITORS
Max Muller
Steve Munt

TEAM COORDINATOR
Vanessa Evans

MULTIMEDIA DEVELOPER
Dan Scherf

INTERIOR DESIGNER
Gary Adair

COVER DESIGNER
Alan Clements

GRAPHICS
Tammy Graham
Laura Robbins

Contents at a Glance

Introduction   1

Part I Getting Started with AppleScript   5

Hour 1   Introducing AppleScript   7

2   Using AppleScript   19

3   Running the Scripts You Already Have   27

4   Getting New Scripts from Apple and Running Them   39

5   Third-party Scripts and Applications That Simplify Your Life   51

6   Looking Behind the Scenes: How These Scripts Work   59

7   Basic Programming Concepts   69

Part II Writing Scripts with Script Editor   81

Hour 8   Introducing Script Editor   83

9   Basic AppleScript Syntax   93

10   Scripting the Finder   107

11   Scripting Mac OS X Applications from Apple   121

12   Scripting Mac OS X Applications from Third Parties   135

13   Interacting with Users   147

Part III Working with AppleScript Studio   157

Hour 14   Introducing AppleScript Studio   159

15   Building a Graphical AppleScript Studio Application   181

16   Writing Code for AppleScript Studio   201

17   Planning and Debugging AppleScript Studio Applications   221

18   Adding Help to AppleScript Studio   241

19   Using Documents and Data Sources with AppleScript Studio   259

Part IV Advanced Scripting   279

Hour 20   Advanced AppleScript Syntax   281

21   Creating AppleScripts to Control Multiple Applications   297

22   Using AppleScript Across a Network   311

| | 23 | Beyond AppleScript: Using Services | 329 |
| | 24 | Beyond AppleScript: Shell Scripts, Perl, and Other Scripting Languages | 341 |

Part V Appendixes   361

Appendix A	Constants and Predefined Variables	363
B	Operators	367
C	Third-party Script Editors	371
	Glossary	381
	Index	385

Contents

Introduction   **1**

Who Should Read This Book 2

How This Book Is Organized 2

Conventions Used in This Book 3

PART I   **Getting Started with AppleScript**   **5**

HOUR 1   **Introducing AppleScript**   **7**

AppleScript Success Stories 8

    Mac OS X 9

    Real Estate and Other Listings 9

    ShowTime 9

    Responding to Disk Insertions with Scripts 10

Scripting Versus Point-and-Click 10

    Using Unused Computer Time 11

    Automating Complex Tasks 11

    Automating Routine but Simple Tasks 11

    Working with Speech Recognition 11

    Watching for Special Cases and Conditions 12

What Makes AppleScript Special:

    Syntactical Scripting 12

How AppleScript Works: Overview 13

    Apple Events 13

    Application Support 13

    Framework Support 14

AppleScript Syntax 14

    Suites 14

    Classes 15

    Commands 15

AppleScript Syntax for Programming 15

    Control Structures 15

    Constants 16

    Variables 16

    Interacting with Users 17

Summary 17

Q&A 17

Workshop 18
    Quiz 18
    Quiz Answers 18
    Activity 18

HOUR 2 Using AppleScript   19

Script Files 20
Applets 21
Droplets 21
Toolbar Scripts 22
Script Menu 22
    Installing the Script Menu 24
    Using the Script Menu 24
    Modifying Script Menu 24
    Removing Script Menu 24
Scripting Additions 25
Where to Get Scripts 25
Summary 25
Q&A 26
Workshop 26
    Quiz 26
    Quiz Answers 26
    Activities 26

HOUR 3 Running the Scripts You Already Have   27

Basics 28
    Scripting Help Viewer 29
    Using Scripts to Navigate the Web 30
    Launching an Application with a Script 30
Finder Scripts 31
Info Scripts 31
Web Services 31
Mail Scripts 33
Navigation Scripts 35
Script Editor Scripts 35
Folder Action Scripts 35
ColorSync and FontSync Scripts 37
Summary 37
Q&A 37

Workshop 38
    Quiz 38
    Quiz Answers 38
    Activities 38

HOUR 4 Getting New Scripts from Apple and Running Them   39

The iPhoto Collection 40
    Photo Summary 40
    Show Image File 41
    Photo to iDVD Background 41
The iDVD Collection 42
    iDVD Companion 42
    Create DVD from Folders, Photos, and More 43
    Other Scripts 44
The iTunes Collection 44
    Installing the iTunes Script Menu 44
    Looking Up Artists on eMusic 45
    Other Scripts 45
The QuickTime Collection 46
    The EMBED Tag Wizard Script 46
    The SMIL Suite 46
    Other Scripts 46
The Toolbar Scripts 46
    Customizing Your Desktop (Snapshot and Set View Options) 47
    Image Manipulation Scripts 47
Summary 48
Q&A 48
Workshop 49
    Quiz 49
    Quiz Answers 49
    Activities 49

HOUR 5 Third-party Scripts and Applications That Simplify Your Life   51

Sites for Scripts 52
    AppleScript Central 52
    AppleScript Info 52
    AppleScript Sourcebook 54
    macscripter.net 55
    ScriptWeb 55
Utility Scripts 55
    iPhoto Librarian 56
    MacSQL 56

Cronathon 56
email.cgi 56
acgi Dispatcher 56
Summary 57
Q&A 57
Workshop 57
Quiz 57
Quiz Answers 57
Activities 58

HOUR 6 Looking Behind the Scenes: How These Scripts Work   59

Blocks 60
Subroutines 61
Using Parameters in Subroutines 61
Using Prepositions with Parameters 61
Handlers 63
Run 63
Open 64
Idle 65
Quit 65
Recursive Processing 65
Summary 66
Q&A 66
Workshop 66
Quiz 66
Quiz Answers 67
Activities 67

HOUR 7 Basic Programming Concepts   69

Units of Control and Definition 70
Conditional Statements 71
Simple Conditional Statements 72
Compound Conditional Statements 72
Multiple Elses 72
Writing Good Conditional Statements 73
Returning from a Handler 74
Repetition 74
repeat forever 74
repeat x times 75
repeat while 75
repeat until 75

          `repeat with/from/to` 76

          `repeat with/in` 76

     Try Blocks 77

     Summary 78

     Q&A 78

     Workshop 79

          Quiz 79

          Quiz Answers 79

          Activities 79

PART II Writing Scripts with Script Editor   **81**

HOUR 8 Introducing Script Editor   **83**

     Finding Your Way Around Script Editor 84

          File Menu 84

          Edit Menu 85

          Controls Menu 86

     Creating a Script 86

     Checking Syntax 86

     Working with Dictionaries 88

     Looking at the Result 90

     Looking at the Event Log 90

     Summary 90

     Q&A 91

     Workshop 91

          Quiz 91

          Quiz Answers 91

          Activities 92

HOUR 9 Basic AppleScript Syntax   **93**

     Tell Blocks 94

          Telling an Application to Do Something 94

          Telling an Object to Do Something 95

          Nesting Tell Blocks 95

          Single-line Tells 96

     Commands 96

          AppleScript Commands 96

          User-defined Commands 97

     Variables 97

          User-defined Variables 97

          AppleScript-defined Variables 99

Expressions 101
Control Statements 101
Optional Words 101
Script Structure 101
   The Basic Script 102
   Using Subroutines 103
Summary 105
Q&A 105
Workshop 105
   Quiz 106
   Quiz Answers 106
   Activities 106

HOUR 10 Scripting the Finder   107

References 108
Inheritance 109
Standard Suite: Terms That Most Applications Support 110
   close 111
   open 111
   count 112
   delete 112
   make 112
   Other Commands in the Finder Standard Suite 112
   Standard Suite Commands Not Implemented in the Finder 112
Finder Basics 113
   Elements 114
   Properties 115
Finder Items 115
Container and Folders Suite 116
Files Suite 117
Window Classes Suite 117
Legacy Suite 117
Summary 117
Q&A 118
Workshop 118
   Quiz 118
   Quiz Answers 118
   Activities 119

HOUR 11 Scripting Mac OS X Applications from Apple   121

Reading a Dictionary 122
   Find the application Class and Its Elements 123
   Look at the Element Definitions 123
   Repeat for Elements Contained Within Elements 124

iCal 124

Help Viewer 125

Mail 126

Address Book 127

TextEdit 128

DVD Player 129

Internet Connect 129

Print Center 129

Disk Copy 130

Image Capture Scripting 130

Terminal 130

Summary 131

Q&A 132

Workshop 132

    Quiz 132

    Quiz Answers 132

    Activities 132

HOUR 12 Scripting Mac OS X Applications from Third Parties   135

Scripting America Online 136

Scripting AppleWorks 137

Scripting FileMaker 138

Scripting Microsoft Office 140

    Word 140

    PowerPoint 141

Scripting Internet Explorer 141

Scripting Photoshop 142

Scripting Retrospect 143

Summary 145

Q&A 145

Workshop 146

    Quiz 146

    Quiz Answers 146

    Activities 146

HOUR 13 Interacting with Users   147

Telling the User Something 148

Asking the User Something 150

Other Ways of Communicating with Users 151

    Speech Synthesis 151

    Using Other Applications for Input and Output 152

Aqua Human Interface Guidelines 152

Summary 154

Q&A 154

Workshop 154

    Quiz 154

    Quiz Answers 155

    Activities 155

PART III Working with AppleScript Studio   **157**

HOUR 14 Introducing AppleScript Studio   **159**

Getting AppleScript Studio 160

What Is AppleScript Studio? 160

    AppleScript Studio's Components 160

    Looking at an AppleScript Studio Application 162

Getting Started with Project Builder 164

Looking at Interface Builder 168

    Designing the Table View 168

    Adding Other Interface Elements 172

    Working with Handlers 174

Summary 179

Q&A 179

Workshop 180

    Quiz 180

    Quiz Answers 180

    Activities 180

HOUR 15 Building a Graphical AppleScript Studio Application   **181**

Writing a Simple AppleScript Studio Application 182

    Create the Project 182

    Set Up Interface Builder 183

    Design the Window 183

    Identify Window Elements 184

    Write the Handler 187

    Run the Application 187

A (Very) Little Programming Background 187

    Properties 189

    Elements 190

Commands 192
Events 192
Summing Up the Programming Details 193
Using Menus 193
Implementing a Menu Command 194
Factoring Your Application 195
Catching Errors 196
Enabling Menus 197
Summary 198
Q&A 198
Workshop 199
Quiz 199
Quiz Answers 199
Activities 199

HOUR 16 Writing Code for AppleScript Studio   201

Working with Tab Views 202
Setting Up a Tab View 203
Using a Pop-up Menu to Control a Tab View 205
Using Pop-up Menus and Combination (Combo) Boxes 207
Using Connections to Get Pop-up Menu Values 208
Using AppleScript to Get Pop-up Menu Values 209
Finding Out About Events 210
Nib Handler 211
Action Handlers 211
Drag-and-Drop Handlers 212
Editing Handlers 212
Key Handlers 212
Mouse Handlers 212
View Handler 212
Special Handlers 212
Using Sliders 213
Using the Color Well and Image Views 214
Using Progress Indicators 214
Using Formatters 215
Summary 218
Q&A 218
Workshop 219
Quiz 219
Quiz Answers 219
Activities 219

HOUR 17 Planning and Debugging AppleScript Studio Applications   **221**

Project Builder Preferences 222
Project Builder Targets 223
 Summary Settings 224
 Settings 225
 Info.plist 226
 Document Types 228
 Build Phases 230
Project Builder Styles 231
Debugging Overview 232
 Who Should Debug Applications? 233
 When Do You Debug Applications? 233
Debugging with Script Editor 233
Debugging with Project Builder 233
Debugging with Project Builder's Debugger 234
 Using Breakpoints 235
 A Debugging Case Study 236
 Debugging Strategies 238
Summary 239
Q&A 239
Workshop 239
 Quiz 240
 Quiz Answers 240
 Activities 240

HOUR 18 Adding Help to AppleScript Studio   **241**

Eliminating the Need for Help with Application Design 242
 Data Entry 243
 Command and Menu Design 246
Catching Errors 247
Providing Documentation 248
Providing Help Tags 248
Providing Button-driven Help 249
 Adding an Image to Your Project 249
 Implementing the Button 252
Interacting with Help Viewer 254
Summary 255
Q&A 256
Workshop 256

Quiz 257
Quiz Answers 257
Activities 257

HOUR 19 Using Documents and Data Sources with AppleScript Studio   259

Working with Table and Outline Views 260
Working with Data Sources 262
Data Source Basics 262
Creating Data Sources 263
Adding Rows to Data Sources 264
Populating New Rows with Data 265
Bulk Additions to Data Sources 267
Extracting Data from Data Sources 267
Exploring the AppleScript Document Template 268
Working with Documents: High-level Approach 272
Storing Data to Disk 273
Retrieving Data from Disk 274
Working with Files: Low-level Approach 274
Storing Data to a File 275
Retrieving Data from a File 275
Summary 276
Q&A 276
Workshop 277
Quiz 277
Quiz Answers 277
Activities 277

PART IV Advanced Scripting   279

HOUR 20 Advanced AppleScript Syntax   281

Script Objects 282
What Is a Script Object? 282
Script Objects as Instances 283
Inherited Script Objects 287
Design Considerations 291
GUI Scripting 292
Summary 295
Q&A 295
Workshop 295
Quiz 296
Quiz Answers 296
Activities 296

HOUR 21 Creating AppleScripts to Control Multiple Applications   **297**

Basic Script Design 298
     getData 298
     createDocument 299
     fillDocument 299
Extracting Data from Address Book and Placing It in Text Edit 300
     getData 300
     createDocument 300
     fillDocument 300
Extracting Data from FileMaker and Placing It in Text Edit 302
     getData 302
     createDocument 303
     fillDocument 303
Extracting Data from Address Book and Placing It in InDesign 303
     getData 303
     createDocument 304
     fillDocument 305
Extracting Data from FileMaker and Placing It in InDesign 306
     getData 306
     createDocument 306
     fillDocument 306
Creating Dynamic Pages with InDesign 306
     getData 307
     createDocument 307
     fillDocument 307
Summary 308
Q&A 309
Workshop 309
     Quiz 309
     Quiz Answers 310
     Activities 310

HOUR 22 Using AppleScript Across a Network   **311**

Mounting Remote Disks 312
     Mounting afp Volumes 312
     Using the Server Name 313
     Ejecting Disks 313
How AppleScript Works Across a Network 313

What You Need to Do on the Client Mac 314

What You Need to Do on the Server Mac 315

    Allowing Remote Connections for File Sharing 316

    Allowing Remote Connections for Apple Events 317

    Setting Up User Accounts for Remote Access 317

Using AppleScript to Process CGI Requests 318

    Creating the HTML 319

    Modifying the Script from Apple 320

Using Web Services 321

    XML-RPC 322

    SOAP 322

Using Web Services with Script Editor 325

Using Web Services with AppleScript Studio 326

Summary 327

Q&A 327

Workshop 328

    Quiz 328

    Quiz Answers 328

    Activities 328

HOUR 23 Beyond AppleScript: Using Services   **329**

A Services Overview 330

How Services Work 332

    Processor Services 332

    Provider Services 332

    Combination Services 332

    Under the Hood 333

Enabling Services with AppleScript Studio 333

Why Use Services with AppleScript Studio? 337

Services from Script Editor 337

    Make New AppleScript 337

    Get Result of AppleScript 337

    Run As AppleScript 338

Summary 338

Q&A 338

Workshop 338

    Quiz 339

    Quiz Answers 339

    Activities 339

HOUR 24 Beyond AppleScript: Shell Scripts, Perl, and Other Scripting Languages   **341**

Using Terminal 342

What Commands Are Available? 343

Using the Command Line 344

The Format of Commands 344

Using Files for Input, Output, and Errors 345

Using Files for Commands 346

Working with Files in Terminal 346

Listing a Directory and Displaying a File 347

Changing Permissions 349

Using sudo 349

Running AppleScript from Terminal 349

Running a Script from Terminal 350

Running AppleScript Commands from Terminal 351

Running AppleScript As Commands from Applications 352

Automatically Running Scripts 353

cron 353

periodic 354

Other Scripting Languages 356

Perl 356

Ruby 357

Python 357

Summary 357

Q&A 358

Workshop 358

Quiz 358

Quiz Answers 358

Activities 359

PART V Appendixes   **361**

APPENDIX A Constants and Predefined Variables   **363**

APPENDIX B Operators   **367**

Arithmetic Operators 368

Boolean Operators 368

Containment Operators 368

Equality Operators 369

Comparison Operators 370

APPENDIX C Third-party Script Editors **371**

Smile 372
Script Debugger 374
PreFab UI Browser 377

Glossary **381**

Index **385**

About the Author

JESSE FEILER is the author of a number of Mac OS X books including *Mac OS X Jaguar: The Complete Reference*; *Mac OS X Developer's Guide*; and *Making Movies, Photos, Music, and DVDs on Your Mac*. He is also the author of *Building WebObjects 5 Applications*, as well as many books on the Web-based enterprise (such as *Database-Driven Web Sites* and *Managing the Web-Based Enterprise*), the Y2K problem, home offices, databases, and FileMaker. He has written numerous white papers for Cutter Consortium. His books on OpenDoc, Cyberdog, Apple Guide, and Rhapsody are now collector's items.

He has worked as a developer and manager for companies such as the Federal Reserve Bank of New York (monetary policy and bank supervision), Prodigy (early Web browser), Apple (information systems), New York State Department of Health (rabies and lead poisoning), The Johnson Company (office management), and Young & Rubicam (media planning and new product development).

His interests in new forms of technical training have led him to MediaSchool (http://www.mediaschool.com), for which he has authored several Mac OS X courses available over the Internet, as well as to Geek Cruises' Mac Mania cruise to Alaska. He is also the first author of a technical book to be published in both a paper version and as an e-book.

His Web site, http://www.philmontmill.com, provides additional information as do his blog pages at http://www.pickwickpixels.com.

Active in the community, he is past president of the Mid-Hudson Library System, chair of the Philmont Comprehensive Plan Board, founder of the Philmont Main Street Committee, and treasurer of the HB Playwrights Foundation. He is a regular on WAMC's Roundtable program.

He lives 100 miles north of New York City in the village of Philmont with a rescued greyhound and a cat. His research into Apple's iLife application has earned him the sobriquet "The Digital Scourge of Philmont."

Acknowledgments

The picture of an author sitting alone in a room day after day may be true for some authors and some types of books, but it's not true for this author or for technical books in general. Many people have provided invaluable assistance to the creation of this book.

First and foremost, the AppleScript team at Apple has developed and, over the years, maintained and improved AppleScript. Together with the people who build and maintain Project Builder, Interface Builder, and the Cocoa framework, they have made AppleScript the mighty tool that it is today.

At Sams, Betsy Brown first brought this book into being. As it was being written, technical editors Max Muller and Steve Munt provided excellent feedback to help make the book as accurate and complete as possible. Under the excellent guidance of development editor Damon Jordan, and project editor Matthew Purcell, they, the proofreader (Katie Robinson), the copy editor (Margaret Berson), and indexer (Ken Johnson) worked to bring this book to fruition.

At Waterside Productions, Carole McClendon provided her usual excellent support and advice on the project.

This book would not have been possible without their assistance, and they—along with the other people listed previously—have the author's deep gratitude. Notwithstanding this, any errors or omissions remain the author's handiwork.

We Want to Hear from You!

As the reader of this book, *you* are our most important critic and commentator. We value your opinion and want to know what we're doing right, what we could do better, what areas you'd like to see us publish in, and any other words of wisdom you're willing to pass our way.

You can email or write me directly to let me know what you did or didn't like about this book—as well as what we can do to make our books stronger.

Please note that I cannot help you with technical problems related to the topic of this book, and that due to the high volume of mail I receive, I might not be able to reply to every message.

When you write, please be sure to include this book's title and author as well as your name and phone number or email address. I will carefully review your comments and share them with the author and editors who worked on the book.

Email: consumer@samspublishing.com
Mail: Mark Taber
        Associate Publisher
        Sams Publishing
        201 West 103rd Street
        Indianapolis, IN 46290 USA

Reader Services

For more information about this book or others from Sams Publishing, visit our Web site at www.samspublishing.com. Type the ISBN (excluding hyphens) or the title of the book in the Search box to find the book you're looking for.

Introduction

Welcome to *Sams Teach Yourself AppleScript in 24 Hours*. This book provides a systematic guide to learning AppleScript; when you're finished, you'll understand what it is, how to use it, and how to extend it with the resources of AppleScript Studio.

In each of the 24 hours, you'll find discussions and examples of AppleScript features. You'll find projects to work on so that you have hands-on experience from the very beginning. Most people will find that a single chapter does take an hour. Thus, the book is comparable in many ways to a three-day AppleScript seminar.

A companion Web site for the book contains the code discussed in this book, so you don't have to retype it. In addition, the projects described in Part III, "Working with AppleScript Studio," are available for downloading as Project Builder projects. There are even a few goodies on the Web site that aren't in the book. You can find it at www. samspublishing.com.

AppleScript has long been an important tool for Mac users. With Mac OS X, it has been transformed into an even more powerful tool. For example, AppleScript Studio, the subject of Part III of this book, brings the entire development environment of Mac OS X into the reach of scripters. This means not only that the full Aqua interface is now available for scripts, but also that you can integrate AppleScript with shell scripts as well as with applications written in C, Objective-C, and C++.

Another recent change is that the basic Script Editor application that has served so well for many years has been updated for Mac OS X. In version 2, released in beta at the end of 2002, Script Editor has been rewritten using the Cocoa framework and a variety of sophisticated interface elements. It is shown in Figure I.1.

FIGURE I.1

Use Script Editor to write scripts.

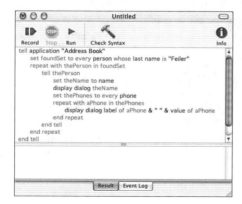

Among the new features is a historical view of the event log that lets you review exactly how your scripts have performed while you're running Script Editor. Saving the events lets you easily check how they've run under different conditions (such as while you're tracking down a bug and making changes). The Event Log and its History drawer are shown in Figure I.2.

FIGURE I.2

Use the history in the Event Log to debug your scripts.

AppleScript syntax has been defined for many years. A very few additions for Mac OS X have been provided. This book describes AppleScript as it is implemented in Mac OS X version 10.2 (Jaguar). Some earlier versions of Mac OS X did not support some of the features described in this book.

Who Should Read This Book

This book is for everyone who wants to learn more about AppleScript. That includes people who want to make the most of the many scripts that come with Mac OS X as well as the thousands (literally!) of scripts that you can download for free from the Internet. It also includes people who want to write their own scripts or who have started looking at scripting and want to become more sophisticated. And it also serves developers and consultants who are looking for an extraordinarily productive development environment.

How This Book Is Organized

In Part I, "Getting Started with AppleScript," you'll find out about the scripts that you already have installed on your computer as part of Mac OS X. AppleScript is used pervasively in Mac OS X: for example, it's the glue that ties together iCal and Mail to alert you and others about upcoming appointments. You're probably already using AppleScript!

You'll also see how to obtain additional scripts from Apple as well as from third parties. After looking at what these scripts can do, the final hour provides an overview of some of the behind-the-scenes terminology and architecture of AppleScript.

Part II, "Writing Scripts with Script Editor," is devoted to writing scripts. You'll see how to use Script Editor, and you'll learn about AppleScript syntax. You'll see how to script the Finder as well as applications from Apple and from third parties.

AppleScript Studio is the topic of Part III. In those hours, you'll learn how to develop full Aqua applications using the templates in Project Builder (downloadable from Apple's Web site). You'll see how to create basic AppleScript Studio applications as well as droplets and even document-based applications.

Finally, in Part IV, "Advanced Scripting," you'll find some advanced topics. You'll see how to use the command line to script UNIX applications, and you'll see how to work with multiple applications as well as networks.

At the end of each hour, there are some questions and answers that discuss the issues raised; you'll also find some quiz questions to recap the high points. Finally, some suggested activities will help you gain hands-on knowledge of AppleScript.

Inside the back cover, you'll find a number of samples of AppleScript control statements. These pseudocode samples can be useful particularly if you are used to other programming languages that may have slightly different syntax for statements such as repeat and if.

Conventions Used in This Book

Certain conventions have been followed in this book to help you digest all the material. For example, at the beginning of each hour, you'll find a list of the major topics that will be covered in that particular hour.

You will also find that icons are used throughout this book. These icons either are accompanied by additional information on a subject or supply you with shortcuts or an optional way to perform a task. These icons are as follows:

Notes include additional information related to the current topic, such as asides and comments.

Tips contain shortcuts and hints on performing a particular task.

PART I

Getting Started with AppleScript

Hour

1 Introducing AppleScript

2 Using AppleScript

3 Running the Scripts You Already Have

4 Getting New Scripts from Apple and Running Them

5 Third-party Scripts and Applications That Simplify Your Life

6 Looking Behind the Scenes: How These Scripts Work

7 Basic Programming Concepts

HOUR 1

Introducing AppleScript

If you're using Mac OS X, chances are excellent that you're already using AppleScript. It's used throughout the operating system and applications that Apple provides. For example, if you use iCal to manage your calendar, you can have it automatically send e-mail messages to remind you and others of meetings. It does so by using AppleScript.

If you use speech recognition, Mac OS X will recognize your speech—and then run AppleScript scripts. You can set your preferences to respond to the insertion of CDs and DVDs—launch specific applications such as iTunes or DVD Player, or run a script. If you use DVD Player, a host of Apple-prepared scripts are provided to help you navigate through the discs.

If you come from the UNIX world that is the basis for Mac OS X, you may be familiar with other scripting languages—Perl, Ruby, shell scripts, and the like. AppleScript is both similar to them and different from them. But it works with them.

It even works with the command line. You can script UNIX commands, and type commands to run AppleScript scripts. Scripting is more important in Mac OS X than it has ever been before in a Macintosh operating system.

This hour introduces AppleScript and provides a brief overview of the terminology and concepts that are described later in the book. It gives some examples of what people have done with AppleScript.

The remaining hours in this part of the book show you in detail how to run the scripts that you have or that you can easily obtain. Then, in Part II of the book you'll see how to write and edit scripts with Script Editor, Apple's basic script authoring tool. In Part III, you'll see how to use AppleScript Studio, Apple's more sophisticated (but still free) script authoring tool. And in the final part of the book, you'll see how to take advantage of advanced scripting.

In This Hour

- AppleScript Success Stories—These stories tell what people have done with AppleScript. Some of these are major achievements that literally run businesses, and others are little scripts that just make life easier.
- Scripting Versus Point-and-Click—How does scripting fit into the world of the Macintosh as you know it?
- How AppleScript Works: Overview—This overview introduces you to the concepts of AppleScript and the basic way in which it works. If you're going to do any authoring of AppleScript scripts, you should know how it works. If you're going to think about what could be done with AppleScript (even if you're not going to be doing the work), this section will help you see the possibilities—and the things that aren't amenable to scripting.
- AppleScript Syntax—You'll find more about AppleScript syntax in Hour 9, "Basic AppleScript Syntax." This section introduces you to the basic terms that will be further defined later on.
- AppleScript Syntax for Programming—A few programming concepts are presented here just to get you started. They will be expanded on in Hour 7, "Basic Programming Concepts."

AppleScript Success Stories

People who use AppleScript swear by it. Some of them have built businesses around it. When you, too, use AppleScript, you will see how much more productive you can be— and how productive your computer can be when you are nowhere in sight.

Mac OS X

Some of the biggest success stories are built right in to Mac OS X. Mac OS X ships with many applications, and a large number of them are scriptable. The scriptable Mac OS X applications include:

- DVD Player
- Finder
- iCal
- iDVD
- Image Capture
- iPhoto
- iTunes
- Mail
- QuickTime Player
- Terminal
- Toolbar Scripts

Real Estate and Other Listings

A common use of AppleScript involves collecting information from a database such as FileMaker and then exporting it into a page layout application such as InDesign or Quark. This process is commonly used for printed listings of real estate, television listings, and catalogs.

ShowTime

One of the more complex scripting applications is used to produce menu listings at the ShowTime network. It starts with a month's worth of program listings. They are imported by hand into an Excel spreadsheet and then saved as a tab-delimited file. (This step is done just to reformat the listings.)

Then, an AppleScript reads the file and, for each listing in the month, produces an Adobe Illustrator file, a Photoshop file, and a TIFF image.

Subsequent AppleScript steps automatically add audio, video, and text to each listing. The final step produces a QuickTime movie with the entire month's listings.

Responding to Disk Insertions with Scripts

There are hooks throughout Mac OS X for you to insert your own scripts. In System Preferences, for example, you can have your own scripts run when you insert CDs or DVDs. You can attach scripts to folders so that they run automatically when the folders are changed. All of this provides a level of sophistication to your computer environment that has not been available in the past.

Scripting Versus Point-and-Click

The graphical user interface you're used to on the Macintosh supplanted earlier and clumsier interfaces that were used on other operating systems. For the first few decades of the computer age, there really was no such thing as a user interface; even with the advent of personal computers, there was no such thing for quite a few years. People had to format their data in accordance with the needs of the computer, and that was that.

For example, a program might expect the first 20 characters of data to be a name and the second 10 to be a telephone number. You would enter data in this way:

```
Tom Paine        5551234567
```

More sophisticated interfaces began to emerge in which the formatting of the data was a compromise between user and computer. It was possible to enter something such as

```
<name>Tom Paine
<telephone>5551234567
```

and have the computer search its list of valid inputs for "name" and then associate "Tom Paine" with that input. This eliminated the need for entering everything in a prescribed order and even counting blank spaces.

The graphical user interface, which has blossomed into Mac OS X today, was a significant further advance. It allows you to point and click your way through an application. You don't have to explain everything in some obscure computer format or language. The instantaneous feedback lets you know what's happening, and if you do make a mistake, the ever-present Undo command in the Edit menu lets you recover.

But point-and-click is not the last word in interfaces. It does provide instantaneous feedback, but that's the drawback: It requires you to sit at your computer, pointing, clicking, and typing (or speaking, with voice recognition turned on). For some tasks this is the best way to work. For others, it's a waste of time.

Scripting allows you to specify the tasks that are to be done, to identify the data involved, and to totally describe the process that is to be completed.

Using Unused Computer Time

Scripting allows you to do other things with your time (such as sleep). Most personal computers are unused for very significant amounts of time every day. Projects such as SETI@home (`http://setiathome.ssl.berkeley.edu/`) seek to harness this unused capacity.

You can harness your unused computer time by running scripts when you're away from your computer. Many people already run automated tasks overnight (such as backups). Scripts help you extend that idea to any scriptable application.

Note that Mac OS X with its UNIX underpinnings supports a variety of scripting and scheduling features. Chapter 24, "Beyond AppleScript: Shell Scripts and Perl," discusses the at and cron UNIX commands that you can use to run scripts at specific times when you are not necessarily around.

Automating Complex Tasks

Scripting is great at automating complex tasks—particularly repetitive ones. A common use of AppleScript is collecting information from a database and then formatting it for publication on the Web or on paper. That's what happens with real estate listings.

It's not worth writing a script to automate a complex task that you'll do only once: It's usually easier just to do it interactively. But if it's a repetitive task, the time spent writing the script is worth it.

Even if it's not a repetitive task, using a script can be valuable, particularly if you don't have to write the script yourself. In iPhoto, you can export selected photos to a Web page that is created automatically for you. What does this? AppleScript.

Apple uses AppleScript extensively for this type of task: tying together various applications. The basics of copying information to the clipboard, cutting or pasting, and executing basic commands are easy to automate in AppleScript.

Automating Routine but Simple Tasks

You can also script very simple tasks. There are all sorts of reasons for doing so. One is that simple tasks are easy to do incorrectly; you pay attention to the complex ones. Also, when you have a script for a task, you don't have to use the keyboard any more. You can ask the computer to do the task for you.

Working with Speech Recognition

The Speakable Items folder contains aliases to documents and applications you want to open. It also contains scripts that carry out tasks you speak. (The name of the script is the command that you speak.)

This is one reason why you might want to automate routine and simple tasks with AppleScript: You can then carry out these tasks without touching the keyboard.

Watching for Special Cases and Conditions

AppleScript and the operating system can watch for certain events to occur and then trigger specified scripts. In System Preferences, you use the CDs & DVDs pane to set actions to take when CDs and DVDs are inserted—both blank ones and those containing photos, music, and movies. One of the actions you can specify is to run a script. Because scripts can do almost anything, you can cause the computer to do almost anything when you insert one of these discs.

Folder actions let you attach scripts to folders; these scripts automatically run when certain types of events occur, such as adding documents to the specified folder. You can attach such a script to a folder on a file server; when files are added to the shared folder, scripts could automatically back them up, print them, send them somewhere, encrypt them, or convert them from one format to another.

What Makes AppleScript Special: Syntactical Scripting

Early scripting languages on personal computers were keyboard- and mouse-automation tools. You described exactly what the user would be doing when interacting with the application, and then these stored commands were executed. Sometimes, they were literally played back: You could see the mouse move in response to the script.

From the beginning in 1992, AppleScript has relied on *syntactical scripting*. This means that it deals with logical, syntactical elements. You can type

```
print document 1
```

into Script Editor; normally you do not type something such as

```
select command 2 of File menu
```

The syntax of AppleScript needs to describe three types of items:

- You need to be able to describe and identify *things*—documents, folders, words, and the like. In natural languages, these are *nouns*.
- You need to be able to describe and identify *actions* to be performed on or by these things. In natural languages, these are *verbs*.
- You need the ability to *control* a script. You may want it to execute once, or you may want it to execute a certain number of times. If it fails, you want it to be able

to recognize the failure and to take appropriate actions. There is no natural-language parallel here, but in programming languages, these are called *control statements*.

AppleScript has been created as a language that is as natural as possible. Its underlying syntax is language-neutral; you can choose to read and write scripts in many human languages.

How AppleScript Works: Overview

You've seen what AppleScript can do, and in the preceding section you learned that its syntactical approach to scripting makes it a powerful language. But how does it work? This section provides a very brief overview of the three key concepts that make AppleScript possible. You'll learn much more about how AppleScript works in Part II of this book.

Apple Events

At the heart of AppleScript are *Apple events*. An Apple event is a command that is directed to a specific item—its *direct object*. (A few commands have no direct object, but most do.) A direct object might be a document or a paragraph within a document; it could also be a database record.

The Apple event may have *parameters*: modifiers for the command. A print command, for example, could have a document as its direct object, and a number of copies as its parameter. Apple events can have more than one parameter.

Apple events may have *return data* associated with them—information that is returned to you. A print event doesn't have return data; however, a command to check spelling would have return data.

Application Support

Apple events are sent to an application in almost all cases. (The exceptions are events that are handled by AppleScript or the operating system itself; and even in those cases there really is an application to which the event is sent.) Thus, you can tell Microsoft Word to print its frontmost document; you can also tell Quark to print its frontmost document.

Applications need to support at least four basic Apple events:

- Open Application (to launch the application)
- Open Documents (to open selected documents in the application)

- Print Documents (to print selected documents in the application)
- Quit (to quit the application)

Applications may support other commands—either standard commands or ones they define themselves. (See the section "AppleScript Syntax.")

Framework Support

Applications built using a framework such as Cocoa from Apple may have AppleScript support provided by the framework. The application itself may not be scriptable, but you may be able to use some of its interface components in AppleScript.

iPhoto is an example of this. It is not scriptable itself; however, you can drag images from iPhoto windows onto AppleScript droplets and have them processed.

AppleScript Syntax

For now, all you need to know about AppleScript syntax is contained in this section. There will be much more in Hour 9, but the information here provides the basic architecture and the terminology you need to get started.

Suites

AppleScript syntax is divided into *suites*—collections of syntactical elements required for specific types of tasks. Some suites are defined by Apple: the Standard suite, which contains the four commands previously cited along with many frequently used commands that most applications implement. Other suites are the Text suite (for text manipulation), the Table suite (for spreadsheets and databases), and so on.

Applications usually implement the commands in these Apple-defined suites in their own ways; however, the use of common suites with common commands means that you should not have to learn different syntax for printing in Quark than you learn for printing in Terminal.

Applications often implement the Standard suites along with relevant other suites, such as Text. Then, they implement their own suite, which expands and extends functionality specifically for their own application. Printing is defined in the Standard suite, but re-indexing a database is likely to be defined in an application-specific suite.

Suites contain various syntactical elements, but the two most important are classes and commands.

Classes

Classes are the objects—nouns—that a suite deals with. For example, the Text suite defines character, word, and paragraph (among others), and the FileMaker suite defines a request class, which is a Find request.

Commands

Suites can also contain *commands*—verbs. The FileMaker suite contains a find command, and the Standard suite contains commands such as save.

You will notice that the FileMaker suite contains both a request class and a find command. This allows you to manipulate a find request (by using the request class) as well as to process a find command.

Commands are defined not only by what they do but also by what their parameters and direct objects are. Some parameters are optional. For example, the save command in the Standard suite requires a direct object—the item to be saved. It has two optional parameters, which allow you to specify the filename and file type for the saved file. If they are absent, the file is saved to its default name and file type.

Sometimes, the direct object or parameters are defined to be a certain class such as a document, word, or list of items. More often, direct objects and parameters are defined simply as *references*. References are parsed by AppleScript and identify objects such as the third word of paragraph 2.

AppleScript Syntax for Programming

The syntax described in the previous section refers to applications. In addition, there is application-independent syntax that you use for programming AppleScript. If you are familiar with programming at all, you will recognize these concepts.

Control Structures

If programming and scripting did not have control structures, all you could do is specify what should be done—once.

These syntax elements unleash the power of programming. They let you group statements together into *blocks* that are executed together. You can execute such a block once, or you can execute it a certain number of times; you also can execute it until or unless a certain condition is met. This is how you can write scripts that change the name of each file in a folder or that indent the first line of each paragraph in a document.

Blocks can also be structured so that they run *when* things happen. Such blocks are called *handlers*. Perhaps the most common use of a handler is to write one that is called when an error occurs. You can also attach scripts to folders as *folder actions*. When a defined action (such as adding an item) occurs, the script you specify is executed.

Tell blocks are blocks of code that are directed to a single application or object.

Constants

AppleScript also defines a wide variety of constants such as `true` and `false`, `pi`, `return` (the keyboard return character), and many date and time constants. The date and time constants include values such as `Saturday` as well as `hours` (the number of seconds in an hour, that is, 3600).

Variables

Variables are used to store data in AppleScript. You do not need to predefine a variable in order to use it, as you must do in some languages. You declare it by using it.

You can get properties of classes by using the `get` command; however, if you want to be able to manipulate those properties, you need to store them in variables using the `set` command. For example with iCal, here is how you get the title of a calendar:

```
get the title of calendar 1
```

If you want to be able to use that information later on, you need to store it. In that case, you would write

```
set myTitle to the title of calendar 1
```

Here you have declared a variable (`myTitle`) and set it to a value—the title of calendar 1.

Variables are one of the most important features of AppleScript. A single script can interact with several applications, and the variables in the script are generally available to the entire script. Here is a very simple AppleScript that gets the name of the first iCal calendar and then puts that name and some introductory text into a TextEdit document:

```
tell application "iCal"
  set myTitle to title of calendar 1
end tell
tell application "TextEdit"
  set text of document 1 to "The name of calendar 1 is " & myTitle
end tell
```

You'll see how to use Script Editor later on in Hour 8, "Introducing Script Editor." If you want, you can get a preview. Enter those lines of AppleScript code into Script Editor and run them by clicking the Run button. Remember that all the code for this book is available on the Web site for this book; you can download it, copy it, and then paste it into Script Editor (www.samspublishing.com).

This is a very simple demonstration, but it is at the core of every AppleScript that moves data from databases into page layout programs and the like. Being able to script across applications is one of the most powerful features of AppleScript. It is made possible by the architecture, which has been designed from the beginning for such interoperability and for the use of standard formats and data structures.

Interacting with Users

The last aspect of AppleScript syntax for programming is a number of interactive commands that let you communicate with users. You could, for example, present the title of the calendar in a dialog. You could ask the user whether or not to delete the calendar. All of these interaction elements are discussed in Hour 13, "Interacting with Users."

Summary

This hour has provided an introduction to AppleScript. You have seen what you can do with it—both in terms of concrete and real examples and in the general nature of tasks that it can address. You can use AppleScript for complex and repetitive tasks as well as for simple and infrequently used tasks. It is particularly useful at tying together various applications because you can use AppleScript to transfer data from one application to another.

Q&A

Q Why don't more people use AppleScript?

A AppleScript is a new way of working with your computer for many people. Because it's an automated, hands-off system, you need to think through what it is that you want to do, and you need to define it in AppleScript. That isn't very hard, but it's daunting for some people. This book will show you how to do it.

Q **Does AppleScript only work with Macintosh applications?**

A Yes and no. AppleScript lets you directly script Macintosh applications, but a number of important technologies allow you to work over the Internet with other platforms and applications. Most important, AppleScript can act as a SOAP Web client so that you can interact with Perl and with Web Services. This is how AppleScript can get stock market quotes, currency exchange rates, the weather, and so forth from Web Services on the Internet. This is described further in Chapter 22, "Using AppleScript Across a Network."

Workshop

The workshop contains quiz questions and activities to help you solidify your knowledge of the material in this hour. Try to answer all of the questions before looking at the quiz answers that follow.

Quiz

1. Do applications have to define basic commands such as Save and Print?

2. What type of syntax do you use to control a script's execution?

3. Where do you store data that you want to transfer from one application to another?

Quiz Answers

1. No, applications use the definitions in the Standard suites as well as optional other suites such as the Text or Table suite. They *implement* those commands, but they do not define them or change their syntax.

2. You control a script's execution with control statements.

3. You store data in variables.

Activity

What types of actions and processes would you like to script? Remember to consider the types of applications that AppleScript is best at performing. (Keep the list for Part II, "Writing Scripts with Script Editor.")

Hour **2**

Using AppleScript

This hour introduces the high-level concepts of AppleScript: the types of scripts, where you can put them (Finder toolbars and the menu bar), and how to get scripts that are ready to run.

When you finish this hour, you should know the different ways you can run scripts and how they can interact with data. You should also know how to place scripts conveniently in the Finder toolbar and in the Script Menu in the menu bar.

In This Hour

- Script Files—Scripts are written as text and are then compiled into runnable applications. This section explains the process.
- Applets—Applets or applications are double-clickable compiled scripts. Most of the scripts that you use are applets.
- Droplets—Droplets are a special type of applet: They are designed to have a file, folder, or standard data element (such as an image) dropped on to them. They then act on some aspect of that dropped data.

- Toolbar Scripts—Toolbar scripts can be any type of scripts; however, they are particularly useful when they act on the selection or target of a window.

- Script Menu—This menu combines all of your scripts into a handy ready-to-run menu. It combines AppleScript, Perl, Ruby, and other scripts; it also merges computer-wide scripts with scripts installed for a single user.

- Scripting Additions—Here is a description of some of the behind-the-scenes technology that helps to make AppleScript so powerful and extensible.

- Where to Get Scripts—You'll find some useful URLs here along with some further comments on the types of places that you can look for more scripts.

> Mac OS X v10.2 (Jaguar) brought a host of new features to Mac OS X including significant advances in the world of AppleScript. Some features (such as the Script Menu) were built in instead of needing to be downloaded separately from the Apple Web site. This book is based on the Jaguar release; if you have an earlier version of Mac OS X, you may want to upgrade to Jaguar for its many new features. If you prefer to stay with an older version of Mac OS X, consult the AppleScript Web page at http://www.apple.com/applescript for information on the various components and how you can obtain them for pre-Jaguar versions.

Script Files

Most of the time, a script starts as text that you type in (or copy and paste). Apple provides Script Editor to help you do this (you'll find out more about Script Editor in Part II). These text files can be opened by any application that can read text, but you'll most often use Script Editor or a third-party editing tool.

These text files have an extension of .applescript. You might not see the extension (you can turn the display of extensions on and off in the Finder), but it's there. Because these text files have their own extension, double-clicking a text file with an extension of .applescript will open it in Script Editor.

> As you will see in Hour 14, "Introducing AppleScript Studio," there are a number of other editing alternatives to Script Editor. Unless otherwise stated, you should interpret references to Script Editor in this book as meaning "Script Editor, AppleScript Studio, or one of the third-party script editing tools you can use."

In order to run a script, you need to *compile* it—convert it to the instructions that AppleScript uses to process your text commands. When you compile a script, you can save it in its compiled form. These scripts contain both the text (so that you can re-edit the script) and the compiled code (so that you can run it). They have a suffix of .scpt.

When you double-click a file with the .scpt extension, it opens in Script Editor. From there you can edit it or run it.

Applets

Applets (sometimes also called *AppleScript applications*) behave like standard applications: If you double-click them, they run. However, you can open them with Script Editor (either by dropping them on to the Script Editor icon or by using the Open command in the Script Editor File menu). When you open them in Script Editor, you can modify them or run them.

You can also save compiled scripts as *run-only* applications. If you do this, only the compiled script is saved: The text is removed. You can do this if you want to distribute a script and not have to worry about someone editing the code. You also may want to distribute a script that has information in it you don't want people to see (a login ID, for example); saving it as run-only provides a minimal amount of this type of security. (A moderately determined person can still find the information from the compiled script because it is not encrypted.)

The word "applet" is not specific to AppleScript. It refers to any small application written in a scripting language or in a language such as Java. Originally, applets were Java programs that could be included in the HTML of a Web page and that would run when downloaded.

Droplets

Droplets are applets onto which you can drag and drop files and folders. The droplet then is launched and it does something to or with whatever was dropped on to it.

Droplets are actually applets that are written to recognize that something is dropped on to them.

Toolbar Scripts

Finder toolbars can contain any document or folder icons that you want. You can customize the toolbar by using the Customize Toolbar command in the View menu, but you can also add folders and documents to the toolbar by dragging them into it. (When you drag a folder or document into the toolbar, an *alias* is placed there—just as when you drag it into the Dock. The original folder or document remains just where it is.) To remove items from the Finder toolbar, just drag them out of it.

You can place compiled scripts, applets, and droplets in the toolbar. This is a convenient place to keep them (but most people find the Dock even more convenient). However, there is one type of script that really does belong in the toolbar: That is a script that acts on the current selection in a Finder window.

As you will see, you can easily get a reference to the current selection (*target*) in the frontmost Finder window. Here is the snippet of AppleScript code that does that:

```
get the target of the front window
```

When you have the target, you can find out lots of information about it. The name, of course, is interesting, and you can obtain it by getting the target as a string:

```
get the target of the front window as string
```

You can also obtain the size of the target as shown here:

```
get the size of the target of the front window
```

And, with that information, it is easy to put up a dialog that informs the user how long and how many CDs it will take to back up the selected item—and then to perform the selected copy. This is a perfect toolbar script because it interacts with whatever happens to be selected in the Finder window. You could create a droplet and drag the relevant folder or document on to the droplet, but this method is simpler because there is no dragging involved.

Script Menu

In Mac OS X 10.2 ("Jaguar"), the Script Menu is distributed as part of the operating system. (If you have an earlier version, you can download the Script Menu from `http://www.apple.com/applescript/script_menu`.) It is a way to organize your various scripts in the menu bar. The Script Menu is shown in Figure 2.1.

FIGURE 2.1

The Script Menu appears at the right of the menu bar.

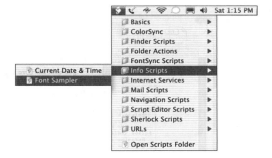

The submenus shown in Figure 2.1 have small arrows to the right to indicate that you can open them. Because the menu bar is built from left to right, this is usually correct. However, for menus that are at the right of the menu bar, the small arrows are at the right, but, as you can see here, the submenus actually open on the left towards the center of the display. This is normal behavior.

As shipped from Apple, the Script Menu has a number of useful scripts in it. Over time these change, and you can add your own scripts to the Script Menu.

In Figure 2.2, you can see one of the scripts that ships with Script Menu. Called Font Sampler, it uses TextEdit (also shipped as part of Mac OS X) to display a standard sentence using each of the fonts installed on your computer.

FIGURE 2.2

The Font Sampler script uses TextEdit to provide samples of fonts.

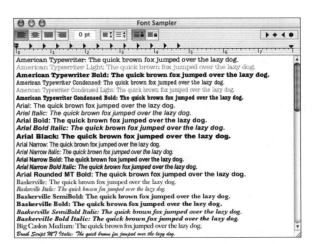

Installing the Script Menu

On most people's systems, the Script Menu is not installed automatically. You can find it in the AppleScript folder, which is located inside your Applications folder. Install it by dragging it to the right-hand side of the menu bar. It will snap into place automatically.

If you want to rearrange the icons at the right side of the menu bar, you can drag them back and forth by holding down the Command key. They slide back and forth to allow you to move them around.

Using the Script Menu

To run a script from the Script Menu, just choose its name.

Before Mac OS X 10.2 ("Jaguar"), a separate application called Script Runner was distributed. You could drag a script onto the Script Runner icon to run it. Now, you can just choose it from Script Menu.

Modifying Script Menu

Script Menu is built dynamically, and you can modify its contents. What Script Menu actually contains is a list of scripts that is merged from two locations: `/Library/Scripts` and `~/Library/Scripts`. The first folder is located at the root of your hard disk; like all other files at that level, its contents are shared among all users of your computer. The second (starting with ~) is located in your home directory (in the Users folder). Each user has a `~/Library/Scripts` folder, and the contents of the various folders are not shared.

If you want to create submenus in Script Menu, you can organize the scripts within your Scripts folders by placing them within folders. Each folder becomes a submenu.

Notice that the word "AppleScript" has not appeared in this section. That is because Script Menu can contain any type of script: AppleScript, Perl, Ruby, or shell scripts. You'll see later in this book how to integrate the various scripting technologies.

Removing Script Menu

If you don't want Script Menu in your menu bar, remove it by Command-dragging it out of the menu bar. It will simply vanish. As with all icons in the Dock or at the right of the menu bar (or in Finder window toolbars), the underlying folder or document will remain where it was. In the case of the Script Menu, it's in the AppleScript folder inside Applications; you can always reinstall it from there.

Scripting Additions

AppleScript has been designed to be enhanced in many ways. Script Menu is one example of how you can manage scripts. Another feature is *scripting additions*. Applications that can be scripted have dictionaries containing the syntax to which they respond. You use a *tell block* to tell a specific application what to do according to its dictionary.

AppleScript itself has commands that it can process. These are normal programming-language types of commands that are found in many languages.

And there is yet a third part of the AppleScript architecture that is important: scripting additions. These are located in /System/Library/ScriptingAdditions. They contain AppleScript syntax dictionaries along with code that executes the necessary instructions. You can use the functionality in scripting additions to add functionality beyond that provided by AppleScript itself and by scriptable applications.

It's rare that you will need to worry about scripting additions; if new ones are needed, they are usually installed automatically with an installer. (If you are still used to moving files around on your computer, remember that under Mac OS X you should really let installers take care of things. "Cleaning up" folders is a prime source of system failure.)

Where to Get Scripts

As you can see from Script Menu, a lot of scripts come with Mac OS X. Scriptable applications often ship with scripts—both demonstration scripts that you can modify and ones that you can use for your own work. A good source of scripts for Adobe products is Adobe Studio Exchange at http://share.studio.adobe.com/.

Probably the best resource for AppleScript is Apple's own AppleScript Web site: http://www.apple.com/applescript. Here you'll find scripts galore as well as links to third-party scripts you can download.

Summary

This hour has provided you with some of the basics of AppleScript: the types of scripts (compiled, applets/applications, and droplets), the locations for scripts (toolbar and Script Menu), and how you can extend AppleScript with scripting additions. You've even seen a few lines of AppleScript code: You'll see much more as the book goes on.

The next hour provides you with a look at the scripts that come installed on Mac OS X. You'll see what they are, what you can do with them, and how you can think about modifying and enhancing them.

Q&A

Q Do you have to restart your computer to add new scripts to Script Menu?

A No, you can add scripts to Script Menu at any time and they will appear.

Q What is the difference between launching a script and launching a regular application?

A None.

Workshop

The workshop contains quiz questions and activities to help you solidify your knowledge of the material in this hour. Try to answer all of the questions before looking at the quiz answers that follow.

Quiz

1. How do you customize the contents of Script Menu?
2. What is the difference between an applet and a droplet?

Quiz Answers

1. Add or remove scripts to or from the /Library/Scripts folder (for the computer) or the ~/Library/Scripts folder (for an individual user).
2. Droplets are applets that are written to interact with a file or folder) that is dropped on them.

Activities

If you haven't done so already, install Script Menu.

Using the Command key, move Script Menu back and forth in the menu bar to change its location.

Add a script to your Finder toolbar. A good one to experiment with is Current Date & Time. You'll find it inside Info Scripts in /Library/Scripts. (The reason this is a good choice is that it only displays data; other scripts rename files and resize images, and until you're more comfortable, you might want to hold off so that you won't change files in ways you don't expect.)

Hour 3

Running the Scripts You Already Have

Over 75 scripts are part of the basic Mac OS X installation in Jaguar. Many of them are installed in Script Menu and are located in /Library/Scripts. Others are part of applications. (iCal, for example, contains four scripts that it uses to send Mail messages to invite people to meetings or to remind you of events.)

This hour shows you each of the Script Menu scripts. It shows you how to use them, and it points out some of the features that you can use in your own scripts when you write them. Remember that each script in this collection comes with its AppleScript code. You can open them in Script Editor to view that code.

Some of the scripts are compiled scripts—with a .scpt extension; those can be double-clicked to open them in Script Editor. Others are saved as applications, but you can open them by dragging them on to the Script Editor icon or by using the Open command from the Script Editor File menu. All scripts in Script Menu—even .scpt compiled scripts—run as applications when you select them in Script Menu.

By the end of this hour, you will have not only seen many of the things that you can do with AppleScript, but you will have discovered new features that are built in to Mac OS X that you may never have known were there!

> The scripts described in this hour are listed in the same groupings that are used in Script Menu. However, in Script Menu the groupings are listed alphabetically. Here, they go from the basic desktop scripts to the Internet scripts and then on to more specific scripts.

In This Hour

- Basics—This is the beginning of your AppleScript adventure. In this section, you'll see how one script works.
- Finder Scripts—Built in to Script Menu are scripts that let you manipulate files and their names. They're described in this section.
- Info Scripts—These scripts use AppleScript's ability to interrogate your computer's environment.
- Internet Services—Moving beyond the desktop, these scripts let you retrieve information from the Internet using Web services.
- Mail Scripts—Mail is a heavily scriptable application. These scripts let you create mail automatically.
- Navigation Scripts—These scripts automatically open Finder windows such as Documents and Applications.
- Script Editor Scripts—Script Editor itself (discussed later in Hour 8, "Introducing Script Editor") is scriptable. These goodies provide fast ways of adding standard code to your scripts.
- Folder Action Scripts—One of the most popular AppleScript features is back. You can be notified when the contents of folders change.
- ColorSync and FontSync Scripts—Finally, these scripts automate vital prepress functions.

Basics

This section presents three scripts that provide a good jumping-off point for learning about AppleScript. The first one opens AppleScript Help, the second takes you to the AppleScript Web site, and the third opens Script Editor.

It's worth taking a look at these scripts, because they can serve as templates for a variety of your own scripts.

Scripting Help Viewer

Help Viewer is the application that displays help for the operating system and applications in Mac OS X. You've probably seen its window, which is shown in Figure 3.1.

FIGURE 3.1

The Help Viewer displays Mac Help.

You can type a word or phrase into the field at the upper right to search for articles relevant to that topic. As you can see in Figure 3.2, a different listing displays the results of that search. In the right-hand column, you can see that Help Viewer has retrieved information from a variety of sources.

FIGURE 3.2

Help Viewer lets you search for help in many locations.

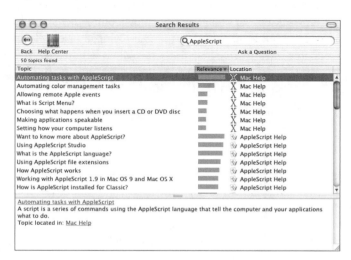

Here's the script for AppleScript Help:

```
tell application "Help Viewer"
  activate
  search looking for "AppleScript"
end tell
```

Although you'll find out more about the full syntax shown here, it's not hard to figure out that what this script does is just what would happen if you typed "AppleScript" into the search field at the upper right of the window.

Want to create an AppleScript to provide information about printers? Change one word so that the third line reads:

```
search looking for "printers"
```

Why would you want to do this? If you're setting up an environment for others to use, you may know how to use Help Viewer, but not everyone else does. Of course you can teach people how to use it, but it might be easier to create several scripts with names such as Printer Help, Network Help, and the like. Then, people need only double-click those scripts (or choose them from Script Menu if they're installed there).

Using Scripts to Navigate the Web

The second script takes you to the AppleScript Web site, and it is only one line long:

```
open location "http://www.apple.com/applescript/"
```

As you can guess, this is exactly the same code that you use to open any Web site in the default browser. If your company has its own online help, you can easily add to Printer Help and Network Help a third script: Our Company Help. These basic scripts require only a double-click to give help to users—albeit help from different types of resources.

Launching an Application with a Script

The third script launches Script Editor; its syntax is the same for any application that you want to launch:

```
tell application "Script Editor" to activate
```

If the application is not running, it is launched. If it is running (either beforehand or as a result of being launched), it is *activated*: brought forward so that it is the frontmost application. When you interact with an application using the mouse and keyboard, it is activated. With AppleScript, you can send commands to an application that is running but not the frontmost process (the equivalent of typing in a window that is behind another window—something you cannot do interactively).

Finder Scripts

The first of the Finder scripts, About Finder Scripts, just puts up the dialog shown in Figure 3.3.

FIGURE 3.3

Scripts can warn you of what they're going to do.

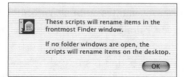

You should be careful running these scripts because they do just what the dialog warns you; they rename selected files in the frontmost window or on the desktop. They're a wonderful way to make wholesale changes in filenames, such as replacing text or shortening them. But after you click OK, they will act on the selected files all together. If you have accidentally left your hard disk icon selected, you could wind up renaming a very large number of files all over your hard disk.

So if you want to experiment with Finder Scripts, create a test file and a test folder, make sure they're selected, and then explore the scripts.

Info Scripts

These two scripts display information in two different ways. Current Date & Time accesses the date, stores it in an AppleScript variable, and displays it in a dialog. This script can serve as a template for storing data in a variable and for using a dialog. Hour 13, "Interacting with Users," is devoted to this type of functionality.

The second script, Font Sampler, displays a standard sentence in each of the installed fonts. (It was shown in Figure 2.2 in Hour 2.) In this case, AppleScript asks another application—TextEdit—to do the data display. It can be used as a template for locating fonts and for setting text and style information in word processing applications.

Internet Services

Sherlock, one of the Apple applications included in Mac OS X, is a wonderful tool for searching the Internet and combining information from a variety of sources in a variety of formats. Movie searches, for example, can show you listings for theaters near a given location and even display QuickTime trailers for the movies.

Sherlock works by taking advantage of a very important new feature of the Web: *Web services*. You are used to using the Web interactively: You click on a link and a new page opens. Often, these are pages written in Hypertext Markup Language (HTML) using text editors or applications such as DreamWeaver or GoLive. However, many pages are built dynamically by applications located on the Web site you are visiting. Such applications are called *application servers* and go by names such as WebSphere (IBM), WebObjects (Apple), and WebLogic (BEA). Even FileMaker can function as an application server. An application server can take a request from a user running a browser and generate an HTML page that is transmitted to the user and displayed by the browser. The actual request is handled with HyperText Transfer Protocol (HTTP)—and you specify it at the beginning of a URL for a Web page as in `http://www.apple.com`.

When the request contains variable information—such as a word or phrase to search for in a search engine—a database is consulted by the application server to provide the information to be returned. The application server merges the information with prepared formatting information, and the HTML is created to be sent to your browser.

Web services take the HTML out of the picture. Instead of sending a request for an HTML page to be returned, an HTTP request is made to return the information. A common way of doing this is to use Simple Object Access Protocol (SOAP), which is an industry-standard for this type of access. It is based on another very important industry standard, extended Markup Language (XML), which is gradually supplanting HTML in many ways.

There is another protocol that is sometimes used, XML Remote Procedure Call (XML-RPC). AppleScript supports both. (Yet another implementation of this type of function is provided by Microsoft in its .Net software, which is still evolving.)

This is a very important advance for Internet processing, and it's a major leap forward for AppleScript. You can sit at your computer and use an online banking Web site to check your balance. If a recent deposit has cleared, you can then decide to pay a bill.

In the United States, most online banking sites update their information after they close the official books of the bank sometime during the evening of each business day. You might not want to wait around for that to happen. You can write a script to check your balance by going to an online banking Web site, but if that script runs automatically in the middle of the night, how will it know whether or not to pay the bill?

With SOAP or XML-RPC, instead of requesting the page with your bank balance, you can request the actual balance itself: a number, not an HTML page. It is very simple for a script to then check if that number is sufficient to cover a payment, and it can then submit the payment—also as a SOAP or XML-RPC request. There is no need for pointing or clicking or for you to read the information displayed on a Web page.

This is a very powerful technology, and it promises many changes in the ways in which Web sites work. For people using AppleScript, it offers an opportunity to retrieve data from the Web and then to pass it on to other applications or back to the Web. This can be done overnight or during the day but without human intervention.

SOAP and XML-RPC work because they are industry standards and because they, like HTML and HTTP, are basically very simple. However, widespread adoption of Web services may take many years—some people have estimated a decade or more. That is because converting many of these systems in banks, corporations, and other large organizations will take time.

If you want to get started with SOAP and XML-RPC, visit `http://www.xmethods.net/`. There you will find a listing of many Web services to which you can link from AppleScript (or any other language that supports the protocols). Looking at the list, you will see various types of services. Some demonstrate random retrieval of information from databases (Joke of the Day, Biblical Quote of the Day, and so forth). Others provide simple verifications of data—you can find one to return whether or not an address in the Netherlands is valid. Still others provide information such as stock quotes or temperatures, and there are yet more services that provide various translation and transfer features (such as those from IBM that convert images from one format to another).

The list of SOAP and XML-RPC services grows daily. Look at the list and you'll get ideas for services that you can use and even for services you might write.

You can look at the two Internet Services scripts to see how this is done: Later, in Hour 22, "Using AppleScript Across a Network," you'll find detailed instructions. But looking at these two scripts will not only give you an overview of how it's done, but will demonstrate a very important feature of AppleScript.

Fully half of each script is identical to the corresponding half of the other one. As you'll see throughout this book, large sections of AppleScript code can be used and reused with minor modifications.

Mail Scripts

Mail is a highly scriptable application. It has to be because applications such as iCal rely on it to send notifications of events via AppleScript. The scripts in Mail Scripts demonstrate the ability to automatically create e-mail messages. Deep in the heart of most of them, you'll find some variation on these lines:

```
tell application "Mail"
  set theSubject to "Test Message"
  set theBody to "This is the message body."
```

```
  set theSender to "yourself@mac.com"
  set theRecipient to "jf@mac.com"
  set newMessage to make new outgoing message with properties ¬
    {subject:theSubject, content:theBody, sender:theSender, visible:true}
  tell newMessage
    make new to recipient at end of to recipients with properties¬
    {name:"Your Friend", address:"friend@mac.com"}
  end tell
  activate
end tell
```

> Lines of AppleScript code are terminated with the Return key. If the code
> requires more than one line, you can continue it on to a second line in Script
> Editor by using the AppleScript continuation character ¬, which is generated
> by the option-l key combination (that's the lowercase letter l, not the
> numeral 1). When you are using AppleScript Studio, Project Builder's format-
> ting handles long lines for you; you simply keep typing and the text will
> wrap onto the next line. At the end of your AppleScript line of code (which
> may span several lines), press Return. In the examples in this book, contin-
> ued lines are presented with the ¬ continuation character so that they can
> be pasted into Script Editor. In Part III, where AppleScript Studio projects are
> presented, the continuation character is not normally shown in the exam-
> ples.

Although AppleScript syntax hasn't been described, you can probably pick out what's
happening here. First, several variables (theSubject, theBody, and so forth) are set to
strings. Then a new message is created, and it is instructed to add a recipient. The reason
for this particular complication is that although a message can have only one subject, it
can have many recipients, and the message needs to manage multiple recipients in a list.

There's another very brief script that uses a different method to create a message. In
Quick Mail, the heart of the script is a single line:

```
open location "mailto:friend@mac.com?subject=Hello"
```

This is the same form of syntax that was used to open the AppleScript Web location.
mailto is as valid an Internet prefix as is http, and so you can use the AppleScript open
location command to create an e-mail message. The difference is that open location is an
AppleScript command, and the previous example required you to use commands recognized by Mail.

Other Mail Scripts use the AppleScript syntax in Mail to report on the status of accounts and mailboxes. Most end by creating an e-mail message that displays the results.

Navigation Scripts

These scripts open common folders—Home, Applications, Favorites, and Documents. The Open Special folder lets you choose from the various folders such as Movies and Pictures that are created automatically in Mac OS X. This script builds a list of folders, and the code at its beginning is an interesting example of how to build an array. (There's more on arrays in Hour 6, "Looking Behind the Scenes: How These Scripts Work.")

Script Editor Scripts

Script Editor scripts are some of the most frequently used control functions and error handlers for scripts. Instead of having to look up or retype these common code snippets, you can simply run these scripts and have the relevant code inserted into the script that you're editing in Script Editor. These will be discussed further in Hour 6.

Folder Action Scripts

Folder actions are one of the most popular features of AppleScript. They are implemented differently on Mac OS X than they were in Mac OS 9, but that rarely concerns you; their purpose is the same.

When scripts are attached to folders, they run automatically when certain events occur. Three standard folder actions are supplied in Mac OS X, and you can add others.

The first folder action lets you know when items have been added to a folder. You receive the notification shown in Figure 3.4, and you have the option to open the folder and see the items highlighted.

FIGURE 3.4

A script can notify you of changes to a folder.

If you're used to working alone at your computer using the keyboard and mouse to control everything that happens, you might wonder why this would matter. But if you're on a network and you allow people to put files into your Public folder, attaching an add action to that folder will keep you updated about their updates about which you would otherwise know nothing.

This is also a useful action to have if you have a background application or script running that will present its results in a file. You can see that it's finished and deal with it whenever you want to.

Another folder action lets you automatically close subfolders when the main folder is closed. If you have folders such as ToDos, Invoices, and Meetings inside your Documents folder, all of them would be closed when you close your Documents folder if you attach such an action to Documents.

Finally, you can use a folder action to display a comment when the folder is opened. Figure 3.5 shows a comment that you can type into the Info box.

FIGURE 3.5

You can type a comment into a folder's Info box.

If you attach an open folder action to that folder, the comment will be displayed whenever the folder is opened, as you can see in Figure 3.6.

FIGURE 3.6

A folder action can show the comment in a dialog when the folder is opened.

To use folder actions at all, you need to enable them on your computer. From Script Menu, use Enable (or Disable) Folder Actions to turn them on and off.

To attach folder actions to a specific folder, use Attach Folder Action. To remove one, use Remove Folder Action. The convenience script, Edit Folder Action, opens the selected folder's action in Script Editor.

You can create your own folder actions to be added to folders by placing them in the Folder Action Scripts subfolder inside either of the two Scripts folders (/Library/Scripts and ~/Library/Scripts).

When you write your own folder actions, you should know that in addition to the three actions that can trigger scripts described previously (open, close, and add), there are two others. You can be notified if items are removed from a folder; you can also be notified if a folder window is moved.

ColorSync and FontSync Scripts

Lastly, these scripts let you take advantage of the tools you need to fix color and to work with fonts in a prepress environment.

Summary

This hour has provided you an overview of the built-in scripts from Apple. You've seen what they are and how to run them. In addition, several of the features of scripting that they demonstrate have been pointed out so that you can see the possibilities of AppleScript.

But there's more from Apple; the next chapter identifies well over a hundred scripts you can download and shows you how to use them.

Q&A

Q Can I modify the built-in scripts?

A Yes, you can open any of the scripts in Script Editor and modify them. If you do, you should make a copy of the script first so that you can go back to it.

Q Can I create new Folder Action scripts?

A Yes, but you cannot create a new folder action. In other words, you can create new scripts that respond to open, close, add, remove, and move window events. But you cannot, for example, create a folder action that is invoked when the folder is renamed.

Workshop

The workshop contains quiz questions and activities to help you solidify your knowledge of the material in this hour. Try to answer all of the questions before looking at the quiz answers that follow.

Quiz

1. Does Mail have to be running to use the Mail scripts?
2. How do you start folder action scripts?

Quiz Answers

1. Any application that is the target of a tell block needs to be running for it to work. AppleScript will launch it if necessary.
2. Use the Folder Actions submenu of the Script Menu to attach actions to the selected folder in the Finder. Thereafter, the folder action scripts are triggered automatically by your interaction with the folder.

Activities

Experiment with the built-in scripts, but remember the caution that the Finder scripts rename selections and can rename all the files in a folder if that is what is selected.

Create a folder and attach Folder Action scripts to it. See what happens as you move files in and out. Think of the folders you normally use that would benefit from having Folder Actions attached to them.

HOUR 4

Getting New Scripts from Apple and Running Them

The scripts described in this hour can be downloaded for free from various parts of the Apple Web site (http://www.apple.com/applescript); you'll find out how to get them in this hour. These scripts include demonstration scripts as well as add-ons and support for major Apple tools. You can use them as is, or base your own scripts on them.

Some of the scripts extend an application's functionality; others merge several applications together. Still others automate repetitive processes so that you can use a single mouse click (or a single drag-and-drop) to step through the process. In short, they do what AppleScript does all the time.

There are literally hundreds of scripts in these collections. In this hour, you won't find all of them. What you will find are key scripts from each of the collections. They're key scripts in some cases because they're ones you might use very often, and in other cases, they're key scripts because they demonstrate features—or use aspects of AppleScript—that you may want to use in other scripts.

Over time, new scripts are added to Apple's Web site. When you explore these scripts, you are very likely to find new treasures to experiment with.

In This Hour

- The iPhoto Collection—Enables you to interact with iPhoto files and move photos to other applications.
- The iDVD Collection—The iDVD companion provides control over the iDVD interface. Other scripts let you quickly convert movies and images to iDVD as content or backgrounds.
- The iTunes Collection—These scripts can control iTunes and your iPod.
- The QuickTime Collection—Use these scripts to play QuickTime movies as well as to convert among various file formats.
- The Toolbar Scripts—These scripts control the Finder; you can easily place them in the toolbar of your Finder windows.

The iPhoto Collection

The iPhoto collection is downloadable from `http://www.apple.com/applescript/iphoto/`. A few of the scripts use Photoshop, but many of them demonstrate the ways in which you can work simply with the Apple-provided applications.

> iPhoto 2, released as part of the iLife suite in January 2003, is directly scriptable. iPhoto 1 was not scriptable. If you need to upgrade, you can purchase iLife or you can download iPhoto from `http://www.apple.com/iphoto`.

Photo Summary

Select some photos in iPhoto and run the Photo Summary script. It will produce a Text-Edit document containing small versions of the images as well as information about them from iPhoto. It opens the resulting summary in Text Edit, as shown in Figure 4.1.

FIGURE 4.1

Photo Summary provides information about selected iPhoto images.

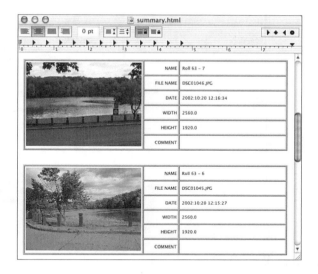

The information displayed here comes from three sources:

- Date, time, and exposure information comes automatically from your digital camera. If your iPhoto images are not downloaded from a camera or if your camera does not support this information, it will not be included.
- The filename for the image file is provided automatically by iPhoto.
- The comments are yours; the name of the photo is yours if you have supplied it. Otherwise it is the iPhoto default name.

Show Image File

iPhoto stores its images inside its own folders with its own naming convention. You can use iPhoto to export files to other formats and locations, but you can also use Show Image File to identify a specific image's file.

Select a photo within iPhoto. Then, run the script. It will locate the file on disk and highlight it in a Finder window. As you can see in Figure 4.2, the names are not intuitive, so this is a great way of locating files for images. You can then copy them or remove them. (You can do both tasks from inside iPhoto, too.)

Photo to iDVD Background

This script lets you select a photo in iPhoto and then import it into iDVD as a background. All you have to do is select the photo and then run the script: Everything else is taken care of for you automatically. This script is an example of how you can use AppleScript to tie two applications together.

FIGURE 4.2
Show Image File locates iPhoto images in the Finder.

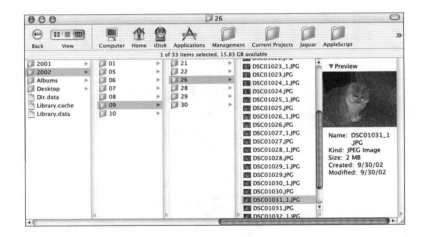

The iDVD Collection

The iDVD collection is available at `http://www.apple.com/applescript/idvd/`. Some of the scripts are described here; feel free to explore the others for new ideas both for your DVDs and for new scripts.

iDVD Companion

The iDVD Companion is an application developed using AppleScript Studio (which is the topic of Part III, "Working with AppleScript Studio"). You can download the application as well as the entire AppleScript Studio project so that you can see how it was developed.

iDVD Companion provides a floating controller to help you tweak your DVD interface. There are three tabs in the controller; the first one is shown in Figure 4.3.

FIGURE 4.3
Use the iDVD Companion controller to nudge interface elements.

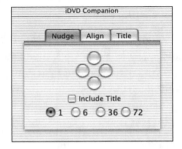

Select one or more interface elements and then move them by using the four buttons on the controller. The radio buttons at the bottom let you set the number of pixels by which to nudge the interface elements.

The next tab, Align, is shown in Figure 4.4. Select two or more buttons and align their left, right, top, or bottom edges by clicking the appropriate button in the controller window.

FIGURE 4.4

Align interface elements.

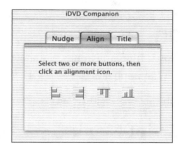

Finally, use the Title tab (shown in Figure 4.5) to set the position of the title on your menu. You can type in the pixel offset from the top-left corner of the screen. If your design features a centered title, this is unnecessary. However, if your iDVD design features a title that is left justified and placed in the same place for several projects, the Title tab will help you achieve consistency.

FIGURE 4.5

Locate the title.

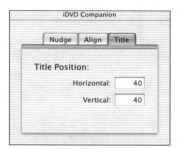

4

Create DVD from Folders, Photos, and More

A number of scripts in the iDVD collection let you drop folders, images, photos, and music onto droplets. They are automatically imported into an open iDVD project.

One of the most powerful is Create DVD from Folder. Set up a folder with movies, photos, and music in it—even arrange them in subfolders if you want. Then, drag the folder onto Create DVD from Folder. It will create the menus for the subfolders and all of the files for you. This is a very quick way to produce a DVD that is mainly for backup purposes. It also works well as a way to capture a project quickly and export it to DVD. Of course, you can always use iDVD to fine tune the default implementation that is created automatically.

Other Scripts

A variety of other scripts let you further manipulate iDVD. In particular, look at Example Scripts, which contains most of the basic AppleScript commands for iDVD.

The iTunes Collection

The iTunes collection is very extensive. It demonstrates yet another aspect of AppleScript: adding a Script menu to an application.

The iTunes collection is located at `http://www.apple.com/applescript/itunes/`.

Installing the iTunes Script Menu

When you download the iTunes scripts, you'll find a folder called Put Contents in Library Folder as shown in Figure 4.6.

FIGURE **4.6**

Add Put Contents in Library Folder to the iTunes folder.

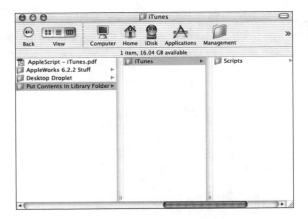

Drag the Scripts subfolder into the iTunes folder that's inside the Library folder in your Home directory. (Do not drag the downloaded iTunes folder into the Library folder because it may overwrite an existing folder there. You just want to move the Scripts sub-folder as shown in Figure 4.7.)

The next time you launch iTunes, a Script menu will appear in the menu bar. If you have Script Menu installed, it will appear at the right of the menu bar; the application Script menu appears with the other application menus at the left (along with File, Edit, and so forth).

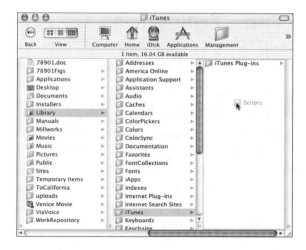

FIGURE 4.7

*Add scripts to your
iTunes Library folder.*

Looking Up Artists on eMusic

Among the iTunes scripts are three that demonstrate how you can integrate a scriptable application on your desktop with the Web. You can select a track in iTunes and then choose from scripts that let you search the emusic.com Web site for the artist, song title, or album that you have selected.

This works because the AppleScript dictionary for iTunes defines properties for artist, song title, and album for the track class. (You'll learn more about this in Part II, "Writing Scripts with Script Editor.") You place the artist name (or album or song title) into a variable and then execute the line of code shown here. (It is split into several lines for readability.)

As long as you know how the search should be structured on the Web site, it's often just a matter of inserting one word or phrase into boilerplate text.

```
set the search_URL to "http://www.emusic.com/aasearch.html?¬
  rtype=search_art&searchterm=" & ¬
  encoded_artist & ¬
 "&cid=emusic"
```

Other Scripts

Other iTunes scripts let you control playback, manage your library, and work with an iPod.

The QuickTime Collection

Perhaps the largest collection of scripts, the QuickTime collection numbers well over a hundred scripts and droplets. It can be downloaded from `http://www.apple.com/applescript/quicktime/`.

The EMBED Tag Wizard Script

If you want to add a QuickTime movie to a Web page, it's not a particularly onerous task. You have to write some basic HTML, which most people copy from the last HTML they wrote to put their last QuickTime movie onto a Web page.

But it's much easier to use the EMBED Tag Wizard script. Double-click it, and it will walk you through the commands and generate the HTML for you. It will place the resulting code on the clipboard or in a file that you specify.

The EMBED Tag Wizard script is an example of using AppleScript to perform a routine but complex operation that has to be done correctly.

The SMIL Suite

This set of scripts lets you work with Synchronized Multimedia Integration Language (SMIL) and with QuickTime. Based on XML, SMIL lets you vastly extend basic QuickTime movies on the Web.

For example, you can add an image or text to your movie. The image or text will appear in front of the movie and it can be hot—a link to another Web page. You can also use a script to create a SMIL slide show.

The SMIL suite is similar to the EMBED Tag Wizard in that it performs a routine but complex operation for you quickly and easily.

Other Scripts

The vast number of other QuickTime scripts let you manipulate playback, create movies, and manipulate movies. They are good examples to use to learn about AppleScript code.

The Toolbar Scripts

Finally, the Toolbar scripts let you script the Finder. This set of about two dozen scripts provides many fill-in features that help to extend the Finder and the desktop. You can drag these scripts into the toolbar in a Finder window so that they're always available.

You can download them from `http://www.apple.com/applescript/toolbar`.

Customizing Your Desktop (Snapshot and Set View Options)

These scripts provide features that many people wanted to have in the Mac OS X Finder and that were not provided directly by the Finder code for one reason or another. Scripts can be an excellent way of extending and enhancing an application and its interface. One reason for extending and enhancing the application with scripts is because the functionality may be idiosyncratic—important only to a small group of people (perhaps only yourself).

Snapshot is a script that identifies the windows you have open and stores their location. You can then run the script to restore those windows to their sizes and locations. When you double-click Snapshot, it asks you if you want to take a snapshot or restore windows.

This is a simple way of customizing your interface—or, from the other perspective—uncustomizing it. If you're running a computer lab, maybe you want a script like Snapshot to run and restore the computers to a known state.

Set View Options sets the options for the frontmost window or the window that's dragged onto it. Those options are stored inside the script, and you can edit them with Script Editor. You can copy this script and make several versions. That way, you can have a Set View Options Columns script that sets up precisely the way you want a Columns view window to look; another one can fine tune an Icons view window.

Image Manipulation Scripts

Image manipulation scripts let you resize or rotate images. You can also use Browse Images to create an HTML page in your browser that shows and identifies images by name.

The scripts discussed in this chapter all have different uses; many of them were also used to demonstrate various aspects of AppleScript. The image manipulation scripts perform that task, too. They use routines that are far down in the operating system (in what is called Core Foundation). These routines operate on images; they are accessed interactively through the Image Capture application.

Inside the ScriptingAdditions folder, a small application called Image Capture Scripting is installed. It is scriptable (unlike Image Capture itself), and it provides access to the Core Foundation routines. You don't have to worry about this. However, if you're a developer, you may want to explore the possibilities of making your application scriptable either directly or through Scripting Additions.

Summary

In this hour, you've seen a few of the scripts you can get from Apple for free. Many of them add functionality to the individual iLife products (iPhoto, iDVD, and iTunes); others help to integrate those applications with one another and with others. How much of your time is spent actually writing text and organizing images—and how much is spent moving data around in order to begin writing text and organizing images? The first task requires your own imagination, but the second—the preparation and setup chores—is ideal for AppleScript.

In addition to scripts from Apple, literally thousands of scripts are available on the Internet, most of them free. The next hour explores some of those scripts and shows you where you can obtain them.

Q&A

Q Why doesn't Apple just build functionality into its applications instead of relying on scripts?

A There are several reasons. The first is that when you use scripts to develop work flows and perform tasks, you can swap scriptable applications in and out. As you can see from the sample scripts on Apple's site, you can use iPhoto as a photo editor—or you can use Photoshop (which is also scriptable). You'll see in the last part of this book how you can place the output from a script in a product such as InDesign or TextEdit.

The second reason is that when you are developing software that integrates two applications, it's cleaner to write a script that is independent of both of them. That way, if either application changes, only the script needs to change—not another application.

Q I think my modification to an Apple-provided script is useful and other people might like it. Where do I go from here?

A To the next hour. Not only will you see how to download scripts, but you'll find sites that are eager to distribute your scripts. The AppleScript community shares a lot of scripts, and you'll find that the Apple scripts form the core of many specialized and sophisticated scripts.

Workshop

The workshop contains quiz questions and activities to help you solidify your knowledge of the material in this hour. Try to answer all of the questions before looking at the quiz answers that follow.

Quiz

1. What is the difference between the Script menu at the left of the menu bar (in iTunes and other applications) and the Script menu at the right of the menu bar?

2. Where does the information in the Photo Summary script come from?

Quiz Answers

1. A Script menu at the left of the menu bar is part of an application's scripting world. It contains scripts only for that application. You'll find such menus in iTunes (if you install the scripts described here).

2. It comes from your digital camera (date, time, and exposure information) as well as from your comments.

Activities

Create a slide show.

Create a movie of your photos.

Apple's Web browser, Safari, has scripts available for it. Download them from `http://www.apple.com/applescript/safari/` and explore their use.

Go to `http://www.apple.com/applescript/apps/` to see a summary of all of the scriptable applications from Apple. Click any one of them to see the scripts that are available. Download and experiment with any that interest you.

4

Hour **5**

Third-party Scripts and Applications That Simplify Your Life

In the previous hour, you saw how to get new scripts from Apple. In this hour, you'll find an introduction to resources on the Web from which you can get other scripts. Many of them are free, some are shareware, and some come with price tags.

In This Hour

- Sites for Scripts—Here are the major AppleScript resources on the Web for literally thousands of scripts—and most of them are free.
- Utility Scripts—A few of the scripts you can download are described here. They're shown to give you an idea of the types of scripts that are available.

Sites for Scripts

A number of sites provide scripts you can use. Most of the scripts are free. Many come with the source code visible so that you can modify them and learn from them.

AppleScript Central

AppleScript Central (`http://www.applescriptcentral.com/`) contains several hundred scripts that are downloadable without charge. The scripts provide all sorts of integration and automation add-ons to applications such as Mail, Entourage, and the other Microsoft Office tools (Safari, Eudora, AOL Instant Messenger, Quark XPress, and more).

AppleScript Info

As you can see from the URL (`http://radio.weblogs.com/0103146/`), this is a blog (Web log). In addition to its continual updates, it contains excellent links to many other AppleScript sites. Figure 5.1 shows part of AppleScript Info.

Do You Blog?

Blogs (short for Web logs) are a relatively new development on the Web. They are Web pages that are updated frequently—often more than once a day—using software that automatically formats text and graphics into prepared templates. Instead of writing raw HTML, the blog author typically uses a Web browser that displays a form in which you can enter a title and text. This is uploaded to a Web site. The resulting blog page may contain a number of such items; many blogs allow for comments and discussions by readers.

As was the case with the Web itself at the beginning, many blogs are personal "what-I-did-today" and "what-my-opinions-are" ruminations. The ease of posting information makes it simple to do this.

That ease of posting also makes it easy to keep the sites up to date. That's why a site such as AppleScript Info can be kept current.

In addition to personal blogs, blogs are used to update information on computer availability at data centers, to distribute and comment on news, and in general to provide anything that needs frequent updating.

Many blogging software products automatically create RSS outputs: XML descriptions of what has changed on the site recently. Many bloggers (blog authors) subscribe to RSS feeds to keep up with what is happening on other blogs and news sources in which they are interested. Thus, information can be disseminated and commented on very quickly.

You can find out more about blogging at—where else?—the author's blog, which is located at `http://www.pickwickpixels.com`.

FIGURE 5.1
*AppleScript Info is
a blog.*

FIGURE 5.1
*AppleScript Info is
a blog.*

Note in particular the first item, a notice of changes to NetNewsWire. NetNewsWire is an RSS reader. An RSS reader (sometimes called a *news aggregator*) checks Web sites to which you subscribe and displays recently changed items. The headline, text, and a link to the item are shown. The NetNewsWire window, similar to the interface of other news aggregators, is shown in Figure 5.2. At the left, a list of subscriptions is displayed. You select a subscription, and the recent changes are shown in the panel at the right.

FIGURE 5.2
*NetNewsWire is an
RSS reader for the
Macintosh.*

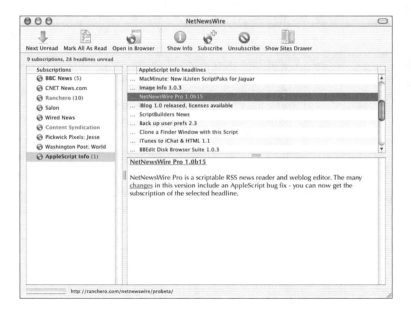

5

NetNewsWire is shown at this point for two reasons. The first is that among the RSS-enabled Web sites to which it lets you subscribe is AppleScript Info. (Radio Userland blogs—like most blogs—are automatically published with RSS subscriptions.) Thus, if you want to subscribe to AppleScript Info using NetNewsWire or another aggregator, you'll get a list of the recent updates to AppleScript Info. This can keep you up to date on what's going on in the AppleScript community, including listings of many new scripts you can download from a variety of sources.

The second reason that NetNewsWire is presented here is that it is a scriptable application.

Do you notice a circularity here? AppleScript Info begets an RSS feed, which is retrieved by NetNewsWire and which, in turn, you can control with AppleScript.

Nothing prevents you from writing a script to retrieve information from NetNewsWire and passing it on either via e-mail or iChat—or even your own Web page or blog. After two decades of point-and-click control of personal computers, automation is coming to the desktop. AppleScript has been a prominent player in the desktop automation world, and in its new features on Mac OS X continues to be a major player along with advanced technologies such as Mac OS X itself and standards such as RSS.

In the last few years, these forces (desktop automation, advanced technologies, and cross-platform standards) have allowed innovative developers to write relatively small applications that address very specific needs. Blogs themselves are a perfect example of very sophisticated technology that builds on standards-based building blocks and that in and of itself is relatively simple.

You'll see later in this book how to use AppleScript to blend applications together. Until now, many of the most compelling examples of such application integration have been in workflow solutions. Now, the most compelling examples of application integration are being found in fields such as RSS syndication and new forms of information dispersal.

AppleScript Sourcebook

AppleScript Sourcebook (`http://www.applescriptsourcebook.com/`) has been in existence for a number of years. It can be a valuable reference to AppleScript history as well as to older scripts.

macscripter.net

The macscripter.net site (`http://macscripter.net/`) is an excellent source of news articles, bulletin board discussions, and a vast array of scripts. The collection of almost a thousand scripts is searchable and provides a host of scripts that you can use either as is or as the basis for your own scripts. (Some scripts are run-only.)

The scripts are organized by category; the following list gives you an idea of the scripts on the site:

- E-Mail
- Finder-System
- Mac OS X
- Multimedia
- Publishing
- Quark XPress
- Script Tools
- Utilities
- WWW

ScriptWeb

Like AppleScript Sourcebook, ScriptWeb (`http://www.scriptweb.org/`) contains information that is not only current, but also includes a variety of historical links.

Utility Scripts

Literally thousands of scripts are available on the Internet. Many are small scripts focusing on very specific issues. A large number are free, some are shareware, and some have a price. A number of suites and packages of scripts are available as well; these frequently are priced products.

These particular scripts have been chosen because they illustrate the range of functionality that AppleScript and Apple events (the underlying technology) can provide.

- iPhoto Librarian—This is an example of a third-party script that adds functionality to an application (in this case, iPhoto from Apple).
- MacSQL—This application shows how a scriptable application can make non-scriptable applications and databases scriptable.

5

- Cronathon—This is an example of an AppleScript that allows you to run the underlying UNIX commands at the heart of Mac OS X without knowing anything about them.
- email.cgi—This script provides form parsing and e-mail generation for a Web browser. It's an example of how you can use AppleScript to write browser additions.
- acgi Dispatcher—This application lets you run AppleScript code from Apache in Mac OS X.

iPhoto Librarian

This script, from Scruffy Software (`http://www.scruffyware.com/products.html`), lets you use multiple iPhoto Library folders and switch among them.

MacSQL

This tool makes a wide variety of databases scriptable. If you are running FrontBase, Microsoft SQL Server, MySQL, Oracle, PostgreSQL, and ODBC (Mac OS 9 only), you can use MacSQL to issue queries and view schema information. It's developed by Runtime Labs, and is described on their site at `http://www.rtlabs.com/macsql/`.

Cronathon

Cronathon, by Thomas Richard of NoName Software (`http://www.nonamescriptware.com/`), runs the periodic background tasks that Mac OS X normally runs automatically overnight. If your computer is turned off or asleep overnight, those tasks won't run.

Running Cronathon on a computer that has been used for a year and that has not been left on overnight (thus not running the periodic scripts) can have significant results. In one test case, 50 megabytes of disk space were reclaimed.

email.cgi

Erik Lease Morgan of Infomotions, Inc. has written email.cgi, which uses AppleScript to parse forms and send e-mail. It's available at `http://www.infomotions.com/email-cgi/`.

acgi Dispatcher

Dispatcher allows the Apache Web server (distributed as part of Mac OS X) to dispatch Apple events. James Sentman is the author; more details are available at `http://www.sentman.com/acgi/`.

Summary

This hour has provided you with an overview of some of the third-party tools and scripts available for your use. Because AppleScript is a mature technology, there are many scripts available. A large number of them come with the source code itself available: You can use them as tutorials or modify them for your own purposes.

The Web sites described here almost all allow you to share your own scripts with other people. If you have a new idea or a little tweak to a process that you've scripted, share it with others.

Q&A

Q Are there risks in using third-party scripts?

A It's always a good idea to test software of any kind before using it. For scripts that simply make your life easier, testing can be straightforward. If you're going to build your business or life around shareware, make sure you test it thoroughly and make sure that it will be around. And do pay your shareware fees; they enable the developers to keep their code up to date.

Workshop

The workshop contains quiz questions and activities to help you solidify your knowledge of the material in this hour. Try to answer all of the questions before looking at the quiz answers that follow.

Quiz

1. Does Apple review the scripts and news items on third-party sites?
2. When you download third-party scripts, can you always examine the code before you run it?

Quiz Answers

1. Apple's "review" is limited to periodically checking that unreleased proprietary information is not disseminated. Scripts and news items are provided "as is."
2. No. Some downloadable scripts are run-only. (This is usually indicated in the description.)

Activities

Look at the Web sites in this chapter to see the sorts of scripts that are available. For applications that you use frequently, use the Search feature available on most of the Web sites to look for scripts you might be interested in.

Make a note that as you become more adept at AppleScript, you should share some of your scripts with other users via these Web sites.

Hour 6

Looking Behind the Scenes: How These Scripts Work

So far, you've only run scripts, not written them. This hour examines the concepts and structures of these scripts in a high-level way. Previously you've seen snippets of code, and there have also been indications of how the scripts use various techniques to get their work done.

In this hour, you'll learn about the structure of scripts. The major organizational structures are described, and you'll see how they impact the running of a script and what it can do. In the next hour, you'll look deeper into some of the programming concepts behind AppleScript. All of this will prepare you for working with Script Editor in the next part of this book.

The process involves looking at scripts at the highest level (in this hour), and then proceeding deeper and deeper into them. When you actually start writing your own scripts in the next part of the book, you'll understand how things will fit together.

In This Hour

- Blocks—These are the basic building blocks of all programs including AppleScript programs. You'll need to know what they are and how they work in order to read the scripts that you see.

- Subroutines—AppleScript uses subroutines to do its work. You create subroutines so that your code is organized and so that you and others can write easy-to-understand code that does your bidding.

- Handlers—Handlers are subroutines that are invoked by AppleScript automatically at predefined times—such as when a script starts up. The handlers are defined here, and you will see why droplets don't run (in the technical sense).

- Recursive Processing—Finally, this section will show you a feature of subroutines that may give you an unpleasant surprise unless you're ready for it.

Blocks

You can write scripts that simply contain AppleScript statements one after another (or perhaps only one). This is how many people start out. However, if you are going to write scripts of any complexity, and if you want to write scripts according to the best practices of programming style, you will want to use *blocks*.

A block of code (in any language) is a set of lines that are executed one after another unless some variation occurs as a result either of an error or of a test carried out during the block of code. (A dialog with two choices for a user to click is such a test.)

Each programming language has its own syntax for delimiting a block of code. In AppleScript, blocks of code usually start with tell, on, or to; and then end with the word end.

Here is a very simple block of code as you could type it into Script Editor:

```
tell application "Finder"
  activate
end tell
```

In Script Editor, the end and the tell are automatically aligned, colored, and shown in bold when you compile or check syntax.

Blocks of code not only organize your code, but they allow you to create structured syntax that can be reused and easily understood. Two types of blocks are described here: subroutines and handlers.

Subroutines

You can create *subroutines*, which are special types of blocks. A subroutine has a name and it may have *parameters*—values or variables that it processes.

Using Parameters in Subroutines

Here is a subroutine that calculates area from length and width:

```
on area given length:l, width:w
  return l * w
end area
```

You can write this another way—a way that may be more familiar to you from other programming languages:

```
on area(l, w)
   return l * w
end area
```

AppleScript is designed to be like a natural language, so the first way of writing the subroutine allows you to later use it in a simple manner. Here is how you could cause the subroutine to be executed:

```
area given width:3, length:2
```

To use the second form of syntax, you would need to write:

```
area (l, w)
```

The difference is that the preferred way of writing uses labeled parameters; as long as you supply the labels, you can enter the parameters in any order. The second way requires that the parameters be entered in a constant order. (Note that the method of using labeled parameters also makes it easy to omit parameters that won't be needed. Unlike some other languages, AppleScript does not require all the parameters to be provided.)

Using Prepositions with Parameters

There is a further refinement to the use of labeled parameters: You get one parameter that, although unlabeled, can be preceded by a preposition. You can thus create a subroutine that is defined as

```
on checkdigit for accountNumber
```

This subroutine could take an account number and perform the arithmetic operations involved in checking whether its final digit (the check digit) is correct—thereby suggesting that the entire account number is correct.

6

If you use this style, you get only one parameter that can be preceded by a preposition (you can follow it with any number of labeled parameters). The prepositions you can use are about, above, against, apart, from, around, aside from, at, below, beneath, beside, between, by, for, from, instead of, into, on, onto, out of, over, since, thru (or through), and under.

You could also define this subroutine as

```
on checkdigit given accountNumber:theAccount
```

The fuss over these forms of subroutine definitions comes from one of the primary aspects of AppleScript: It is designed to let you use its syntax to produce a new linguistic syntax that people can use naturally in writing their own scripts. In choosing names for subroutines and the ways in which you define the parameters, don't think of the subroutine you're writing; instead, think of what way it will be used. If you allow a script writer (including yourself) to write

```
checkdigit for accountNumber
```

you begin to create syntax that is natural, easy to remember, and easy to use.

 Many programmers revert naturally to the unlabeled form of subroutines. In part, this is because they are used to that way of working. Also, a programmer who switches among several languages might try to use the most common syntax available. If you are working primarily with AppleScript—and particularly if your code will be shared with others—opt for the most intelligible format, which usually is labeled parameters.

As the code in the subroutine suggests, it returns a value. You can invoke the subroutine in the ways shown here, but that will not do anything with the result that is returned. It will simply be discarded. To use the subroutine as it was designed to be used, you can take the return value and place it in a variable, as in

```
set x to area given width:3, length:2
```

Why bother with all this? The most common reason is that you can define a subroutine once in a script and then use it repeatedly. You will often find subroutines that handle utility conversions (such as Unicode to plain text) called repeatedly throughout a script. Furthermore, by placing those common routines in a subroutine, you can embed that same subroutine in many scripts.

Without knowing anything more about AppleScript, you can now look back over the scripts that have been described and see their structure. It's not hard to find the subroutines, especially because Script Editor indents them and colors them.

Normally, subroutines are located either at the beginning or end of AppleScript files. That's not a requirement; rather, it's an individual preference of the person creating the file. It makes it easier to read the file when all subroutines are together.

Handlers

Subroutines are *handlers*: They handle a command that consists of the name of the subroutine along with any parameters that are used in the subroutine. Certain commands are built in to AppleScript and you can write handlers to support them. The difference between a handler and a subroutine is that with a subroutine, you define the subroutine and also invoke it; with a handler, you define the handler and it is invoked when AppleScript chooses to do so. (AppleScript documentation makes subroutines a special case of handlers.)

There are four basic handlers that AppleScript can invoke: run, quit, open, and idle. They are described in this section, and you'll see more details about them when specific code is described in Part II. More handlers are described in AppleScript Studio: They are invoked as a result of actions such as mouse clicks in the interface as well as when interface elements are loaded at runtime.

Run

When a script is run, its run handler is invoked. If you write a handler named run, that code is what will be executed. For most simple scripts, a run handler is the same as the script. In other words, these two scripts function identically:

```
on run
  beep
end run

beep
```

Using a run handler makes your script easier to read. But it also lets you distinguish between an applet and a droplet. In order to discuss run handlers further, it is important to look at how you save and then run scripts.

When you save a script in Script Editor, the Save dialog shown in Figure 6.1 appears. (Depending on the format you choose in the second pop-up button, the bottom of the dialog will change.)

6

FIGURE 6.1
The Save dialog lets you select a name and format for your script files.

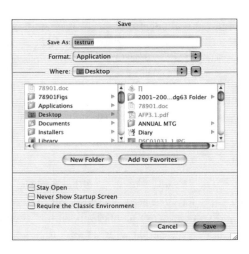

In the Format pop-up menu, you can choose the saved format. If you save it as a compiled script, double-clicking it will open it in Script Editor. You can then run it by clicking the Run button in the script window.

If you save it as an application, double-clicking it will launch the script and show the window that appears in Figure 6.2

FIGURE 6.2
The Run dialog is shown for compiled scripts.

If you choose Never Show Startup Screen, the window shown in Figure 6.2 does not appear, and the script begins to run right away.

In each of these cases, you run the script and the run handler is executed. But what happens if you save the script as an application and drop documents, folders, or disks on it?

Open

The open handler is invoked when you drop documents, folders, or disks on a compiled script. The run handler is not invoked in these cases. In a number of the scripts provided by Apple, this distinction is used to let you set preferences. If you double-click the script, the run handler is invoked and you are queried for preferences. If you drop something onto the script, those preferences are used to carry out an action.

The open handler is what lets you distinguish between an applet and a droplet: Both are compiled scripts, but the droplet has an open handler. In fact, droplets (with open handlers) can also be applets (with run handlers).

The open handler has a single parameter, which is a list of the items dropped on to it. Later, in Hour 7, "Basic Programming Concepts," you'll see how to handle lists of items. For now, just appreciate the fact that the open handler has access to the items dropped on to it and can access the data within them.

Idle

If you look back at Figure 6.1, you can see that one of the choices at the bottom is Stay Open. This means that when the script finishes running—either at the end of its code or at the end of its open or run handler, it remains active. In that case, its icon appears in the Dock, and its menu bar is visible. It continues to run until you choose Quit from its application menu (or until you click a button on its interface that causes it to quit).

In this way, you can keep a script running. It can wait for further input. It can periodically check to see if something has happened. The idle handler is what takes care of this. It is called periodically while the script is running, and you can place code in the idle handler to check whatever issue you want to know about, such as, "Is a file present?" "Has a sequence of events finished?" and the like.

Quit

Finally, the quit handler is called (as you might expect) when the script receives a Quit command—either from the user or when the script is finished running. This is the place where you can execute clean-up operations, bid the user farewell, and otherwise exit the script cleanly.

Recursive Processing

As you begin to work with subroutines, there's one feature you should be aware of (it is a feature, not a bug, but the first time you hit it you might not realize this). Subroutines can call other subroutines; they can even call themselves. When a subroutine calls itself, it executes the code just as if it had been called by another subroutine. Then, when it hits the place where it calls itself, it calls itself again—for a third time, then a fourth, and so on.

There are times when you want to call a subroutine *recursively* (as this is called). However, sometimes a typo means that you accidentally call a subroutine in this way. If you do, the script will appear to freeze as it continuously calls itself over and over. This is called an *infinite loop*. (If you're a collector of trivia, you may like to add to your collection the fact that when Apple built its headquarters in Cupertino, California, the new street on which it was located was named Infinite Loop. Apple's corporate address is 1 Infinite Loop, Cupertino, CA 95014.)

When you have a subroutine that is deliberately designed for recursive processing, it must have some method to stop those calls. In the next hour, you'll see how conditional statements can help you do this.

Summary

The concepts in this hour are the basics of all programming languages. Rather than start with simple lines of code, the technical hours begin with this chapter that helps you look at scripts—even the biggest ones—and see how they're organized.

Q&A

Q How different is AppleScript syntax from that of other programming languages?

A AppleScript uses a highly structured syntax that is similar to that used in most modern programming languages.

Q Does it really matter if I use labeled parameters?

A Many people hold the position that you are writing not for the user (who actually never sees your code) but for the programmer who—years from now—may need to modify your code. For that reason, it should be as clear and understandable as possible. Labeled parameters help meet that goal.

Workshop

The workshop contains quiz questions and activities to help you solidify your knowledge of the material in this hour. Try to answer all of the questions before looking at the quiz answers that follow.

Quiz

1. After a script starts to run, you have no control over it. (True or false?)
2. Do you have to identify scripts as droplets before saving them?
3. Prepositional parameters (preceded by of, from, and so forth) are equivalent to labeled parameters (preceded by given). (True or false?)

Quiz Answers

1. False. If you have a `run` handler, you can control what happens as the script starts up.

2. No. A droplet is defined when you add an `open` handler to it.

3. False. You can only have one prepositional parameter, and it must precede any labeled parameters.

Activities

Look at the scripts in `/Library/Scripts` by opening them in Script Editor. See if you can identify the subroutines and handlers (hint: they're indented automatically and color-coded).

Take one of the longer scripts such as Stock Quote and lay out its structure. On a piece of paper, list the handlers and subroutines; from their names you can probably tell what they do. Go back to the full script and see where each handler and subroutine is called.

Drag a photo (or any TIFF, PICT, or JPEG file) onto Mail iPhoto Images to see how an e-mail message is created. Then quit. Now, double-click Mail iPhoto Images and see how you are prompted to set preferences. Open Mail iPhoto Images in Script Editor. Look at the `run` and `open` handlers to see how these different behaviors are implemented.

6

HOUR 7

Basic Programming Concepts

This hour introduces the control mechanisms that programmers use in writing programs. Whereas the previous hour looked at the overall structure of a script with blocks, subroutines, and handlers, this hour looks within those architectural elements to see what happens inside them.

These concepts are common to all scripting and programming languages. After you have mastered them, you'll be ready to proceed into the next part of the book to look at individual lines of AppleScript code, which you combine into the elements you have seen in the previous hour and in this one.

In This Hour

- Units of Control and Definition—Scripts can get very long and complex. One way of managing the complexity is to use subroutines and handlers and to limit where variables are used.

- Conditional Statements—The heart of programming languages, these statements let you test whether conditions are true or false and then take alternative actions.

- Repetition—Computers are great at handling repetitive tasks. AppleScript provides a number of built-in features that let you do things repetitively—to each item in a list, until a condition is met, and so forth.

- Try Blocks—These are a sophisticated tool that all good programmers use. Instead of testing whether or not something has succeeded or failed, you just go right ahead and assume all is well—while providing explicit code to execute if AppleScript encounters an error. In other words, let AppleScript test for an error condition; you just provide the code.

> Handlers and subroutines are basically the same with the sole difference being that handlers are called by AppleScript and you call your subroutines yourself. In this chapter, they are grouped together as handlers; the references to handlers apply also to subroutines.

Units of Control and Definition

Subroutines and handlers can contain AppleScript statements; they also can contain definitions of variables. These definitions can be explicit or implicit: An implicit declaration occurs when you use a variable. The following example implicitly declares the variable theDate and sets it to the current date (an AppleScript construct):

```
set theDate to current date
```

You can then refer to the variable theDate and use it for calculations, in dialogs, and so forth. There are actually four types of variables in AppleScript: variables, globals, properties, and locals. (There is more on variables in Hour 9, "Basic AppleScript Syntax.")

What matters for now is that the variables you declare in your scripts may or may not be shared throughout the script. Here is how it works.

When you declare variables in the outermost part of a script (that is, not inside a handler), they can be used throughout the script. However, if you have a run handler, you cannot declare a variable outside it for use in the entire script. You can declare a property.

When you declare variables inside a handler, they are recognized only within that handler. They cannot be used in other handlers or in the outermost part of the script.

This allows you to use the same name for different variables. If the variable username is declared in each of three handlers, it is three separate and unrelated variables. To let the three handlers share a single variable, it must be declared at the outermost part of the script as a global or property.

> There are other ways of sharing variables. You can pass them back and forth as parameters of handlers. You'll see that not only in the sample scripts you've already looked at but also in Part II, "Writing Scripts with Script Editor."

This concept is referred to as the *scope* of variables—the area within which a variable is recognized. Programmers also speak of a *namespace*, which is the area within which names are unique.

The issue of the scope of variables is very important in structuring scripts (just as it is in structuring applications). Today, most programmers follow a few simple rules in naming and creating variables.

First of all, declare variables at the lowest possible level: In most cases, that means within a handler. If the variable needs to be passed to another handler, try to pass it as a parameter. This strategy means that the code is quite clear about what variable is being used.

To make the code even clearer, avoid duplicate names even if the scopes of variables make them different. For example, if you have a handler that contains a variable called username, you can have another handler with the same variable. Whether or not they are the same depends on whether the definitions are inside the two handlers or outside them. If they are two distinct variables, consider naming them loginusername and verifiedusername (or some other pair of names that indicates the difference).

Above all, if you are using variables that have the same names but are different, use a comment in AppleScript to point this out. Ambiguity in the use of variables is a common cause of bugs, and it is particularly difficult to catch—especially if you are tired.

> This hour focuses on basic programming techniques. Hour 9, "Basic AppleScript Syntax," explains the specific types of variables and properties available in AppleScript.

7

Conditional Statements

Normally each line of code in a program or script is executed sequentially. One exception to this is when conditional statements (or if statements) are encountered.

Conditional statements are implemented slightly differently in various programming and scripting languages. Here is the AppleScript implementation.

Simple Conditional Statements

The simplest `if` statement is a test for a condition; if the condition is true, some code is executed. Here is an `if` statement:

```
set thedate to (current date) as string
if "Monday" is in thedate then
  display dialog "Did you have a good weekend?"
end if
```

In some programming languages, the test needs to be enclosed in parentheses. You can do this in AppleScript, but it is not required.

Compound Conditional Statements

The test can be complex. You can join two tests together, as in this test:

```
if "Monday" is in thedate and "May" is in thedate then
```

Joining the two tests with `and` means that both must be true. Joining them with `or` means that either must be true. To improve the readability of your scripts, you can handle compound tests in several ways. First, break them into several lines. The continuation character (¬) makes several separate lines of code into a single AppleScript command.

Another strategy is to perform the tests outside the `if` statement. You can write this line of code, for example:

```
theTest = "Monday" is in thedate and "May" is in thedate
```

Your `if` statement would then read:

```
if theTest then
```

You can even build up your `if` statement from more than two tests. In that case, you might write the following:

```
theTest = "Monday" is in thedate and "May" is in thedate
theTest = theTest and "2002" is in the date
```

Although this will take slightly longer to execute, it can improve the readability of your script.

Multiple Elses

There is another way to perform multiple tests; you can use an `else` clause. With an `else` clause, you have two choices: If the test succeeds, one statement (or group of statements) is executed; if it fails, another statement is executed. Here is an `else` clause in an `if` statement.

```
set thedate to (current date) as string
if "Monday" is in thedate then
  display dialog "Did you have a good weekend?"
else
  display dialog "Good morning"
end if
```

And there is still a further refinement: the `else if` statement. This allows you to continue testing as the statement is executed:

```
set thedate to (current date) as string
if "Monday" is in thedate then
  display dialog "Did you have a good weekend?"
else if "Friday" is in thedate then
  display dialog "Have a good weekend"
else
  display dialog "Good morning"
end if
```

This type of code is often implemented in other languages as a `switch` or `case` statement.

Writing Good Conditional Statements

You can use the various forms of `if` statements to control execution, prevent errors, and make your scripts more powerful. However, beware of going too far. If your `if` statements are unduly complex—either in their tests or in their `else if` clauses—your code can become hard to read. It is hard to see what is happening in these very complex cases.

One way to simplify complex conditions is to consider whether or not to reverse the tests. Often, as you approach a problem and look at the possibilities, you come up with a wide variety of cases that you need to test for. Sometimes, when you have laid out all of those cases, you can find a different way of phrasing the question (perhaps using a test for a negative case). Note also that you can have empty clauses. The following is a perfectly valid conditional statement:

```
set thedate to (current date) as string
if "Monday" is in thedate then
else
  display dialog "Good morning"
end if
```

7

If the day is not Monday, a dialog is shown; if it is Monday, nothing happens. This is a very effective way of testing for a negative and preserving your code's readability.

Returning from a Handler

One common statement that can occur in a conditional statement is a `return` statement: It stops execution of the handler and transfers control back to the place where the handler was called.

A `return` statement (described further in Hour 9) can return a value or a variable. Thus, any of the following are valid `return` statements:

```
return
return 4
return theResult
```

Repetition

Another exception to the general rule that statements are executed sequentially is *repetition statements*. In these, one or more statements are executed repeatedly as specified in the statement. There are six types of repetition statements, and they are all described in this section. (Repetition statements are sometimes called *loops*.)

Each repetition statement allows an `exit` statement to be used within it. If an `exit` statement is encountered, the repetition is immediately stopped and control passes to the first line of code following the repetition statement. You can also jump out of a repetition statement in a handler by using a `return` statement: In that case, control is transferred totally out of the handler to the place where the handler was called.

`repeat` statements all are terminated with an `end` statement.

repeat forever

`repeat forever` is the simplest form of a repeat statement. It repeats forever:

```
repeat
  set x to x + 1
end repeat
```

The repetition statement shown here does, indeed, repeat forever. The way in which you get out of a `repeat` statement is to use an `exit` statement. Normally, you perform a test with a conditional statement, and if it succeeds (or fails, depending on the circumstances), you exit from the loop.

Some programmers use these infinite repetition statements to wait for something to happen—for a disk to be inserted, perhaps. You test if the disk is there, and if it is not, you loop around and test again until the disk is inserted and you can exit.

In almost all cases, this type of program structure is a bad idea. If you need to loop continuously, don't use a `repeat` statement. Rather, use an `idle` handler, which will be called periodically by the system. Let the operating system and AppleScript handle the repetition; you just do your test in the `idle` handler. If the test succeeds (the disk is inserted), you can then call your own subroutine to process the data. If the disk is not there, the `idle` handler exits until the next time it is called. This is much more efficient and improves throughput on the computer enormously.

repeat x times

This form of repetition statement repeats the number of times specified. It's commonly used in preparing output where you want to repeat a set of instructions (perhaps a printing layout) several times. You can use either a variable or a constant in such a loop. Here is one example:

```
counter = 10
repeat counter times
  ...
end repeat
```

repeat while

In this and the following repetition statement, you can combine conditional statements with repetition statements. This form performs the test; if it succeeds, the body of the repetition statement is executed. Then, the test is performed again, and the process is repeated. When the test fails, the loop exits.

The `repeat while` statement is useful in processing a known number of unnumbered items such as records in a database. Here is some sample code:

```
repeat while numberOfRecordsRead ≤ numberOfRecordsAvailable
  ...
  numberOfRecordsRead = numberOfRecordsRead + 1
end repeat
```

repeat until

This repetition statement is the complement of the preceding one: It executes while the condition is false and terminates when it's true. You can usually rewrite one statement to the other by reversing the test. Here is the previous statement rewritten in this way:

```
repeat until numberOfRecordsRead > numberOfRecordsAvailable
  ...
  numberOfRecordsRead = numberOfRecordsRead + 1
end repeat
```

7

In AppleScript, the test is executed before each repetition of the loop—even the first. Thus, if the condition is true, the loop will not even execute once. In some other programming languages, such a situation would let the loop execute a single time.

 In reversing the test, note that in one case you test for less than or equal; in the other you test for greater than (not greater than or equal).

repeat with/from/to

This form of repetition loop provides you with a counter. In the two previous loops, you kept track of your own counter (`numberOfRecordsRead`). You can execute a similar loop with this code:

```
repeat with numberOfRecordsRead from 1 to numberOfRecordsAvailable
   ...
end repeat
```

AppleScript takes care of incrementing the counter. You can use the counter's value within the loop, and you can change any of the values (the counter value, from, and to). However, those changes will not affect the loop's processing: It reverts to its own values. In some programming languages, it is possible to get out of a loop by setting the counter to a value greater than the end value. That doesn't work in AppleScript (use the `exit` command instead).

You can also add a `by` clause to the end of the `repeat` statement. In that way, the counting will not be by one:

```
repeat with value from 1 to 100 by 25
```

This statement will execute four times, with values of 1, 26, 51, and 76.

repeat with/in

The final form of a repetition statement lets you process the items in a list in order. There are no counters involved—they are just processed as they are encountered. You can use this form of repetition statement to process files that are dropped on a droplet: Each one is handled, and you don't really care what their numbers are. Here is a common droplet section of code:

```
repeat with theFile in droppedFilesList
```

As you can see, you can use these repetition statements in various ways. Some are matters of personal preference: You can use a `repeat with/in` statement or a `repeat with/from/to` to handle a list of items. It's your choice.

Try Blocks

The last type of control statement covered in this hour is the try block. It's one of the greatest contributions to code readability. A try block is a conditional statement with a twist; the condition is error-free execution. Here is a sample try block

```
try
  --read a record
on error number errnum
  if errnum = -39 then
    exit repeat
  else
    display dialog "Error reading file"
  end if
end try
```

This code is getting complex. Don't worry; the next part of the book will let you see how it works. For now, just read it as if it were natural language.

The first part of the try block is the code where you attempt to read a data record. You can write this code without any conditional statements. You also don't need to use a repetition statement to read each record in the file: You just go ahead and read.

If an error is encountered, the on error clause is executed. You test if the error is -39 (end of file), and if so, you simply exit. (Remember that you can exit from any loop with the exit statement regardless of conditions and counters.) Although you did encounter an error, it is legitimate: You have read all the records. If it is not an end-of-file error, it is, indeed, an error, and you need to alert the user.

The reason that try blocks are so useful is that the straightforward code—the code you execute when all is well—is clear. It's not cluttered up with tests for error. All the exception handling is in the on error clause.

> You can speak of both exception and error handling in the context of try blocks: Both refer to processing other than the routine operation of the code in most cases. Many people prefer to speak of exception handling because some exceptions (such as end-of-file) are often not errors.

Looking ahead to Part II, there's one other feature that you should know about. You can use the error statement to indicate that an error exists. You'll see more about this later. Thus, you can execute the on error clause not only when an error known to AppleScript occurs, but also when one that you have defined occurs.

7

Try blocks are a relatively recent addition to programming languages, and they are used frequently by good programmers to improve code readability.

 Have you noticed how many times "readability" appears? Get in the habit of making your code clear so that it can be maintained. In the late 1990s, when the Y2K problem loomed, companies around the world pored over their computer programs to see if there would be problems with their date routines. This process was very costly—and many errors were found and repaired before they caused problems. But two lessons emerged clearly. First, you never know when the code will need to be examined for potential flaws of one sort or another. Second, even seasoned computer professionals were amazed at the age of the programs. Whole programs—and very commonly parts of programs—were several decades old. It was not uncommon to find code from the 1960s still running with a few patches and modifications in 2000. So document your code, and write it clearly. Your children may be reading it long after you've retired!

Summary

This hour concludes the first part of the book. You've seen how AppleScript works, some of the things that it can do, and you've looked inside scripts to see how they are structured.

In particular, this hour has shown you the basic programming concepts of scope and control, conditions, repetition, and error handling. All the basic concepts of AppleScript and programming have been presented, so it's time to move on to the next part of the book to actually begin to write scripts from the ground up.

Q&A

Q How different is AppleScript from other programming languages?

A It's very similar in its control structures.

Q If I have a simple script to write, is it really worth using handlers, subroutines, and try blocks? Isn't it easier just to write the code and test for errors?

A There are two answers. First, when you get used to good programming practices, they don't take more time. Second, remember the comments about readability. "Simple scripts" have a tendency to grow as needs change and you see more that you can do with them. Start from the most structured environment you can.

Workshop

The workshop contains quiz questions and activities to help you solidify your knowledge of the material in this hour. Try to answer all of the questions before looking at the quiz answers that follow.

Quiz

1. How do you escape from a repetition statement?
2. Can you change the values in a `repeat with/from/to` statement as it is executing?
3. What is the limit of `else if` clauses in an `if` statement?

Quiz Answers

1. Use the `exit` or `return` statements.
2. You can change them, but when the loop recycles, the previous values will be used. You can't jump ahead by resetting the counter within the loop. If you need to do this, use a `repeat while` or `repeat until` loop and do your own counter management.
3. There is no limit.

Activities

You've seen the control structures of AppleScript. Take the Make Audio Slideshow script and analyze its structure. Don't worry about what all the script statements do (although you can probably figure them out). The `run` handler contains `if` statements, `try` blocks, and repetition statements. Trace through how control passes within the `run` handler.

Imagine that you're going to write a script that calculates a grade for each student in a class based on five tests. The grade is the average of the five scores. How would you structure the program with repetition statements, try blocks, and conditional statements? (You may not need all of them.) If a student only took four tests, you can average those; but if the student only took three or fewer tests, you have to give an "Incomplete" grade.

7

PART II

Writing Scripts with Script Editor

Hour

8   Introducing Script Editor

9   Basic AppleScript Syntax

10   Scripting the Finder

11   Scripting Mac OS X Applications from Apple

12   Scripting Mac OS X Applications from Third Parties

13   Interacting with Users

HOUR **8**

Introducing Script Editor

The first part of this book helped you understand what AppleScript is, how to find and use scripts, and the basic programming concepts and structures that you'll use. This part of the book goes into AppleScript itself. You'll find the syntax itself, and you'll see how to script the Finder, Apple's own applications, and applications from third parties.

This hour starts you off. You'll see how to use Apple's Script Editor tool, how to create a script, and how to use the dictionaries that are at the heart of all scriptable applications. You'll see how to monitor and debug your scripts with the Result and Event Log windows.

In This Hour

- Finding Your Way Around Script Editor—This is the basic editing tool that comes as part of Mac OS X. You'll see how to use it.
- Creating a Script—Creating a script is just a matter of typing in the AppleScript commands.
- Checking Syntax—Script Editor checks your syntax for you so that you can see if your script will run. It also formats the script for easy reading.

- Working with Dictionaries—Dictionaries are at the heart of applications' scriptability. They contain the commands and classes for suites supported by the application.
- Looking at the Result—As you run scripts in Script Editor, you can monitor the result of each AppleScript command.
- Looking at the Event Log—In addition to looking at the result of each script step, the Event Log lets you monitor the flow of execution of the script.

Finding Your Way Around Script Editor

The first tool you'll probably use to write scripts is Script Editor. It's part of the basic installation of AppleScript that you find in the AppleScript folder located inside Applications in the Mac OS X installation. There are a number of third-party tools for authoring scripts; they will be described later in the book. In addition, you can use Project Builder to write and edit scripts. Project Builder is discussed in Part III, "Working with AppleScript Studio."

The script editing window is shown in Figure 8.1. An empty window opens when you launch Script Editor. You can create new scripts with the New Script command from the File menu. As you can see in the figure, you can type your script into the window.

FIGURE 8.1

Type your script into the Script Editor window.

The Script Editor menus are simple and provide access to basic commands. The Script Editor application menu provides the standard commands that all applications provide in their application menu (including Quit); the Window menu provides the list of all windows just as it does in other applications. They are not discussed here.

File Menu

The File menu contains the standard file opening, closing, saving, and printing commands you expect from any application. Two points are worth noting.

First, Script Editor can open two types of files: scripts and dictionaries. Thus, there are two Open commands: Open Script and Open Dictionary. Not only are there two Open commands, but if you drag a file on to Script Editor in the Finder, it will behave appropriately: If you drag a script on to Script Editor, it opens in the editing window, and if you drag an application on to Script Editor, its dictionary is opened for you. If there is no dictionary, the application is not scriptable, and you will get an error message.

Second, you can save scripts as run-only scripts. Thus, there are Save and Save As commands for saving scripts in any of the following formats: text, compiled script, or application. (You select from a Format pop-up menu in the Save dialog.) To save a script as run-only—that is, without the text of the script—use the Save As Run-Only command.

At the bottom of the File menu is a useful command, Set Default Window Size. Create an editing window and then size it to the size that you like. Choose this command, and then all newly created windows will be this size. (The default editing window size is small.)

Edit Menu

The Edit menu contains the standard Cut/Copy/Paste commands. An additional command, AppleScript Formatting, lets you choose how Script Editor displays your scripts. That command opens the window shown in Figure 8.2.

FIGURE 8.2

Set AppleScript formatting for scripts.

Select the syntax element you're interested in (as shown in Figure 8.2) and then change its formatting by using the commands in the Font and Style menus. Those menus are used solely for this purpose; they contain fonts and font sizes (Fonts) and styles such as bold, italics, and colors (Styles). They are not discussed further in this section.

Note that you can change the formatting of syntax elements, but you cannot change the default indentation that Script Editor uses.

Controls Menu

Commands in the Controls menu let you record, run, and stop scripts. You can also use the buttons in the center of the editing window to do so. Also in this menu are commands to open the Event Log and Result windows. They are discussed later in this chapter.

Creating a Script

To create a script, just type it in as shown previously in Figure 8.1. AppleScript commands take a single line each: You cannot combine two commands on one line.

If you must extend a command over two or more lines, use the ¬ character (Control-l or option-Return) at the end of all lines except the last.

There's one other point to mention about typing in a script. Any text following -- (two dashes) is treated as a comment. Every good programmer and script author uses comments extensively. Use comments to remind yourself what you're doing—the next time you read this script might be six months or more from now.

Comments are the exception to the line continuation described in the previous paragraph. A comment that ends with ¬ will not cause the next line to be treated as a continuation—that is, as part of the comment. However, if you want to extend a comment over several lines, you can start it with (* and end it with *). Everything between will be treated as a comment, and you do not need any special continuation characters at the ends of the lines within it.

Checking Syntax

When you have finished typing in your script, check its syntax. You can check the syntax by clicking the Check Syntax button at the right of the middle of the editing window; alternatively, you can run it and the syntax will be checked before it runs. (If the syntax check fails, the script won't run.)

When Script Editor checks the syntax, it reformats and restyles the script in accordance with the AppleScript Formatting settings you provided through the command in the Edit menu. Figure 8.3 shows a script that is syntax checked and formatted.

If the syntax check fails, Script Editor will highlight the line in question and show you an error message as you see in Figure 8.4.

Sometimes the error is obvious and you can fix it easily. Other times, the error is harder to find. A particularly nasty form of error involves mismatched quotation marks.

FIGURE 8.3

Check your syntax.

8

FIGURE 8.4

Syntax errors are flagged.

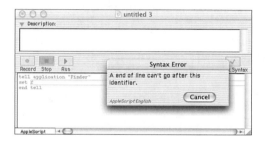

For example, the following line of code generates the error message that appears next:

```
set x to hello"
```

```
Expected end of line but found "
```

There's nothing wrong with the end of the line: The problem is a missing quotation mark before hello. Whenever you get error messages you can't figure out, check for mismatched quotation marks.

Just because error messages occasionally are misleading, that's no reason not to read and understand them. A surprising number of people just register the fact that an error has been found and then they start poking around trying to fix it. The compiler always attempts to give you an explanation of the error, and that's a good starting place to look. Also, in the case of complex errors, take a moment to consider whether your possible solution could fix the problem. There are many people who just take a trial-and-error approach to solving syntax errors when a few moments of deliberation would pay off handsomely.

Working with Dictionaries

Dictionaries show you the syntax for any scriptable application. You can open a dictionary by dragging an application on to Script Editor: If it is scriptable, the dictionary will open.

You can also use the Open Dictionary command in the File menu to open a dictionary. When you choose the command, Script Editor looks for all of the scriptable applications that it can find (this may take a moment or two). The window shown in Figure 8.5 opens and you can select which application you want to see.

Sometimes you will see multiple listings for the same application. In this case, there are two listings for Address Book. If you scroll to the right of the window, you'll see where the application is located. In this case, you can see that one copy is located in /Applications/—where it should be, and the other is located in /Volumes/Mapp/ Applications/—another disk mounted on this computer. It is the first one you would use.

FIGURE 8.5

View a dictionary to see its AppleScript syntax.

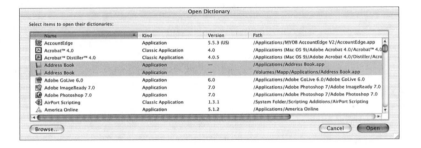

If the application you want to view is not listed, you can use the Browse button in the lower left to open a standard Open dialog that lets you locate any file on disk.

When you open a dictionary, it appears as shown in Figure 8.6. This is the dictionary for Retrospect, one of the leading backup products.

Dictionaries are divided into *suites*; each suite is a logically related set of syntax. Some applications implement more than one suite: Mail, for example implements the Apple-defined Standard and Text suites as well as its own Mail and Message suites. Figure 8.6 shows the Retrospect suite, which is solely confined to its own needs.

Inside a suite, you will find two sections: commands and classes. Commands precede classes. (A suite must have either commands or classes or both—it cannot be empty.) You can use the scrolling list at the left of the dictionary window to look at individual commands or classes; or, you can click the suite's name to show all of its commands and classes as in Figure 8.6.

FIGURE 8.6

Retrospect dictionary.

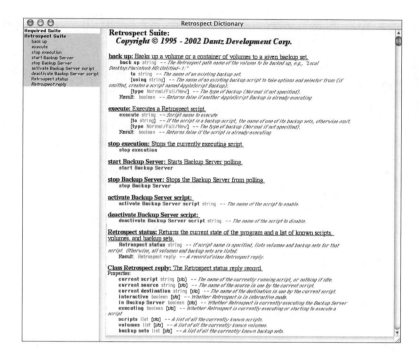

8

Commands are shown and defined. For example, the first command in the Retrospect
suite is back up. In the syntax that follows the description of the command, you can see
that it takes one parameter: a string. The string is defined as being the path to the volume
to back up.

Sometimes parameters are optional; in those cases, they are enclosed in square brackets.
In the execute command, you can see three parameters: The first is required, and the second
and third are optional.

If you look at the Retrospect Status command (toward the bottom of the list), you'll see
yet another element: a result. If a command returns a result, it is described here.
Sometimes a result is a number or a string; other times it is a complex structure—
perhaps one defined in the suite. That is the case here.

Following the commands, one or more classes may be defined. Commands are like
verbs, whereas classes are like nouns. In the Retrospect suite, there is one class:
Retrospect reply. It is the result of the Retrospect Status command. It contains information
that you can query using AppleScript; you'll see how to do this in Hour 12,
"Scripting Mac OS X Applications from Third Parties."

You'll find out more about dictionaries in the remaining hours of this part of the book when you work with them.

Looking at the Result

If an AppleScript command returns a result, you can use it in your script. But sometimes you want to look at the result as you're developing a script. Choose Show Results from the Controls menu to open the Result window, which is shown in Figure 8.7.

FIGURE 8.7

The Result window shows the result of an AppleScript command.

Looking at the Event Log

The Result window contains a single result. Each time you execute an AppleScript command, the Result window's content changes. Thus, if you're debugging a script, it's hard to track what's happening. To follow the events, use the Controls menu to open the Event Log window, which is shown in Figure 8.8.

FIGURE 8.8

The Event Log window lets you monitor a script's progress.

As you can see, the entire script is shown; when a result is returned, it is indicated by -->.

Summary

This hour has provided an introduction to Script Editor, the basic AppleScript editing tool that is provided as part of the standard Mac OS X installation. You've seen how to use Script Editor to create a script and check its syntax. You've also seen how to work with dictionaries as well as how to monitor your scripts with the Result and Event Log windows.

In the next hour, you'll explore AppleScript syntax and start to write your own scripts with Script Editor.

Q&A

Q **Why does my Script Editor window look different?**

A As noted in the Introduction, Apple released a beta version of Script Editor 2 at the end of 2002. It provides the same functionality with a slightly different look and feel. Preferences in the Script Editor menu, for example, are used to control syntax formatting. The results and event log windows are incorporated into tabs at the bottom of the main window although they can also be opened separately. Also, the text editing engine is changed so that lines of code wrap automatically. But the functionality is the same.

Q **Are there script-writing tools other than Script Editor?**

A Yes. From Apple, AppleScript Studio (discussed in Part III of this book) is a powerful tool that provides the same tools that developers use to create full-blown applications. In fact, it is the tool that Apple itself uses to create its software—everything from iPhoto and iCal to Mac OS X itself. In addition, there are third-party tools. You can find them on Apple's site at `http://www.apple.com/applescript/resources/`.

Q **Are all the words necessary in the commands?**

A No. Words such as "the" are optional; they are included here to improve the readability of the scripts. There are also synonyms in AppleScript: = and `is` are treated the same.

Q **Where can I find out more about AppleScript syntax?**

A The bible is *AppleScript Language Guide* from Apple. You can download a PDF file from `http://developer.apple.com/techpubs/macosx/Carbon/pdf/AppleScriptLanguageGuide.pdf`; an HTML version is available at `http://developer.apple.com/techpubs/macosx/Carbon/interapplicationcomm/AppleScript/AppleScriptLangGuide/index.html`.

Workshop

The workshop contains quiz questions and activities to help you solidify your knowledge of the material in this hour. Try to answer all of the questions before looking at the quiz answers that follow.

Quiz

1. What happens if I can't find an application's dictionary?

2. How do I get my scripts nicely formatted as in the figures in this chapter?

3. What is the result of a command?

4. What do the square brackets in dictionaries mean?

Quiz Answers

1. It means that the application is not scriptable. The dictionary is generated from the AppleScript code within the application that actually will carry out the script.

2. Run the script or click the Check Syntax button. If there is an error, the script will not be formatted properly until you correct the error.

3. Every command can return a result. It can be a number or text; it can also be an instance of a class that is defined in the dictionary.

4. Parameters within square brackets are optional.

Activities

Look at the list of script ideas you prepared in Hour 1, "Introducing AppleScript." Will they work? Can you build any of them with the knowledge you have so far?

You can tell the Finder to get the current selection as a string. Write that script, open the Result window, and then run the script. Experiment with different selections in the Finder and run the script again.

 Save the scripts that you write in this part of the book. In the last hour, you'll see how to interact with users. You'll come back to these scripts and have them display data in a dialog rather than using the Result window.

Hour 9

Basic AppleScript Syntax

In Hours 6, "Looking Behind the Scenes: How These Scripts Work," and 7, "Basic Programming Concepts," you saw the basic programming elements that let you write scripts with AppleScript. Those elements are common to most programming languages. In this chapter, AppleScript-specific syntax is presented. By the end of this hour, you should be able to write basic scripts using the syntax described here, the programming elements from Hours 6 and 7, and Script Editor, which was described in Hour 8, "Introducing Script Editor."

The scripts you'll be able to write are basic, but the techniques are the same as you'll use in sophisticated scripts. In the next two hours, you'll see how to write really useful scripts for Apple and third-party applications.

In This Hour

- Tell Blocks—This construct lets you address commands to specific applications or objects.
- Commands—These are the heart of AppleScript, the instructions that are executed.

- Variables—As in other programming languages, you can store data in variables while the script is running.

- Expressions—Expressions are the components of statements; they yield the values that are stored in variables.

- Control Statements—These statements let you manage control of your script with conditional statements, repetition, and the like.

- Optional Words—AppleScript provides optional words that you can add to scripts to improve readability.

- Script Structure—Finally, you'll see a script written in three different ways as you explore the use of subroutines in structuring scripts.

Tell Blocks

You've seen tell blocks in many of the examples so far. A tell block is a section of a script that is addressed to a specific application or object.

Telling an Application to Do Something

When you tell an application to do something, that application's dictionary and its terms are available for use along with the standard AppleScript commands and syntax. For example, you can tell Photoshop to activate itself. (This brings it forward if it is running; if it is not, the script launches it and brings it to the front of the screen.) Here's how you could write that script:

```
tell application "Photoshop"
  activate
end tell
```

AppleScript will attempt to find the application and send the message to it. If AppleScript can't find it, it will ask you to locate it as you see in Figure 9.1.

FIGURE 9.1

Locate an application for AppleScript.

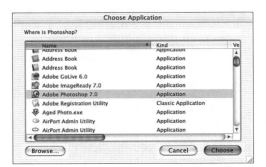

You can select the application from the list shown; if it is not visible, use the Browse button in the lower corner to find it. (This is the same way in which you opened a dictionary in Hour 8.) After you select the application, AppleScript proceeds with the script. In this case, it also modifies the script to read:

```
tell application "Adobe Photoshop 7.0"
  activate
end tell
```

As in this case, sometimes the name of the application is quite different from what you expect. If you're poking around in the *P* section of the application list, you'll never find Photoshop because its actual name is Adobe Photoshop and it's listed under *A*.

Telling an Object to Do Something

You can also address a tell block to an object, as in this snippet:

```
tell window 3
  move to front
end tell
```

This is a very common practice when there are several windows, documents, or other objects in use.

Nesting Tell Blocks

You can nest tell blocks within one another, as follows:

```
tell application "Finder"
  tell window 3
    move to front
  end tell
end tell
```

When you check syntax or run the script, AppleScript will indent the tell blocks as shown here. Sometimes, you can accomplish your task in alternate ways. The code shown next moves a window to the front by telling the window to move itself. Another way of writing this is to tell the Finder to do the work:

```
tell application "Finder"
  move window 3 to front
end tell
```

Single-line Tells

Yet another way of writing a single line such as this is

```
tell application "Finder" to move window 3 to front
```

Commands

Commands are instructions that AppleScript carries out. Most commands have a *direct object*—the object on which the command acts. In the code at the end of the last section, the direct object is `window 3`. (Direct object is used here in exactly the same way it is used in natural-language grammar.) Some commands—such as `quit` or `beep`—have no direct object.

Commands are directed to a *target*: the entity that responds to the command. In the previous examples, the target has been the Finder or the window in the case of the `tell window` block.

There are four types of commands:

- *AppleScript commands* are those that are defined and implemented in AppleScript itself.
- *Application commands* are implemented in specific applications; they may be part of standard AppleScript suites that are defined as part of AppleScript, but they are implemented in applications. You will see many of these in the two hours that follow this one.
- *User-defined commands* are just that: commands that you define. The subroutines shown previously are user-defined commands.
- *Scripting addition commands* extend AppleScript. You can use them as if they were AppleScript commands. The only distinction is that they are distributed in separate files, which are normally installed automatically for you as part of the installation of the application that is being extended.

AppleScript Commands

The AppleScript commands are the most basic elements of the language. Three of them (`get`, `set`, and `copy`) are used to work with variables as described in the following section. The `count` command is used to count items as in the following:

```
tell application "Finder"
  count the windows
end tell
```

The `run` command is used to run scripts or applications. The `error` command is used to signal that an error has occurred. It is described in Hour 20, "Advanced AppleScript Syntax."

User-defined Commands

When using user-defined commands or subroutines, there is a syntactic rule you must follow if they are used within a tell block. In the following code, the user-defined command `displayName` needs to be invoked:

```
tell application "Finder"
  displayName()
end tell
```

If you use this code, the command `displayName` will be sent to the target of the tell block: the Finder. The Finder does not recognize that command, so you will get an error. The solution is to let AppleScript know that you are invoking a user-defined command from within your script. The correct syntax is either of the following:

```
my displayName()
displayName() of me
```

Variables

Variables are used to store information in a named location. All programming languages use them. Some programming languages require you to declare variables before you use them; in the declaration, you specify what *type* or *class* of data will be stored in the variable. You can have variables that store numbers, others that store strings, and so forth.

User-defined Variables

In AppleScript, you declare and type variables by using them. For example, if you write

```
set theName to "Aristotle"
```

AppleScript creates a variable called `theName`, and it is a string.

Sometimes, you want to manipulate the type of a variable. For example, you can set a variable to the number 742; you can also set it to the string "742." Here is how to set it to the number:

```
set x to 742
```

Either of the following two lines will set `y` to a string:

```
set y to 742 as string
set y to "742"
```

When you use the first form (as string), you are *coercing* the value to another type. AppleScript automatically does coercion for you when it can. For example, in the following code, the string is coerced to a number and the correct addition is performed:

```
set x to 742
set y to 742 as string
set z to x + y
```

Sometimes you need to explicitly do your own coercion. Most commonly, that occurs when there is ambiguity and AppleScript chooses the wrong coercion.

Variables that you declare can be referenced throughout the *scope* of the script in which they are declared. If you declare a variable within a tell block or a subroutine, you can use it within that tell block or subroutine. (Remember that declaring a variable usually means using it for the first time.)

The variable cannot be used in another block or subroutine. If you use a variable with the same name in another block or subroutine, it is a different variable. (This is one of the most common programming bugs.)

To create a variable that you can use throughout a script, use it outside a block or subroutine. It can then be referenced from anywhere in the script.

Such variables—called *global* variables—can lead to problems. It is much better to explicitly pass variables into blocks and subroutines as parameters than to use them globally. You will see examples of this throughout the later hours of this book.

Variables are assigned values either by the set command or the copy command. The syntax is

```
set x to (5+7)
copy (5+7) to x
```

As you can see here, you can set variables to the results of expressions (described later in this hour) as well as to specific values.

You use the value of a variable by using its name or by using the get command, which you have seen before. You cannot use a variable—either with its name or with a get command—before you have assigned it a value. Thus, the following lines of code are both wrong if nothing has been assigned to x:

```
set a to x * 2
get x
```

Properties are a special type of variable; their value is retained after the script has run. If you modify a property during a script's execution, the modified value is what is used the next time the script is run. When you recompile the script, the property is set to the value that you have specified. A property is declared in this way:

```
property maximumScore : 0
```

The names of variables must begin with a letter; they can contain upper- and lowercase letters, numbers, and the underscore character. They are not case sensitive, which means that these are three references to the same variable:

```
myname
MyName
myName
```

The use of uppercase letters within variable names made up of compound words is for readability only.

You can begin and end a variable name with vertical bars; if you do so, you can use other characters within the name. However, you may sacrifice readability in these cases.

 There's one further rule to remember: Variable names cannot be the same as reserved words in AppleScript—constants and syntax elements. If you want a counter for a loop, you can't call it `repeat` because `repeat` is a syntax element. You can call it `myRepeat` or `repeatCounter`.

Table 9.1 shows some examples of legal and illegal variable names.

TABLE 9.1 Legal and Illegal Variable Names

Legal	Illegal	Comment
x3	3z	Must start with a letter.
x_3	x-3	Underscores are legal characters within names; hyphens are not.
x	2	Must start with a non-numeric character.
x3	x 3	Cannot contain a space.
|x 3|	x 3	Vertical bars delimit variable names that include special characters.

AppleScript-defined Variables

In addition to using a specific value or an expression to set a value for a variable, you can use a *constant*. AppleScript defines a number of constants for you. One is the common trigonometric term *pi*. A number of others are text characters that represent certain keys. If you pressed these keys while typing your script, they would distort your script.

For example, the Return key terminates a line of AppleScript code. If you want to use the Return character in your script, you've got to use a constant rather than the keystroke, which would terminate the statement.

These are the AppleScript string constants:

- `tab`
- `return`
- `space`

They have the same meaning as the corresponding keys on the keyboard.

Other constants are provided; they are listed in Appendix A, "Constants and Predefined Variables."

Commands can return a *result*. It can be the result of a `set` or `copy` command, or it can be a value explicitly returned from a subroutine with the `return` statement. (You saw how to view results in the preceding hour.) You can reference this value directly as in the following:

```
set x to 17
display dialog the result
```

Another important constant is *missing value*. It is just what it says: a missing value. You can use it in lines of code such as the following:

```
set x to missing value
if x = missing value then set x to "Unknown"
```

Note that `missing value` is an AppleScript syntax element; it is not enclosed in quotes even though it is two words.

Using `missing value` is good programming style and can prevent nasty problems. A major part of the Y2K problem was the use of 99 as a year to indicate missing data or some other anomaly. When applications were written in the 1960s and 1970s, 1999 seemed a long way off, and it was safe to use it as a special flag. Likewise, the year 2000 (00) seemed unimaginable; it, too, was commonly used in this way. Much of the large cost of converting programs to the new millennium consisted of removing these nondate dates from the code.

In some cases 0 can be interpreted as a missing value; in other cases, a blank is a missing value. It's far simpler to use the actual syntax `missing value` because there's no question about what it means—and what valid values mean.

Expressions

You have seen expressions throughout this hour and the previous ones. Expressions produce values that you can use to set variables; you can also use them in conditional statements. They can produce numeric, text, string, date, or other valid AppleScript types.

Examples of expressions are

```
length * width

accountBalance > 0

current date + days
```

> The final example may require some explanation. It uses the days constant to add one day to the current date and yields tomorrow's date.

Control Statements

The final element of AppleScript is its control statements, `tell`, `if`, `repeat`, `exit`, and `try`. `tell` has been described previously in this chapter; the others have been described in Hour 7. You'll see them used again in the final section of this hour, "Script Structure."

Optional Words

Finally, you should know that AppleScript allows you to add words to your scripts that improve readability. The most common is `the`. The following two lines of code are identical:

```
set today to the current date
set today to current date
```

There are also synonyms that you can use to improve readability. These two lines are identical:

```
set theCalendars to calendar where title is "Personal"
set theCalendars to calendar whose title is "Personal"
```

Script Structure

You can write a script as a sequence of lines that are executed one after another. As you have seen, you can include conditional code that is executed only if a test passes or fails; you can also include various repetition segments. This section examines a single script and shows how it can be structured in a variety of ways.

The Basic Script

Here's a basic script that displays all events from today forward from an iCal calendar named "Personal":

```
tell application "iCal"
  set theCalendars to calendars whose title is "Personal"
  if (count of theCalendars) > 0 then
    tell first item of theCalendars
      set futureEvents to events where start date ≥ (current date)
      repeat with theEvent in futureEvents
        display dialog summary of theEvent as string
      end repeat
    end tell
  end if
end tell
```

The entire script consists of a single tell block addressed to iCal. Within that, two major things happen:

- First, a set statement retrieves the list of calendars titled "Personal" and stores the list in theCalendars. Although the syntax could retrieve multiple calendars with that title, the semantics of iCal—the way in which it works—doesn't allow duplicates, so you'll know that you have at most one calendar returned.

- Second, check to see if there are any items in the list. If there are, you retrieve the first (and only) item of the list, and tell it what to do. This tell block extends over six lines.

Within the tell block, two other things happen:

- First, you set a variable (futureEvents) for the events with a start date of today or later.

- Second, a repeat loop iterates through each event and displays it in a dialog.

It's worth noting that you do have to test whether or not a calendar has been returned; if there are no items returned from the first set statement, your script will fail when attempting to issue the tell command to the first (nonexistent) item. On the other hand, you don't have to test whether or not any futureEvents have been returned. If there are none, the repeat statement will simply not execute.

Using Subroutines

Cleaner, easier-to-read code consists of subroutines and handlers. The preceding script can be rewritten as follows:

```
tell application "iCal"
  set theCalendars to calendars whose title is "Personal"
  if (count of theCalendars) > 0 then
    tell first item of theCalendars
      set futureEvents to events where start date ≥ (current date)
      repeat with theEvent in futureEvents
        my displayEvent(theEvent)
      end repeat
    end tell
  end if
end tell

on displayEvent(whichEvent)
  tell application "iCal"
    display dialog summary of whichEvent as string
  end tell
end displayEvent
```

The difference here is that a subroutine is used to display each event. That may not seem like a big deal, but it will allow you to expand this script easily. One example is adding the date to the summary of the event. You know exactly where to make the change:

```
on displayEvent(whichEvent)
  tell application "iCal"
    tell whichEvent to display dialog (start date as string) & " " ¬
      & summary as string
  end tell
end displayEvent
```

You can further refine the script in the following way:

```
tell application "iCal"
  set theCalendars to calendars whose title is "Personal"
  if (count of theCalendars) > 0 then my displayFutureEvents(first item of ¬
    theCalendars)
end tell

on displayFutureEvents(aCalendar)
  tell application "iCal"
    tell aCalendar
      set futureEvents to events where start date ≥ (current date)
      repeat with theEvent in futureEvents
        my displayEvent(theEvent)
      end repeat
    end tell
```

9

```
    end tell
end displayFutureEvents

on displayEvent(whichEvent)
  tell application "iCal"
    display dialog summary of whichEvent as string
  end tell
end displayEvent
```

At first glance, you may notice only that this code is longer. However, it is written in a way that ultimately makes it easier to modify and maintain. There are only two lines of code that are executed directly; they are the first two lines of the script. The two subroutines that precede them are called from those lines of code.

What the script does is defined in those two lines of code; how it does it is defined in the subroutines. This style of programming is called *structured programming*, and it is the norm today. AppleScript allows you to write subroutines and code in any order. Some people prefer the structure shown here with the subroutines last and the actual code at the beginning; other people prefer to put the executable code last: It's your choice. What is definitely misleading is to mingle subroutines and executable code together. It's legal, and AppleScript won't complain, but anyone who attempts to read the script will have problems.

> Structured code using subroutines makes complex programs much easier to read. Because the scripts shown in this book are very brief demonstrations, the advantage of structured code is not immediately obvious. However, as soon as a script is more than a few lines long—certainly more than one page long—the structure makes it easier to read.

There's one final point to be made about script structure: Use comments. Unless you're writing a one-shot script, you'll need to come back and look at it sometime in the future. Your comments will help you remember what you were doing.

Comments work very well in structured scripts like the following code. Instead of getting the name of the selection from the Finder, you could write a script to query a database for the address associated with a name. Here's what that script might look like:

```
set theAddress to getAddress("Claude Debussy")

on getAddress(theName)
  --query the database
  return "Claude's address"
end getAddress
```

The getAddress subroutine has a comment in it reminding people that the database query has to be written. For now, it returns a standard string. This is a very convenient way to develop a script: Write dummy subroutines, and then write the code that calls them. You can then check that the basic logic of the script works. After that, you go through and work on each subroutine in turn. Instead of winding up with a long script that you have to work on for some time, you wind up with a lot of small, self-contained subroutines that are easy to write (and debug).

Summary

This hour has been devoted to the basics of AppleScript itself. You've seen the structure of scripts, and learned about tell blocks, commands, variables, expressions, and control statements. There are other aspects of AppleScript besides these, but these are the most important. Other concepts, such as records and lists, will be introduced in the chapters that follow as they are needed to explain the code that is presented there.

Q&A

Q What is the biggest difference between AppleScript syntax and that of a programming language such as C?

A Programming languages such as C require that variables and subroutines be declared before being used. In addition, those languages generally allow you to write a program that is composed of several separate files. In AppleScript, a script is contained in a single file.

Q Why can't I write x = 14? Why do I have to write set x to 14?

A In AppleScript, the = operator is used only for the test of equality. This prevents the confusion that occurs in some languages when it serves both purposes. For example in C, you can write if x = 14, but it will not do what you probably want. It will set the value of x to 14, and then it will test that value. If you are used to other programming languages, getting your fingers to type set may be one of the hardest tasks you have at the beginning. Rest assured that you'll quickly get used to it.

Workshop

The workshop contains quiz questions and activities to help you solidify your knowledge of the material in this hour. Try to answer all of the questions before looking at the quiz answers that follow.

Quiz

1. How do you declare a variable in AppleScript?
2. What is the difference between a property and a variable?
3. How do you invoke a user-defined command or subroutine?
4. What is the difference between these variable names: `myData`, `Mydata`, and `my_data`?

Quiz Answers

1. You don't declare variables. You just use them.
2. A property is defined in a script using the syntax shown in this hour. Its value is defined there, and it remains set at that value unless it is changed when the script runs. The changed value is retained in the script over time. To reset the value, you need to recompile the script.
3. You use its name and parameters. If it is inside a tell block, you need to use `my` or `of me`.
4. The first two are the same variable: Capitalization doesn't matter in AppleScript. The last is an illegal variable name because AppleScript variable names can consist only of letters and numbers, and must start with a letter.

Activities

Write a script to count the windows open in the Finder. Open the Result window to monitor your script.

Count the letters in the title of the front-most window.

Open the Event Log window so that you can see several results at a time. Now use the programming techniques from Hour 7 to get the title of every window in the Finder.

HOUR 10

Scripting the Finder

The script syntax you've seen so far has been general AppleScript syntax, available at all times. You've also seen a few tell blocks that direct commands to specific applications, but the emphasis has been on the general syntax.

Now it's time to start scripting individual applications. The Finder is one of the most important of these, and it is the subject of this hour. The first section examines the Standard suite in great detail. The Standard suite is implemented by most applications that are scriptable. Each one implements it in a slightly different way. Some of the commands have the same syntax and functionality across all applications; others vary depending on the needs of the applications.

The suites described in this chapter (particularly the Standard suite) are described in much more detail than the other suites that you'll see in this part of the book. This is just to get you used to looking at suites. By the end of this hour, you should be able to understand dictionaries on your own.

In This Hour

- References—References allow you to specify objects for AppleScript to act on. You've seen them before; this section provides full details.
- Inheritance—This concept is at the heart of the dictionary class structure in AppleScript.
- Standard Suite—These are the commands and classes that most applications implement in one way or another.
- Finder Basics—In this suite, you'll find the commands and classes specific to the Finder.
- Finder Items—This small suite defines Finder items from which other Finder classes are derived.
- Container and Folders Suite—These classes let you work with disks and folders.
- Files Suite—The heart of your work with the Finder is the files on your disk.
- Window Classes Suite—You can manipulate the windows that display your files with these classes.
- Legacy Suite—Finally, there's a suite of commands that were implemented in old versions of the Finder and AppleScript: They will still work, thanks to the Legacy suite.

References

In the discussions of AppleScript syntax so far, you have seen references in use, but they have not been described. In order to proceed, it is necessary to discuss the concept.

A simple line of AppleScript code such as the following behaves as you would expect; its result is "now."

```
set x to word 1 of "now is the time"
```

In fact, what happens is that a *reference* (word 1 of "now is the time") is evaluated, and its value—"now"—is returned.

A reference can be defined simply as an AppleScript phrase that identifies one or more objects when it is executed. Much of the utility of references comes from the fact that rather than specifying an object when you write the script (the name of a file, for example), you can specify an object that you describe when you write the script and that is identified at runtime (the selection, the front-most window, and the like).

A reference consists of three parts:

- It identifies the `class` or `type` of the object in question. (Class and type are used synonymously in this sense.) In the example given here, `word` is the class of the object; other common classes used in the Finder suite are `files`, `folders`, `windows`, and `disks`.

- It specifies where to find the object. This may be referred to as a container. The container may be named or it may be an expression. In the example shown here, it is an expression (`"now is the time"`). The location may be implicit in a tell block: telling the Finder to get the front-most window means selecting from its set of open windows.

- Finally, a reference contains distinguishing information (a *reference form*) to resolve ambiguities. In the example shown here, `word 1` consists of a class and a reference form. The reference form may be complex and scattered throughout the reference as in `word 3 of paragraph 2 of selection`.

Sometimes you don't want the value; you want the reference itself. The Finder suites are full of uses of references; the very first entry uses a reference, and it shows why they're useful.

Inheritance

Inheritance is a concept of object-oriented programming that is used extensively in AppleScript. As used in AppleScript, it means simply that you can define a class, specify its properties, and then define a second class based on the first one. The second class is said to *inherit* the first class's attributes.

You'll find an example in the Finder suite with the `container` class. The `container` class is an abstract class that exists nowhere in the operating system. Finder containers can contain folders and files; they can be expanded or not. The abstract class serves as the ancestor for two real classes: `disks` and `folders`. Each of those inherits from the `container` class. Because they share this common background, the AppleScript code that you write to identify a file or folder on a disk is the same code that you write to identify a file or folder within a folder. The `disk` class defines additional properties (such as `capacity`) that are not relevant to folders.

Inheritance can extend over several generations. The `container` class itself is a descendant of the Finder `item` class. Inheritance is shown in a dictionary as follows in this line from the `container` class:

```
<Inheritance>  item  [r/o]  -- inherits some of its properties from the item ¬
   class
```

10

This means that the properties of the `item` class (defined in the Finder Items suite) are inherited by this class: If a property is a property of the `item` class, it is a property of the `container` class. This makes for a very nice structure of objects, and it can be carried further, as it is in this case.

Standard Suite: Terms That Most Applications Support

Most scriptable applications support some or all of the commands in the *Standard suite*. The commands in the Standard suite are defined by AppleScript, but they are implemented in each individual application. Although they have the same meaning in each case, what they actually do may vary.

If you open the Finder dictionary using Script Editor, you will see the window shown in Figure 10.1. You can click on the name of any suite in the left-hand scrolling list to see its syntax. For example, click on Standard Suite to see this display.

FIGURE 10.1

The Finder Standard suite provides many application functions.

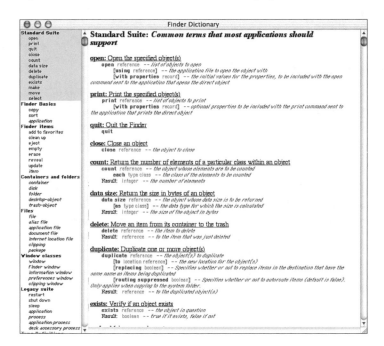

You can also click on a single item at the left to see its syntax rather than an entire suite's syntax. This is shown in Figure 10.2.

FIGURE 10.2

Click its name to see the syntax for a single item.

 In old documentation, you may find references to a *Required suite* that all scriptable applications needed to support. It consisted of the run, quit, open, and reopen commands that are now part of the Standard suite.

10

You saw how to open dictionaries in Hour 8, "Introducing Script Editor." As a reminder, suites consist of commands and classes. The syntax for commands shows optional parameters in square brackets. You'll see that in this section, and it is pointed out in the first few entries.

Commands in the Standard suite are listed here, and their purposes are described. The syntax for each one is available in the Finder dictionary using Script Editor, so it is not repeated here. Some examples of usage are provided; however, such examples are not part of the dictionary. Not all of the commands in each suite are presented. You'll see some of the representative ones, and the other commands will be presented in a list at the end.

close

Here's the full entry for the close command in the Finder dictionary:

```
close: Close an object
  close  reference  -- the object to close
```

At runtime, the reference you pass in will be evaluated as described previously in this hour. If the reference evaluates to something of the wrong class, you'll receive a message such as this:

```
Handler can't handle objects of this class
```

open

The close command takes a direct object that is a reference to the object to close. open works the same way.

count

Use the count command to count items in a reference as in these lines:

```
count the words of "now is the time"
```

As you would expect, the result is 4. The count command takes a reference as its first parameter. If you examine the syntax, this is the general form:

```
count "now is the time" each character
```

delete

The delete command moves the object pointed to by a reference to the Trash.

make

The make command specifies a type class, which is what to make. For example, use this within a tell block to the Finder to create a new Finder window:

```
make new Finder window
```

You can set properties for the object that you create:

```
make new Finder window with properties {current view:list view}
```

You'll see more about properties in the next section, "Finder Basics," which discusses File classes.

Other Commands in the Finder Standard Suite

The Finder Standard suite contains a variety of other commands:

- duplicate
- exists
- move
- print
- quit
- data size
- select

Standard Suite Commands Not Implemented in the Finder

As noted previously, each application implements the Standard suite for itself because each command may have a different meaning in different applications. This design means that the syntax for commands such as duplicate is the same across all applications.

However, some commands in the Standard suite (and in other suites) don't make sense for all applications. Accordingly, they are not implemented. The rule is: If you implement a command, the syntax must be standard, but you don't have to implement all commands.

Here are the Standard suite commands that are not implemented in the Finder. They are defined in Apple's documentation, and they may or may not be implemented in other applications.

- launch
- run
- save
- reopen
- set
- get

10

Finder Basics

The Finder Basics suite consists of two commands, copy and sort, as well as one class: application. This is the first class that you'll examine in depth; its description is used to help show you how all classes are defined in AppleScript.

The application in question is the Finder itself. The Finder Basics suite is shown in Figure 10.3 with the application class highlighted.

FIGURE 10.3

The Finder Basics suite defines the application class for the Finder itself.

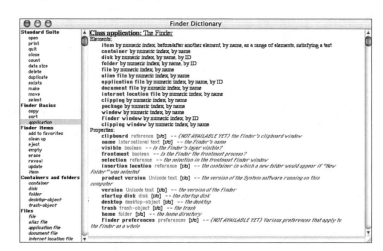

Elements

Elements are objects contained within a class. There can be many, one, or no instances of a single element. Here is the AppleScript dictionary entry for the element `file` of the application class:

file by numeric index, by name

All of the elements of the application class are identifiable by their names. In some other classes, definitions need to be provided as comments when the names are not self-explanatory.

In the definition shown here, the element `file` is defined. The syntax that follows it shows how a `file` element can be referenced. Because there may be multiple instances of a single element, you need ways to distinguish among them. In this case, there are two: numeric index and name.

To use a numeric index, you use a number (or an expression that evaluates to a number). Here is the code to get the fifth file on the Finder desktop:

```
tell application "Finder"
  get file 5
end tell
```

To get an instance of an element by name, you use syntax such as this:

```
tell application "Finder"
  get file "78901r.doc"
end tell
```

Unless otherwise noted, the commands in this hour are targeted to the Finder. To save space, the `tell` and `end tell` lines are omitted from the scripts after this point.

The most generic element of the application is `item`. An instance can be identified by other methods, as you can see from its definition:

item by numeric index, before/after another element, by name, ¬
    as a range of elements, satisfying a test

The syntax for getting an instance before or after another is simple:

```
get item before item "2001-2002 budg63 Folder"
```

And, to get a range of elements, use this code:

```
get items 1 thru 5
```

Another form of a range is

```
items item1 thru item2
```

where `item1` and `item2` are specific items in an ordered list that you select.

Finally, you can get items that satisfy a test such as

```
get items where name ends with ".tiff"
```

This command will return all the files that have a .tiff extension. A complete list of AppleScript operations is provided in Appendix B, "Operators."

Properties

Properties differ from elements in that they are unique to a given class object. The Finder application may have dozens of files, but it has only one name and one selection, one clipboard, one desktop, and so forth. All AppleScript classes have a name, but their other properties differ depending on what they are.

Properties can be strings, numbers, or Boolean (true/false) values. For example, the Finder application has Boolean properties `visible` and `frontmost` that let you find out if it is visible (that is, not hidden using Hide from the Finder application menu) and whether it is the front-most application.

Finder Items

The next Finder suite is Finder Items. It contains commands and a class to help you work with the file system. Commands such as `add to favorites`, `clean up`, `eject`, `empty` (trash), and `erase` are self-explanatory. Two others help illustrate the difference between working with the mouse and writing a script.

The `reveal` command makes an item visible. When you work with the mouse, you click a folder, window, or other interface element to select it, and then you work on it with a menu command or the mouse. By definition, the items you are working with are selected and visible. With AppleScript, you can identify the items to work on with a script (by identifying elements as described previously), and you can go about working on them without the user being able to see what is happening. That may be fine, but when you are finished, you often want the affected window, document, folder, or the like to be visible to the user. The `reveal` command scrolls it into view or brings it forward—whatever is necessary to show it.

The `update` command updates the display to reflect changes you have made via the script. Again, this is something that has no analog in the point-and-click world: The display is automatically updated.

The single class is the Finder `item` class. It is used as an abstract class for other Finder items, and it defines properties that are common to those items. For example, because `information window` is a property of the common Finder `item` class, it need not be defined in descendant classes such as `container`, `disk`, or `folder`. But it's there through inheritance, and for any objects in those classes, you can tell the Finder

```
open information window of container 1
```

Container and Folders Suite

The Container and Folders suite is one of the most important Finder suites. It consists of elements that can contain other elements or other instances of themselves: folders, disks, the Desktop, and the Trash. Figure 10.4 shows the dictionary for the `container` class, one of the classes in this suite.

FIGURE 10.4

The dictionary for the container *class shows disks, folders, desktop objects, and trash objects.*

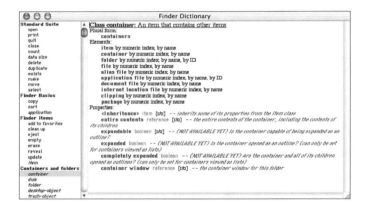

At the top of the definition, you'll see a new type of entry: the plural form. AppleScript can let you use a plural form of a name. English is one of the languages with many variations of plural forms (oxen, geese, and sheep being three examples from the animal world), so being able to specify a plural is useful in all of the languages with this problem.

The other classes in this suite—`disk`, `folder`, `desktop-object`, and `trash-object`—are descendants of the `container` class. Thus, they inherit `container` and `item` properties. In fact, `folder` and `desktop-object` have no properties of their own. The `trash-object` has one property: `warns before emptying`. Other than that, it's just a container as far as properties are concerned.

Files Suite

Like the Containers and Folders suite, the Files suite contains no commands, just classes. These classes are `file`, `alias file`, `application file`, and `document file`. Three other classes are of interest:

- `internet location file` is a file containing an Internet location. This class can help you to write code that accesses information in similar ways whether it is on your disk or the Internet. Because `internet location file` is a descendant of `file`, you can write code that manipulates an object of this class identically to a file object.
- `clipping` is a Finder clipping file created when you drag content out of a window.
- `package` refers to a folder usually containing an application and its resources that appears as a single file on the desktop.

Window Classes Suite

The Window Classes suite defines the `window` class and its subclasses such as `finder window`, `information window`, `preferences window`, and `clipping window`. You can set properties such as `position` and `bounds` to locate the window and to set its size. Other properties for specific types of windows let you find the current panel of preferences for windows, the current view of Finder windows, and so forth. You can also set many of these properties in order to create an automated user experience.

Legacy Suite

The Legacy suite illustrates yet another aspect of what you can do with AppleScript. The commands and classes defined here used to be part of the Finder on Mac OS 9 and earlier, but on Mac OS X, they are handled by other parts of the operating system. The implementation of these commands in the Mac OS X Finder dispatches them to the appropriate places. Thus, old AppleScript code written for Mac OS 9 and earlier continues to work.

Summary

This hour has combined the syntax described in previous hours into your first in-depth exploration of a single application's scripting. The Finder is scriptable both with regard to its underlying data (files, folders, disks, and the like) as well as its interface (windows). You've seen how the concepts of references and inheritance play out in the syntax of this hour; rest assured that they will retain a prominent role in the rest of this book.

Scripting the Finder is all well and good for routine tasks; however, you can move on and script applications from Apple to significantly increase your productivity. The next hour shows you how.

Q&A

Q Why are there so many Finder suites?

A Breaking up an application's scripting support into several suites can make it easier for you to work with what would otherwise be a large suite.

Q How much of this do I really need to remember?

A Very little. Remember, the dictionaries for scriptable applications are always at hand in Script Editor. What you should remember is the sort of things you can do; consult the dictionary for the actual syntax.

Q How often do the dictionaries change?

A The implementation of commands changes periodically as the applications change, but Apple and other developers attempt to minimize changes in the script syntax itself. (That's why the Legacy suite exists.)

Workshop

The workshop contains quiz questions and activities to help you solidify your knowledge of the material in this hour. Try to answer all of the questions before looking at the quiz answers that follow.

Quiz

1. What is the Legacy suite?
2. What are references?
3. What is the difference between elements and properties?

Quiz Answers

1. The Legacy suite consists of commands that formerly were implemented in the Finder but are now handled by other parts of the operating system. In order to provide compatibility with Mac OS 9 and earlier scripts, they remain in the Finder dictionary. They are no longer implemented by the Finder, but they will be processed as they were before.

2. References are pointers to objects or data. They are not the objects themselves. Many of the Finder commands take references as their direct object.

3. A class can have many instances of its elements, but only one value for each property. The Finder, for example, has many instances of its windows element, but it has only one clipboard.

Activities

With the Desktop visible in List or Column view in the Finder, try getting the various elements defined in the Finder application class. View the results in the Event Log or Result window.

The following activity combines a number of different skills that you've learned. The end result is purely for practice (who cares what the average length of the words in your window title is?), but rest assured that this type of iterative processing is common to programming.

Count the number of characters in the title of each window in the Finder and add them up. This task will require you to use the control structures described in Hour 7, "Basic Programming Concepts," and you will need to access the window titles as you did in the activities for the previous hour. You'll also need to use the count command as described in this hour.

Repeat the previous activity, but now make it a little more complex: Find the average length of the words in all the window titles by dividing the number of words by the number of characters.

10

Hour 11

Scripting Mac OS X Applications from Apple

This hour examines many but not all of the scriptable applications from Apple. Some are installed automatically as part of Mac OS X; others are downloadable from Apple's Web site. One of the most exciting aspects of Mac OS X and its AppleScript support is the way in which these small applications can be put together in new and innovative ways by people like you. All you need is the AppleScript glue.

In discussing these applications and their scripting features, the focus is on those that make the application special as well as those that interact particularly well with other applications both from Apple and elsewhere. In addition, examining the syntax of these applications helps to introduce additional features of AppleScript that have not been discussed previously.

As this part of the book continues with third-party applications in the next hour, you'll begin to learn more about building scripts. This won't come so much from explicit instructions about how to write more complex scripts; rather it will come from seeing these scripts as they are presented to you.

In This Hour

- Reading a Dictionary—Here's the most effective way to approach a new dictionary with AppleScript syntax.
- iCal—In addition to the iCal examples shown previously in Hour 9, "Basic AppleScript Syntax," this section shows another way of searching for events.
- Help Viewer—You can integrate Help Viewer assistance automatically using AppleScript.
- Mail—The Mail code shown previously in Hour 3, "Running the Scripts You Already Have," is now rewritten as a subroutine that you can use in more general cases.
- Address Book—The Address Book sample code shown here provides the basic few lines that let you loop through all items found in a search.
- TextEdit—This section shows you two ways of scripting TextEdit.
- DVD Player—You can automate almost all of DVD Player's functionality using AppleScript.
- Internet Connect—You can script the application to connect to the Internet.
- Print Center—Print Center supports no commands, but you can use AppleScript to query the status of printers and queues.
- Disk Copy—The scripting commands for Disk Copy can be used to create and burn CDs and DVDs overnight as part of complex work flows.
- Terminal—You can script the command line in Terminal. In addition, this section shows you how to use the clipboard to communicate between Terminal and Aqua applications.

Reading a Dictionary

You've seen what's in a dictionary in previous hours. You'll be relying on dictionaries as you explore these and other applications. This section provides a guide to how to get the most out of a dictionary when you approach it for the first time.

The iCal dictionary is shown in Figure 11.1. (The final class—event—is not visible at the bottom of the window.)

You know how a dictionary is laid out. Here's how to put it together. This recipe for reading a dictionary works in almost all cases. (The exceptions are some complex dictionaries.)

Figure 11.1

The dictionary for the iCal suite shows its syntax.

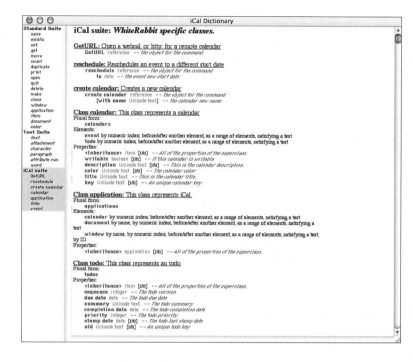

Find the `application` Class and Its Elements

To start with, look for the `application` class. It represents the application itself. The `application` class is about halfway down the screen shown in Figure 11.1.

Look for its elements. Here there are three: `calendar`, `document`, and `window`. Go to the definitions of the elements (`calendar` is above the `application` class.)

Look at the Element Definitions

Most of the time, you only want to deal with a calendar. As you can see, you can access calendars by numeric index, before/after, as a range, or satisfying a test. (This is the common set of accesses.) So now you know that you can write this script:

```
tell application "iCal"
 get calendar 1
end tell
```

Look at the properties of `calendar`. Among them is `title`; that means you can write this line of code:

```
get title of calendar 1
```

Of course, you can also get any of the other properties of the calendar.

Next, look up the `calendar` class to see what its elements are: They are `event` and `todo`. You can access them in the same ways that you access calendars within the application. So now you can write this line of code:

```
get last todo of calendar 1
```

> Although you can write this line of code, it is not guaranteed to execute correctly in all cases. If there are no to-dos in the calendar, there is nothing to get. Hour 20, "Advanced AppleScript Syntax," goes into error handling for cases such as this.

And finally, if you look inside the `todo` class, you'll see that among its properties is `summary`. So you can write this:

```
get summary of last todo of calendar 1
```

Repeat for Elements Contained Within Elements

Repeat the process as necessary until there are no more elements to explore.

To recap:

1. Go to the application and see what its elements are.
2. For any elements that interest you, go to their class definition to see what their properties and elements are.
3. Repeat until you find what you need to do your work or until you find a class with no elements in it (thus no inner objects for you to continue tracing through the dictionary).

iCal

You saw in Hour 9 how to find calendars and events within them based on dates. Using the iCal dictionary, you can search on words or phrases in event summaries as shown here:

```
tell application "iCal"
 set theCalendars to calendars whose title is "Personal"
 tell item 1 of theCalendars to count (events where summary contains "Anni")
end tell
```

The iCal dictionary demonstrates another tip you should remember in look-ing at dictionaries: Look for commands that modify data rather than chang-ing properties yourself. In this case, there's a `reschedule` command. Use it to change an event. By using a command, you can ensure that an application does any related processing; simply changing an attribute's value may not do that.

Help Viewer

The next application dealt with in this hour is Help Viewer, and its scriptability enables you to do some very impressive things. First, take a look at the Help Viewer suite shown in Figure 11.2.

FIGURE 11.2

The dictionary for the Help Viewer suite pro-vides its syntax.

By now you've seen several AppleScript dictionaries, so you should be able to make your way through this one on your own. There are commands and a class for the applica-tion; the class inherits from the main AppleScript application class.

As will frequently be the case, many of the commands may seem daunting at first. Don't worry: Just focus on what you understand easily. For example, take a look at the search command. That's simple enough. Here is a little script that searches Help Viewer for `"ink jet"`.

```
tell application "Help Viewer"
 activate
 search looking for "ink jet"
end tell
```

The result of this script is shown in Figure 11.3.

Think for a moment what this means. Using Help Viewer to get help isn't particularly hard. But this means that you can write a script to search with Help Viewer on any text you choose. If you're writing an AppleScript application, you can put a Help button in a window (using AppleScript Studio) and have that button automatically search for a string that you prepare based on what your window does.

You can also write your own interface to Help Viewer. As you'll see in Hour 13, "Interacting with Users," you can pose dialogs and get information from users. You could then use that text in the search command in your script.

FIGURE 11.3
Automatically search for `"ink jet"` *using a script.*

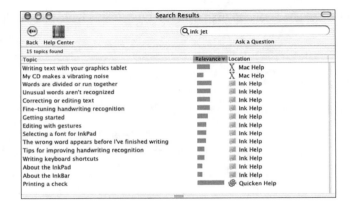

Mail

You saw in Hour 3 that Mail was highly scriptable. You may want to look back at the script shown there that creates a Mail message. Now that you've learned more about the AppleScript language, you should be able to see how the script actually works.

Here's a variation of that script that you can use in many places. Rather than the inline code shown in Hour 3, this script uses a subroutine to actually create and send the message. Here's the subroutine:

```
on createMailMessage given subject:theSubject, content:theContent, ¬
    sender:theSender, recipientName:theRecipientName, recipientAddress:¬
    theRecipientAddress

  tell application "Mail"
    set newMessage to make new outgoing message with properties ¬
    {subject:theSubject, content:theContent, sender:theSender, visible:true}
    tell newMessage
      make new to recipient at end of to recipients with properties ¬
      {name:theRecipientName, address:theRecipientAddress}
    end tell
```

```
   send newMessage
 end tell
end createMailMessage
```

As compared to the script in Hour 3, there are no constants involved; you pass them in as parameters. Thus, to invoke this subroutine, you need to set the parameters either using interaction with the user, by retrieving data from a database, or with code such as this:

```
set theSubject to "Test Message"
set theContent to "This is the message body."
set theSender to "yourself@mac.com"
set theRecipientName to "A Friend"
set theRecipientAddress to "friend@mac.com"
```

Then send the message by calling the subroutine:

```
createMailMessage of me given subject:theSubject, content:theContent, ¬
  sender:theSender, recipientName:theRecipientName, ¬
  recipientAddress:theRecipientAddress
```

Address Book

You can work your way through the Address Book dictionary in a similar manner to the way you looked at the iCal dictionary. There's something special in this dictionary—and it's something that you will run across periodically in dictionaries of scriptable applications. Look at the person class from the Address Book suite as shown in Figure 11.4.

11

FIGURE 11.4

The person class is in the Address Book suite.

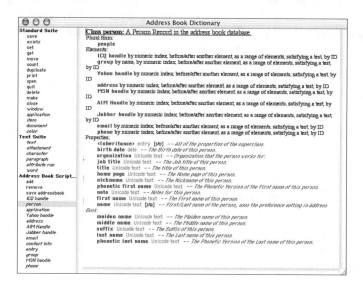

Here's a script that gets all of the people with the last name Harris and displays their first names. If you reuse this script, most likely you will replace the display with some other processing. Three points are worth noting here:

1. As you can see in Figure 11.4, the plural of person is people. Although persons would make sense in English, you need to use the AppleScript plural form—people.

2. This type of code is quite common when you want to loop through a list of returned records. The `repeat` clause format shown here is one of the commonly used AppleScript syntax structures.

3. Also, note that the `first name` property of the `person` class is Unicode text according to the dictionary. The `display dialog` command cannot display Unicode text, but you can convert it to a string—which can be displayed.

```
tell application "Address Book"
 set foundSet to people whose last name is "Harris"
 repeat with theperson in foundSet
  display dialog first name of theperson as string
 end repeat
end tell
```

TextEdit

TextEdit implements a very small suite of its own with its own application and document. It relies on the standard Text suite in AppleScript to do the work. Here's a short script that creates two paragraphs in a document.

```
tell application "TextEdit"
 activate
 set text of document 1 to ¬
  "The quick brown fox jumped over the lazy black dog."¬
  & return
 tell document 1
  make at end new paragraph with data "Next paragraph." with ¬
   properties {size:14}
 end tell
end tell
```

The first paragraph is created by the script in the same way you would create it with the keyboard: text followed by a return character. The second paragraph is created by the script using AppleScript syntax that creates a paragraph instance and fills it with data. Note that in this case you don't need to supply the return: TextEdit knows that a paragraph class needs to be followed by a return character.

The AppleScript `make` command (part of the Standard suite) is used so often that it's worthwhile to point out its syntax. You see its full version in the preceding script. You can omit the `with data` section (creating an empty object), and you can omit the `with properties` section (or use some or all of the properties defined for a class). You also can use these two sections in either order.

In this case, the second paragraph reads `"Next paragraph"` and its font size is `14`.

DVD Player

DVD Player has a very simple suite, which includes the commands you would expect, such as `play dvd`, `stop dvd`, and so forth. Two other commands open up some very interesting opportunities for scripting multimedia presentations, training tools, and more. You can use the DVD menu system to automatically navigate using the following sets of commands:

```
go to main menu
go to title menu
go to subpicture menu
go to audio menu
go to angle menu
go to ptt menu/return to dvd

press up arrow key
press down arrow key
press left arrow key
press right arrow key
press enter key
```

11

Internet Connect

Internet Connect has a dictionary containing only its own suite: No Standard suite is defined. If you are using dial-up access to the Internet, Internet Connect is easy enough to use. But there are cases where you want to make things even simpler. If you write an AppleScript Studio application, for instance, you can have someone fill in a form in a window. You can add a button that runs a script to launch Internet Connect and connect to the Internet for further processing of the data.

Print Center

The Print Center suite has no commands; it just has three classes. The application itself contains `printers`, and those contain `jobs`. You can use Print Center scripting to query status and provide reports, but you cannot start or stop jobs or printers from there.

Disk Copy

Sometimes a small application with only a few AppleScript commands can play a major role in an AppleScript workflow. Disk Copy is one example. It has only a few commands, but two, BurnCD and BurnDVD, will probably be important for you if you're building AppleScript solutions to run in off hours or overnight. You can pop a blank disc into your computer before you go home, let AppleScript collect the data, and then, whenever it's finished, burn the disc.

Image Capture Scripting

Here's another small application with just a few commands that can come in handy—and even work with Disk Copy. Image Capture Scripting lets you open and close image files. After they're opened, you can use the scale and rotate commands to modify the image. When scaling an image, you can scale it by a factor or to a given size; when rotating, you can rotate to any angle (even a fraction of a degree).

With Disk Copy and Image Capture Scripting, you can create a folder with image files in it and write a script to rotate or scale every image, copy it to a CD or DVD, and then burn it.

Terminal

Finally, Terminal is scriptable, and in scripting it, you can do some very interesting things. Terminal is the interface to the UNIX command line that is normally hidden from the user's view. Rather than pointing and clicking, you type in commands and they are executed by the core of Mac OS X.

One common UNIX command is date, which returns the date. Figure 11.5 shows what Terminal looks like when you type in **date** and press Return.

FIGURE 11.5

The date *command in the Terminal window.*

Instead of typing it into the Terminal window, you can run the command using Terminal's do script AppleScript command: Here's the code. The result is exactly the same.

```
tell application "Terminal"
 activate
 do script "date" in window 1
end tell
```

But you can do even more, and that's where things get interesting. In UNIX, you can use the output of one command as input to another. You do this by placing a | between the two commands to *pipe* the output of the first into the second.

In Mac OS X, Apple has added some Mac OS X commands to the UNIX commands available on the command line. One such command is pbcopy: It takes whatever is sent into it and puts it on the clipboard. (The "pb" in the command comes from the internal programmer terminology of "pasteboard," which refers to what users call the clipboard.)

This means that you can write date | pbcopy, piping the output of the date command into the pbcopy command. This copies the output of the UNIX command onto the Mac OS X clipboard from where the Finder can fetch it.

```
tell application "Terminal"
 activate
 do script "date | pbcopy" in window 1
end tell
```

What you have just seen is how to use AppleScript to run a UNIX command (or, indeed, a script consisting of several UNIX commands), paste the output on the clipboard, and be able to use it in the Finder or other applications.

11

Summary

This hour has shown you some of the scripting features in Apple's applications. Not all of them have been covered, but you now know how to open dictionaries and read them, so you can find out about them on your own.

Mail, iCal, and Address Book all interact with one another. You can create sophisticated and personalized AppleScript applications to combine them in your own way. (You'll work on one such application in Part III of this book.)

The final section of this hour, showing you how to script the command line in Terminal, is one of the most important aspects of AppleScript on Mac OS X. All of the scripting languages that are available on Mac OS X can interact through the command line, pipes, and the clipboard.

Q&A

Q I can't find script commands for some of the things I want to do with the Apple applications. Are they working on them?

A Apple has been seriously enhancing its AppleScript support. In some dictionaries, you'll see syntax that is marked as not yet implemented.

Q Where can I learn more about the command line in Terminal?

A For any given command, there's a man (manual) page. To find out more about a command, type `man` and the command name.

Workshop

The workshop contains quiz questions and activities to help you solidify your knowledge of the material in this hour. Try to answer all of the questions before looking at the quiz answers that follow.

Quiz

1. When scripting the command line in Terminal, how do you get output from UNIX commands back into AppleScript?

2. Why would you want to script DVD Player when the user can just as easily use the onscreen controller?

3. How do you find an application's elements?

Quiz Answers

1. One way is to pipe the output into `pbcopy`, which puts it on the clipboard from where you can access it.

2. You can write an AppleScript that lets people access specific items in Help Viewer and in DVD Player without knowing where they're located or even which application has the information they need.

3. Go to the application class in the dictionary. Find its elements. For each element, find its class definition until you come to an element that contains no further elements.

Activities

Create an e-mail message that contains a value from a spreadsheet.

Search an e-mail message for a given word. (View the results in the Result or Event Log window.) One way of doing this is to use a `repeat` loop to examine each word. Another is to use a text operator as shown in Appendix B, "Operators."

Look at the Count Messages in All Mailboxes script, which is inside Mail Scripts in the AppleScript folder inside Applications. In its repetition, it does something similar to what you did in the previous activity. It's much more complex, though, because it's doing more work, and it's written using subroutines and other good programming techniques. You should be able to read that script now and understand it.

11

Hour **12**

Scripting Mac OS X Applications from Third Parties

You've seen how to script the Finder and how to script many of Apple's applications that come with Mac OS X or that can be downloaded from the Apple Web site. Now it's time to move on to third-party applications.

As in the preceding hour, the applications discussed in this hour have been chosen not only for their importance, but also to demonstrate still more features and aspects of AppleScript. So even if you don't use a particular application, read through its section so that you can see what it can do and how you may be able to use that information in other applications.

For example, the section on Scripting Retrospect delves into lists and records, concepts of AppleScript that you've seen in use, but which have not been discussed at length.

One important use of third-party applications and AppleScript is to move data from one environment to another. You'll see in Hour 21, "Creating AppleScripts to Control Multiple Applications," how to use InDesign to format information retrieved from applications such as FileMaker (described in this hour) and Address Book (described in the preceding hour).

In This Hour

- Scripting America Online—You can script your log on to your AOL account.
- Scripting AppleWorks—Scripts in this section show you how to create word processing and spreadsheet documents and how to manipulate their data.
- Scripting FileMaker—You can script FileMaker in several ways. This section shows you how to run FileMaker scripts as well as how to use AppleScript to carry out a Find in FileMaker.
- Scripting Microsoft Office—You'll see how to script Microsoft Office both with AppleScript and with Visual Basic.
- Scripting Internet Explorer—You can navigate the Web using AppleScript commands.
- Scripting Photoshop—Photoshop uses its own scripting engine, but it's available through AppleScript.
- Scripting Retrospect—This section shows you how to use Retrospect's dictionary and how to interpret result classes declared in any dictionary.

Scripting America Online

You can write scripts to log on and log off to America Online. One reason you might want to do this is if you want someone to check your mail while you're gone, but you don't want to give out your password. Write a script like the following one, and save it as run-only (that is, without the text). Although someone could poke into the script to pull out your password, that's beyond the skills of most people.

```
tell application "AOL"
  activate
  Sign On screenname "jessefeiler" password "jf"
end tell
```

This scenario is for demonstration purposes only. The safest way to actually do this is to change your password before you leave, reveal the new password to your friend, and then change it back again when you return.

Scripting AppleWorks

AppleWorks is Apple's all-purpose application that lets you work with spreadsheets, databases, presentations, drawing and painting documents, and word processing documents. It's bundled with some Macintosh models (generally the iMac and iBook models).

At one point, it was spun off into a separate company, Claris, but it's now back at Apple. It's included in this hour as a third-party product because it is available for sale in retail outlets separately from Macintosh computers (as well as installed on some of them).

Scripting support is extensive in AppleWorks. This section covers a few of the highlights including how to get started.

Because AppleWorks can deal with so many different types of documents, you need to be able to distinguish among them. They are all documents for AppleWorks; the document kind property is used to distinguish among them as you can see here:

```
tell application "AppleWorks 6"
  activate
  make new document at front with properties¬
   {document kind:text document, name:"Things to Do Today"}
end tell
```

Just to recap what you learned in the past hour, this information is found by looking in the dictionary for the application class. Remember that there can be more than one. Look at the most specific one—use the Standard suite application only if there is no other one. That is the case with AppleWorks.

Look for the elements of the application class; in this case there are two—documents and windows. Look in the document class and there you'll find the document kind property:

```
document kind¬
  drawing document/text document/spreadsheet document/¬
  database document/painting document/presentation document
```

In the past hour, you also learned how to tell a newly created TextEdit document to create a paragraph at the end of its text. The code in AppleWorks is identical:

```
tell application "AppleWorks 6"
  activate
  make new document at front with properties ¬
   {document kind:text document, name:" Things to Do Today"}
  tell document 1
    make new paragraph at end with data "Laundry. Shop for present for Gail."
  end tell
end tell
```

12

This isn't an accident: This is the point of having suites declared with common syntax. In the case of asking a text-editing document to create a new paragraph, the syntax can be identical.

However, in the case of creating a new document, the code is not the same. It's similar, but the properties are different, reflecting the different designs of the applications. In fact, creating a new paragraph is the same in the simple case shown here, but there are different properties in the two applications (and in others). So if you are setting properties, you may need to consult the application's dictionary to find out what they are and what their names are.

Making a spreadsheet is just as easy. Spreadsheets don't have paragraphs; instead they have cells. The cells don't need to be created, but you need to set and get their data. Here's a script that creates a new AppleWorks spreadsheet and sets cell A1 to 14. Next, it copies that cell to the clipboard and pastes its value into cell B1.

In the past hour, you saw how to use pipes in the Terminal to get data from UNIX tools that you can run via AppleScript and paste the data onto the clipboard. Here you see how to copy data to the clipboard and paste it into a document. Nothing prevents you from copying output from a UNIX tool via the clipboard into a spreadsheet or other document with AppleScript. In fact, that's one of the most exciting areas that has opened up with the implementation of AppleScript on Mac OS X.

```
tell application "AppleWorks 6"
  activate
  make new document at front with properties¬
  {document kind:spreadsheet document, name:"My Spreadsheet"}
  tell document 1
    set cell "A1" to 14
    copy to clipboard cell "A1"
    select cell "B1"
    paste values
    recalculate
  end tell
end tell
```

Scripting FileMaker

FileMaker is owned by Apple, but it is its own corporate entity, FileMaker, Inc. FileMaker is one of the easiest-to-use databases available on any platform; it is now implemented on Windows and Macintosh, with a FileMaker Mobile version available for cell phones and PDAs.

Because FileMaker is scriptable, it is a common application used in workflow solutions where database data is moved into a scriptable page layout application such as Quark

XPress or InDesign. This is all discussed in great detail in Hour 21. FileMaker can also be scripted to import data from other applications. You can write a Perl script to parse data from the Internet or other sources and then import it into FileMaker with AppleScript.

One of the most common things that you want to do is to manipulate a database by searching for information. That's easy to do with FileMaker and AppleScript. Use the show command to perform a find as the following code demonstrates. The only thing you need to know is that what FileMaker calls a field in its own world becomes a cell in AppleScript. This script finds records from the Inventory database template that ships with FileMaker.

```
tell application "FileMaker Pro"
  show (every record of database 1 where cell "Location" = "Lab")
end tell
```

The problem with this script (and with many similar scripts) is that it can fail not because of syntax errors but because there is no data available. Either case produces an error. Look back at the control statements in Hour 7, "Basic Programming Concepts." You can add a try block to this script so that if an error is encountered, no message is displayed.

```
tell application "FileMaker Pro"
  try
    show (every record of database 1 where cell "Location" = "x")
  end try
end tell
```

This solves the problem of producing an error message when no records are found; but the solution comes at the expense of hiding all error messages. The solution is to only hide the error message for no records being found. Here's how you do that.

Test to see if the error number is -1728 (the no records found error). If it is, do nothing; otherwise, take some other action such as posing a dialog (which you'll see how to do in the next hour).

To find the error number, you can look in the FileMaker documentation. A quick-and-dirty way of doing so is to test the code and temporarily insert a dialog into the error handler to display the number (which you have stored in a variable called theNumber). When you have its value, you can write this code:

```
tell application "FileMaker Pro"
  try
    show (every record of database 1 where cell "Location" = "x")
  on error number theNumber
    if theNumber = -1728
      --take no action because no records found isn't an error
```

12

```
      else
        --report the error
      end
    end try
  end tell
```

FileMaker is an example of an application that supports several types of scripting. It has its own scripting language that you can use to write scripts. You can then invoke them via AppleScript by using the doscript command. The following script sets a data element of a FileMaker record in the current database to a value; it then runs a FileMaker script to reformat the data.

```
tell application "FileMaker Pro"
  set data cell "Street" of record 1 to "14 Hudson Street"
  doscript "reformatAddress"
end tell
```

One reason why some applications support their own scripting languages is that it makes it easier for them to support multiple platforms. You can access FileMaker scripts from Visual Basic on Windows as well as from AppleScript on the Macintosh. Some applications only support their platform-independent scripting languages; others support their scripting languages as well as one or more platform-specific scripting languages.

Scripting Microsoft Office

The applications in Microsoft Office can be scripted using Microsoft's Visual Basic; they can also be scripted using AppleScript. If you want to run a Visual Basic script, you use the do Visual Basic command:

```
do Visual Basic "nameOfScriptToRun"
```

In addition, you can use other AppleScript commands in Word and Excel.

Word

The standard word processing script that has been used with TextEdit and AppleWorks runs as well on Word:

```
tell application "Microsoft Word"
  activate
  make new document
  tell document 1
    make new paragraph at end with data "Demonstration"
  end tell
end tell
```

As you browse the Word dictionary, you'll find that many of the formatting commands are available to you. You use the same logical structure you've already used to identify the objects to tell as in this code:

```
tell paragraph 1 of document 1
  set justification to center
  set size to 14
end tell
```

When you look in the Word dictionary, you'll see that the paragraph class inherits from both the character and section classes. In the preceding code, justification is a property of the paragraph class, and size is a property of the character class. Because paragraph inherits from character, all of the character properties are available for setting at the paragraph level.

This is the first time you've seen an example of *multiple inheritance*, where there are two ancestors. Their properties and elements are combined in the resulting class. Sometimes, as in the case of paragraphs, the properties and elements are simply merged. Other times, some do not apply in certain circumstances.

It is also worth noting that although the inheritance statement is often the first property in a class description, it is not always so. The Word dictionary places the inheritance statements last.

PowerPoint

PowerPoint is also scriptable, but its scripting is limited to the do Visual Basic command.

Scripting Internet Explorer

12

Internet Explorer, like Netscape, is scriptable. Both support the standard GetURL and OpenURL commands. OpenURL allows you to specify the window or file where the URL data should be placed. Although this is a very simple script, you should see the GetURL command now because it will be used in the next part of the book.

```
tell application "Internet Explorer"
  activate
  GetURL "http://www.philmontmill.com/"
end tell
```

Netscape supports a do JavaScript command, whereas Explorer supports a do script command, which also runs JavaScripts.

Scripting Photoshop

Photoshop is scriptable via its own scripting language. (Photoshop refers to its scripts as *actions*.) The Photoshop do script command is presented in its entirety from the Photoshop dictionary to show you a common type of issue with commands.

Particularly when used in droplets, some commands generate dialogs and other messages from the application. Because scripts need to run in unattended environments, you need to be able to suppress such messages. The do script command is an example of the sorts of messages you can suppress.

```
do script  string  -- Name of action or actual action to execute
  [with  a list of alias]  ¬
    -- List of files on which to run the action.  ¬
    -- If this parameter is not present, the script is run on the active ¬
    -- document *for use only by droplets*
  [override open  boolean]  ¬
    -- Override open commands in the action *for use only by droplets*
  [include subfolders  boolean]  ¬
    -- Process subfolders of folders dropped on the droplet ¬
      *for use only by droplets*
  override save  boolean]  ¬
    -- Override save commands in the action *for use only by droplets*
  [save and close  boolean]  ¬
    -- Save processed files over originals *for use only by droplets*
  [save to  alias]  ¬
    -- Save processed files to this folder *for use only by droplets*
  [log  alias]  -- Error log file *for use only by droplets*
```

AppleWorks has a similar issue with its open command. When you open a document that is protected by a password, a dialog opens asking you to enter the password. Likewise, if a document needs data conversion, another dialog opens. A third opens if you are open-ing a non-AppleWorks document and you need to decide what type of AppleWorks docu-ment you want it opened as. Thus, here is the open command syntax for AppleWorks. It lets you specify this information in advance so that your script is not stopped by a dialog:

```
open alias  -- list of objects to open
  [using translator  international text]  ¬
    -- the name of the translator to use to open the file
  [as document type  drawing document/text document/¬
    spreadsheet document/database document/painting document/¬
    presentation]  ¬
    -- the type of AppleWorks document as which to open the file
  [with password  string]  -- the password to use
```

If you're not very familiar with an application that you're scripting, make sure you run it before writing a script. (Believe it or not, this advice is needed by some people!) Also, look for options in commands that may seem strange to you. Many people don't know that they can password protect AppleScript documents, for example. Not only will you learn something about the application, but you'll start to think about conditions that could occur when your script is running at 3 a.m. with no one around. These issues are much less important if you are writing a script just for your own use. If you are processing files and data from other people, their idiosyncrasies may be no greater in number than yours—but they will probably be different.

Scripting Retrospect

Finally, the popular Retrospect backup software from Dantz is presented. It allows you to look more closely at two data structures that you have seen before but not examined in depth: lists and records.

Retrospect lets you control backups from scripts. It also lets you examine the status of an individual script of all backups. Here is the Retrospect status command from the dictionary:

```
Retrospect status  string  -- ¬
   If script name is specified, lists volumes and backup sets for that script. ¬
   Otherwise, all volumes and backup sets are listed.
Result:   Retrospect reply  -- A record of class Retrospect reply.
```

The result of the command is a Retrospect reply, a class defined elsewhere in the Retrospect suite. Until now, most of the commands that have been examined have returned standard AppleScript types such as Booleans, text, or references to objects. Often, developers create classes to be used as a reply, as is the case with Retrospect reply in Retrospect. Here is the class:

```
Class Retrospect reply: The Retrospect status reply record.
Properties:
   current script  string  [r/o]  ¬
    -- The name of the currently running script, or nothing if idle.
   current source  string  [r/o]  ¬
    -- The name of the source in use by the current script.
   current destination  string  [r/o]  ¬
    -- The name of the destination in use by the current script.
   interactive  boolean  [r/o]  ¬
    -- Whether Retrospect is in interactive mode.
   in Backup Server  boolean  [r/o]  ¬
    -- Whether Retrospect is currently executing the Backup Server
   executing  boolean  [r/o]  ¬
    -- Whether Retrospect is currently executing or starting to execute a script
```

12

```
scripts  list  [r/o]  ¬
  -- A list of all the currently known scripts.
volumes  list  [r/o]  ¬
  -- A list of all the currently known volumes.
backup sets  list  [r/o]  ¬
  -- A list of all the currently known backup sets.
```

The primary reason for creating a class for a result is that a result is a single object: one number, a text string (which can be long), and the like. If this command were to return a long text string with the status in it, you could parse it using AppleScript operators searching for keywords, or you could just display it. However, returning it as a class makes it easier for you to use the information.

In the make command, you've seen how you specify properties:

```
make new document at front with properties¬
  {document kind:text document, name:"Things to Do Today"}
```

The properties form a *record*, which is a common AppleScript syntactic element. You specify the properties in a record as shown in the make command. You've already seen how to access properties from a class, and that's the way you retrieve values from a record.

```
name of document 1
```

This code returns "Things to Do Today" when executed after the preceding make command.

When you execute the Retrospect status command, you can examine the properties of the result. In this script, the variable status is set to the result of the Retrospect status command. The variable currentScript is set to the value of that item from the class returned.

```
tell application "Retrospect"
  set status to (Retrospect status)
  set currentScript to current script of status
end tell
```

You access properties of classes and items within a record by name. Another AppleScript construct, lists, allows you to access items by number. The Retrospect status command demonstrates that with its scripts, volumes, and backup sets properties: Each is returned as a list.

The following script gets the status and then stores the list of scripts into a variable called theScripts. It then stores the name of the first script into a variable called firstScript. This is the syntax for working with lists. (In addition to numbers, you can use ranges and constants such as first and last.) See Appendix A, "Constants and Predefined Variables," for the various ways of identifying items in lists.

```
tell application "Retrospect"
  set status to (Retrospect status)
  set theScripts to scripts of status
  set firstScript to item 1 of scripts of status
end tell
```

Summary

This hour has shown you how to deal with scripting in a variety of applications. You've seen how to use AppleScript to create paragraphs in AppleWorks, TextEdit, and Word; they all function in very much the same way. You've also seen how to combine AppleScript with other scripting languages in applications such as FileMaker, Word, and Photoshop.

Finally, in examining Retrospect, you saw the Retrospect reply class and learned the difference between lists and records. (You'll learn other aspects of AppleScript in other hours as they occur so that by the end of the book most of the language will have been revealed.)

Q&A

Q For applications that offer a choice of scripting languages (Visual Basic and AppleScript in Word, FileMaker and AppleScript in FileMaker), which is better to use?

A The choice is easy if what you want to do is only available in one of the scripting languages. However, there are many actions that can be carried out in either language. The primary consideration should be whether or not your script needs to run on Windows as well as on the Macintosh. If that is the case, use FileMaker or Visual Basic scripting because they run on both platforms.

Q I'm sure I've got the syntax right, but my script doesn't work.

A Double and triple check your syntax looking carefully for mismatched quotes and parentheses. But sometimes, there are bugs in the implementation of AppleScript code. Other times, the dictionary is provided before all of the AppleScript code is implemented in an application. If you're sure your syntax is right, try getting more information. Look on the vendor's Web site for support information. (If there's a search function, try searching on "AppleScript" or "scripting.") Log on to http://www.apple.com/support and search the discussions for the product name. Another approach is to reimplement the task using a slightly different technique if possible. It may solve or at least bypass the problem.

12

Workshop

The workshop contains quiz questions and activities to help you solidify your knowledge of the material in this hour. Try to answer all of the questions before looking at the quiz answers that follow.

Quiz

1. How many different types of documents does AppleWorks support?
2. What AppleScript command can you use to perform a find in FileMaker?
3. Why would you use a try block?

Quiz Answers

1. In AppleScript terms, there is only one kind of document. The `document kind` property determines whether it is a text, spreadsheet, or other type of document.
2. You can use the `show/where` command.
3. When an error could occur and you want to handle it yourself (such as in finding no records that satisfy a database query).

Activities

If you have FileMaker, update a database with data from a spreadsheet in Excel or AppleWorks.

Write a script to report the values in a spreadsheet using TextEdit.

Use Script Editor to find which of your applications are scriptable. Use the `Open Dictionary` command; Script Editor will browse your applications and list those that are scriptable. Open the dictionaries of applications you have and use regularly that are not discussed here and try to script them.

HOUR 13

Interacting with Users

The last hour of this part of the book adds a major piece of functionality to your AppleScript knowledge: interaction with users. Although you've seen a few dialogs right at the beginning of the book, you haven't seen the details of how to create them and how to use them effectively. This hour covers that subject. No longer do you have to use the Result or Event Log windows to see what's going on in your scripts: You can display the results for yourself and your users.

Following the discussion of AppleScript dialogs, you'll find an introduction to the Aqua Human Interface Guidelines for Mac OS X. As you move on into the next part of the book, you'll be able to create dialogs and windows from scratch, putting the buttons where you want to and designing them the way you want. Before doing so, you should know what the guidelines are. Following them makes your AppleScript application easier to use because it will behave the way users expect applications to behave on Mac OS X.

In This Hour

- Telling the User Something—From results of scripts to warnings and errors, you often need to tell users something.

- Asking the User Something—You frequently need to get input from users; this can be data on which to operate or it can be an okay to continue with a task.

- Other Ways of Communicating with Users—Dialogs aren't the only way of communicating. You can use speech synthesis as well as other applications to communicate with users.

- Aqua Human Interface Guidelines—Finally, here's a look at some of the issues to consider as you build more complex interfaces to your scripts.

Telling the User Something

The `display dialog` command lets you communicate easily with users. It puts up a dialog such as the one seen in Figure 13.1.

Figure 13.1

You can use an AppleScript dialog to display information.

The command is an AppleScript scripting addition, which means that it can be used inside any tell block—or on its own. The single line of code shown here is a complete AppleScript that puts up the dialog just shown. It relies on the AppleScript `current date` routine.

```
display dialog "Today is " & (current date)
```

The text to be displayed can be the result of an expression or it can be text that you enclosed in quotes. It can consist of both. In this case, the string `"Today is "` is concatenated to the result of the `current date` routine. (*Concatenate* is the term used for combining characters in sequence. From the Latin for chain, it is widely used in the computer world; in AppleScript the symbol for concatenation is `&`.) Note that in concatenating the two, there is a space after `is` so that the resulting dialog is properly spaced.

The dialog is automatically sized to accommodate the text you provide. For example, Figure 13.2 shows part of the first paragraph of this chapter in a dialog.

FIGURE 13.2

AppleScript sizes the dialog for the content you provide.

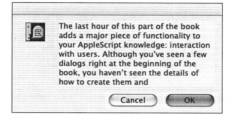

As you see at the left in Figure 13.2, you can add icons to a dialog. You do so by specifying a known icon for AppleScript to use. Figure 13.2 shows the Note icon. You use it by adding this code to the end of the `display dialog` command:

```
with icon 1
```

The other icons, Stop (`icon 0`) and Warning (`icon 2`) are shown in Figures 13.3 and 13.4.

You can specify the names for the buttons in your dialog. Here, one button is specified, and the Stop icon is used. The result is shown in Figure 13.3.

```
display dialog "Today is " & (current date) buttons {"Yes"} with icon 0
```

FIGURE 13.3

Provide button names if you want.

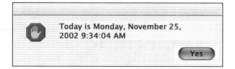

If you provide more than one button, you can specify which one is the default. The buttons are numbered from left to right, starting at 1. Here is the code to put up the dialog shown in Figure 13.4, which also demonstrates the Warning icon.

```
display dialog "Today is " & (current date) buttons ¬
  {"That's Wrong", "I Agree"} default button 2 with icon 2
```

FIGURE 13.4

Create multiple buttons and set the default.

13

As you would expect, the code to create the dialog shown in Figure 13.5 differs only by specifying `default button 1`.

Figure 13.5

Change the default button.

The last part of this hour is devoted to Aqua Human Interface Guidelines, but it's not jumping the gun to describe some of the interface concerns you should think of when designing dialogs.

First, limit the number of buttons; three is the practical maximum. Second, arrange them properly and choose the default button wisely. The default button should be the natural and most obvious choice (such as OK), unless its inadvertent use could cause damage. If the dialog asks, "Do you want to print a report?" the OK button is fine for a default. Because the user can click the OK button by pressing the Return key on the keyboard, it's easy for a typist to continue without reaching for the mouse. If, on the other hand, the dialog question is, "Do you want to erase the disk?" the default button might well be No so that the user has to make a conscious effort to erase the disk.

Finally, note that the icons shown in the dialogs here are a remnant of Mac OS 9 and earlier. In Mac OS X, their use is discouraged.

Asking the User Something

The previous section showed you how to tell the user something. Now you'll see how to get information from the user. That information can take two forms: the name of the button that was clicked and text that is entered in the dialog.

If you run the script for the dialog shown in Figure 13.5 and look at the Result window, you'll see that after you click a button, the result is this:

```
{button returned:"I Agree"}
```

This is a record consisting of one named element, and you access it just as you saw in the past hour:

```
if button returned of the result = "I Agree" then
  --do something
else
  --do something else
end if
```

You can create a dialog like the one shown in Figure 13.6 in order to get input from a user.

FIGURE 13.6

Get user input with a dialog.

You display this dialog with the following line of code:

```
display dialog "Enter Account Name" default answer "last, first"
```

The `default answer` section is optional; it is useful if there could be ambiguity in the formatting of the data to be entered. You can set the default answer to an empty string—`" "`. Do this in order to provide a data entry field in the dialog with nothing in it. Without a `default answer` clause, there will be no data entry field in the dialog.

To access the text, you use the `text returned` item of the result. Here is the code to confirm data entry:

```
display dialog "You entered " & text returned of the result
```

> You can use the text that is returned in any way that you want. In the previous hour, you saw how to set text in word processors, spreadsheets, and databases. You can design an AppleScript front end to such applications to make data entry easy.
>
> One reason for doing this is so that you can customize the interface for yourself and your users. No one has to be aware that you are storing the data in a database or a spreadsheet. And, in fact, you can switch from database to spreadsheet for storage without anyone knowing: They will just continue to use the interface that you've designed.

Other Ways of Communicating with Users

13

Dialogs are certainly not the only way of communicating with users. Speech synthesis and other applications are also available.

Speech Synthesis

Mac OS X has built-in speech synthesis. You can use the AppleScript `say` command to confirm the data that was entered using the following code:

```
say text returned of the result
```

Using Other Applications for Input and Output

You saw in previous hours how to set data. You can assemble data in any format you want using any of those applications. TextEdit is part of the standard Mac OS X installation, so you know that you'll have it available (unless someone has removed it). Because TextEdit is scriptable, you can create documents, style them, and print or save them from AppleScript.

In Hour 11, "Scripting Mac OS X Applications from Apple," you saw how to create text in TextEdit. You can use those scripts in conjunction with dialogs to create a document. Likewise, you can create a new person in Address book using information from dialogs. Here's a basic script that asks for the first and last name, and then creates a new Address Book entry.

```
display dialog "Enter First Name" default answer ""
set firstName to text returned of the result
display dialog "Enter Last Name" default answer ""
set lastName to text returned of the result
tell application "Address Book"
  make new person with properties {last name:lastName, first name:firstName}
end tell
```

You can also proceed in the reverse way: Instead of asking users for data with a dialog, you can retrieve data from other applications. You saw in the previous hour how to search the Address Book; you can use a dialog to specify what to look for as in this modification of a script from Hour 11:

```
display dialog "Last name to look for" default answer ""
set searchName to text returned of the result
tell application "Address Book"
  set foundSet to people whose last name is searchName
  repeat with theperson in foundSet
    display dialog first name of theperson as string
  end repeat
end tell
```

Aqua Human Interface Guidelines

Aqua is the graphical user interface to Mac OS X. Its design is not just a matter of making the interface attractive; it also is carefully engineered by Apple to make the interface easy to use.

Dialogs are a very useful way of interacting with users, but they are limited. They are ideal for brief messages and relatively small data entry tasks. Until the advent of AppleScript Studio at the end of 2001, that's where matters rested. With AppleScript Studio, however, everything changed. You can use it to create windows and dialogs using the same tools that developers use when they develop applications for Mac OS X. AppleScript Studio is the subject of the next part of the book.

Because you'll be moving on to a world with more sophisticated data entry tools, it's worth looking at the principles of the Aqua Human Interface Guidelines so that your AppleScript application is consistent with other applications, is easy to use, and looks as good as it can.

 The Apple Human Interface Guidelines are available for download as a PDF file from `http://developer.apple.com/ue`. This is the User Experience site, and you'll find additional information there that may be of interest to you.

Many of the guidelines are automatically implemented for you when you use AppleScript Studio. As you'll see in the next hour, Interface Builder has palettes of standard interface controls such as buttons and text fields; they automatically adhere to the guidelines. Interface Builder itself has spacing guidelines built into its interface so that you can position items properly.

Among the guidelines that you should consider are feedback, communication, consistency, and forgiveness. These give the user the sense of being in charge and of knowing what's going on. The concepts are all self-explanatory, but the last one—forgiveness—merits a brief discussion.

The user should be able to recover from mistakes, and the interface has a lot to do with that. Let the user know what is happening with appropriate feedback, and warn (with a dialog or alert) when something irreversible may happen.

If your application is over alerted (that is, you keep warning the user about potential problems), maybe the interface is wrong. Don't let the user get into situations that may be troublesome. As you know from your own use of applications, menu commands are always visible, but they're not always available. With AppleScript Studio, you'll have control of the menu bar, and you'll be able to dramatically improve your AppleScript interface.

Finally, remember this statement from the guidelines: "Apple reserves the right to change terms and guidelines at any time." Interfaces evolve in response to new technologies and to new expectations and experiences on the part of users.

13

Summary

This hour has shown you how to interact with users. First, you saw the `display dialog` command in all of its guises, and then you saw how to use speech synthesis to communicate in another way. Finally, the Apple Human Interface Guidelines were discussed. You'll need to keep them in mind as you move on to the next part of the book, in which AppleScript Studio is discussed and you have access to all of the Aqua Interface tools.

Q&A

Q Why are the interface guidelines so important?

A The primary answer has nothing to do with aesthetics. The more alike programs are in their behavior and controls, the easier it is for users to switch from one to another and to use unfamiliar applications.

Q When do you use the icons in dialogs?

A On Mac OS X, their use is discouraged. If you are modifying scripts that were written for Mac OS 9 and earlier, you may want to remove them as part of your maintenance work. (If the scripts need to continue to run on Mac OS 9 and earlier, you may want to postpone this.)

Q If I need to get two pieces of information from a user, do I have to use two dialogs?

A Unless one of the pieces of information can be conveyed by knowing which button was clicked, the answer is usually yes. If you need two small pieces of information and if they are logically related (such as first and last name), you can get them in one dialog and split them apart based on a space, comma, or other delimiter.

Workshop

The workshop contains quiz questions and activities to help you solidify your knowledge of the material in this hour. Try to answer all of the questions before looking at the quiz answers that follow.

Quiz

1. How do you control the size of a dialog?
2. How do you determine the default button?
3. How do you format the text in a dialog?

Quiz Answers

1. AppleScript sizes it automatically to accommodate its content.

2. It is the most commonly used choice (such as OK). This allows a user to "click" it by pressing the Return key on the keyboard. The exception is when that choice could cause serious and irreversible damage.

3. You can't.

Activities

Rewrite the FileMaker error handler from the previous hour so that in the case of all errors except -1728, the error message is displayed in a dialog that you create.

In each of the hours in this part of the book, some of the activities required you to use the Result or Event Log window to monitor your script. Modify those scripts to display the information in a dialog.

For scripts in which you hard-coded values, modify them to use a dialog window to get data from the user.

13

PART III

Working with AppleScript Studio

Hour

14 Introducing AppleScript Studio

15 Building a Graphical AppleScript Studio Application

16 Writing Code for AppleScript Studio

17 Planning and Debugging AppleScript Studio Applications

18 Adding Help to AppleScript Studio

19 Using Documents and Data Sources with AppleScript Studio

HOUR 14

Introducing AppleScript Studio

Part III, "Working with AppleScript Studio," of this book focuses on AppleScript Studio, a suite of tools and technologies that expands AppleScript and the other Mac OS X development environments in a powerful way. This hour provides an introduction to the technologies and architecture that you'll use, and it gives you a preview of what's to come.

AppleScript Studio leverages Apple's developer tools, its Cocoa application development framework, and AppleScript itself to provide you with a rapid application development environment for projects that can become very complex. You can use AppleScript Studio to build such big projects; however, you can also use just a few of its tools to provide an Aqua interface to scripts that you have already written.

This hour provides background as well as a high-level look at AppleScript Studio. You'll see the sorts of things that you can do. In the following hours in Part III, you'll find detailed step-by-step approaches to specific parts of the process that is presented in this hour.

In This Hour

- Getting AppleScript Studio—You'll need some (free) software from Apple to get started.

- What Is AppleScript Studio?—This is the basic description of AppleScript Studio. You'll learn the terminology that is used throughout this part of the book.

- Getting Started with Project Builder—Of the two basic AppleScript Studio tools, Project Builder is the one you use to write code and manage your application.

- Looking at Interface Builder—The other basic tool, Interface Builder, is the graphical editing tool for your interface. As you'll see, Project Builder and Interface Builder are tightly integrated.

Getting AppleScript Studio

AppleScript Studio is part of the developer tools that come with Mac OS X when you purchase it as a shrink-wrapped product. It may also come preinstalled on your Macintosh with Mac OS X.

If it is not preinstalled, you can obtain it through the Apple Developer Connection (ADC) on the Web at `http://developer.apple.com`. You can join ADC in a variety of ways. Some memberships are available for students and online users; others are geared for professional developers. Online memberships can be free, and you can download the tools. If you want the tools on CDs or DVDs, you will normally need to register for one of the paid memberships.

If you are a member of an educational institution, check to see if the developer tools are available on your server or through a coordinator.

What Is AppleScript Studio?

AppleScript Studio is a collection of technologies that work together with Mac OS X to let you produce applications that incorporate AppleScript as well as all of the developer tools that Apple provides.

AppleScript Studio's Components

Specifically, the components of AppleScript Studio are the following:

- AppleScript itself is the core. The language that you have seen described in the first part of this book provides the entrée to all of these tools.

- Project Builder is one of the two primary applications in Apple's developer tools. It is an integrated development environment (IDE) that combines editing, compiling, building, and managing applications. Project Builder has been modified slightly to respect AppleScript syntax and to automatically format AppleScript code.

- Interface Builder is the other primary application in Apple's developer tools. It enables you to build and manage your application's graphical user interface using its own graphical interface. You draw the interface that you want using tools and controls from an Interface Builder palette; Project Builder then fills in the basic code structure, and all you have to do is provide any customization your application requires. Interface Builder has been modified to allow you to specify AppleScript settings for common interface elements such as buttons, windows, and data-entry text fields.

- The Cocoa application framework (derived from OpenStep and, before that, NeXTSTEP) is a robust and sophisticated object-oriented framework. It consists of two separate frameworks that work together: The *Foundation* framework manages objects, memory, and various data storage concerns; the *AppKit* (or *Application Kit*) provides support for and implementation of interface elements such as views, windows, and buttons as well as menus, documents, and the clipboard. Cocoa has been modified to support AppleScript access to many of its interface elements.

As you can see, AppleScript Studio is not a separate application; rather, it is a combination of modifications to Apple's existing development tools and environments. (The fact that this could be pulled off in this way gives you an indication of how sturdy those tools and environments are.)

Any Cocoa application is potentially scriptable using AppleScript Studio. With Interface Builder, you can assign names and other attributes to interface elements such as buttons and windows. Cocoa contains code that parses references such as these:

```
tell table view "tableData" of scroll view "tableScrollView" to update
```

This is AppleScript code. You use Interface Builder to provide AppleScript names for standard interface elements—tableData and tableScrollView are such names. When this line of AppleScript code is executed and directed at the application that you build with AppleScript Studio, the appropriate view is updated.

The process described in this hour requires the identification of the interface elements with AppleScript names or with known ID numbers, and it also requires that the underlying application be built with Cocoa, which can interpret the code. It does not require the application to be scriptable in the sense in which that term has been used until now in this book.

14

Throughout the rest of this part of the book, you'll find details of building AppleScript Studio applications. This hour gives you a high-level overview of what you can do, how to do it, and why you would want to do so. Don't worry that it is a high-level overview: You'll find details and step-by-step tips later in this hour and in those that follow.

The main example that you'll see in this chapter is a simple AppleScript Studio application that displays a two-column table of food and wine. Two data entry fields below the table let you type in names of new foods and wines; when you click the Add button, those new entries are added below the existing table entries. There's no editing, no deletion, no sorting—this is a barebones example of the power of AppleScript Studio.

Want to experiment with the application? Want to get your hands on the code? It's located on this book's Web site (http://www.samspublishing.com) in the folder called Hour 14. You'll find the project inside that folder in its own folder called TableView Project. The TableView application is also in the Hour 14 project; you can run it by double-clicking it.

Looking at an AppleScript Studio Application

To start, look at Figure 14.1, which shows the TableView AppleScript Studio application in action. Compare it to the figures that show AppleScript dialogs previously in this book. Right away, you'll find a number of differences.

FIGURE 14.1

TableView is an AppleScript Studio application in action.

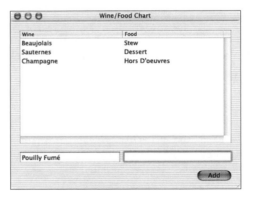

The biggest difference is that this is a standard Aqua interface window with a variety of elements in it. Traditional AppleScript dialogs contain displayed text, perhaps a single data entry field, and one or more buttons. This interface is much more complex.

It consists primarily of a sophisticated data manipulation and display structure called an NSTableView. The view contains two columns: One is labeled "Wine" and the other is labeled "Food." The table view manages the display of tabular data with a minimum of effort on your part.

The table view is contained within a scroller; if there were more lines than could be seen in the window, a scrollbar at the right would be enabled automatically. As you'll see, Interface Builder packages this all up for you automatically so that you just drag a single object (scroller containing table view) into your interface.

Below the table view are two data entry fields. ("Pouilly Fumé" is entered in the first one.) Below and to the right of the data entry fields, a button labeled "Add" is provided.

A word on nomenclature is in order at this point. The actual Cocoa framework classes are frequently prefixed with "NS" as in NSTableView. This reflects the origin of Cocoa in NeXTSTEP. Even classes developed totally at Apple after its acquisition of Next, Inc. (such as NSDocument) adhere to this naming convention. When referencing a class in code (which you may rarely need to do), you will need to use the appropriate class name. When discussing an interface element, its descriptive name is used: Often that is a variant on the formal class name without the prefix. Thus, in the figures shown here, the table view (descriptive name) is implemented with an NSTableView Cocoa class; the button (descriptive name) is implemented with an NSButton Cocoa class.

This window works as described previously. It's a simple demonstration, but it is a practical example that you can modify for other purposes. (When you combine it with the code in Hour 19, "Using Documents and Data Sources with AppleScript Studio," that lets you save and restore data to and from disk, you have a handy little data manager.)

The functionality of the interface elements is quite sophisticated, and it is provided automatically by Interface Builder and Cocoa. The editing of data in the text data entry fields is managed for you. More impressively, the table view itself supports a number of interface features with no work on your part. Figure 14.2 shows how you can reorder the columns just by dragging their titles to new positions.

14

FIGURE 14.2

Reorder columns in a table view.

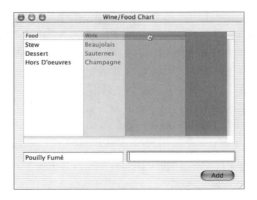

Getting Started with Project Builder

Project Builder provides an environment for you to develop applications. It is a very powerful tool: You can use it to develop tiny one-shot AppleScript Studio applications, and you can also use it to develop the biggest Mac OS X applications you can think of. (Apple uses it for all of its Mac OS X software development; it is powerful enough to build the operating system itself, although that is not necessarily the most complex application.)

This section walks you through the steps in creating a very basic AppleScript Studio application. Then, you'll move on to the Table View application that you saw previously.

Project Builder comes with a variety of templates that you can use as a jumping-off point for many types of applications. You'll find Project Builder in the Applications folder inside the Developer folder at the root level of your hard disk. (If it's not there, see the previous section in this hour on obtaining the developer tools.) Choose New Project from the File menu to create a new AppleScript Studio project. You'll see the window shown in Figure 14.3. You may need to use the disclosure triangles to open the Application section to select AppleScript Application. (The list of templates varies depending on which particular templates have been installed on your computer; WebObjects, for example, is a separate development product from Apple.)

After choosing a template, you need to select where its files will be located. Project Builder manages all of your project files within a folder. You can choose to place it within your Documents folder, as shown in Figure 14.4.

FIGURE 14.3
Choose a template.

FIGURE 14.4
Choose your project's location.

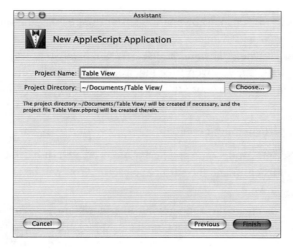

After a few moments, the project window will open, as shown in Figure 14.5. It will display the files that are part of your project. The files are organized into groups; you can use the disclosure triangles to inspect the contents of each group.

Several points need to be made here. First, the specific layout of Project Builder windows depends on preferences that you can set in its application menu. You can choose various styles of windows: a single window with all project information in it, many windows, or some combination thereof. Thus, your window might not look exactly like the one shown here.

14

FIGURE 14.5

Project Builder creates your project's files.

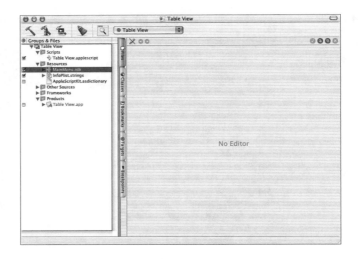

In the Groups & Files pane shown at the left of Figure 14.5, the files are combined into logically related groups. You can drag files from one group to another: Project Builder will keep track of where they are on disk. (If you open your project folder in the Finder, you'll see the files, but you won't see the groups.) As you become more adept at using Project Builder, you may choose to modify the default structure, but for now, leave it as is.

Three files in particular are important:

- In the Scripts group, an AppleScript file is created. It has the project name (Table View in this case) and the suffix applescript. You will be able to create additional files if you want.

- A *nib file* is created to contain your interface elements. There is more about nib files in Hour 15, "Building a Graphical AppleScript Studio Application"; for now it is sufficient to know that MainMenu.nib contains your application's menus and windows. If you open the disclosure triangle, you will see that you have files within the nib file that correspond to various languages. Compare the Project Builder structure to that of files in your project folder on disk. In the project folder, you'll see a folder like English.lproj, which contains a nib file. In Project Builder, the nib group contains an English nib (which corresponds to the nib file within English.lproj). Don't worry about this remapping of files; it works.

- Finally, in the Products group you'll see the application file—in this case TableView.app. It will be shown in red or some other highlighted color to indicate that it does not yet exist.

Project Builder is closely integrated with Interface Builder, the graphical tool that helps you build the interface, which is stored in a nib file. Double-click MainMenu.nib to open the nib file in Interface Builder. You'll see something like Figure 14.6; remember that preferences you set in Interface Builder will affect what you see.

FIGURE 14.6

Nib file in Interface Builder.

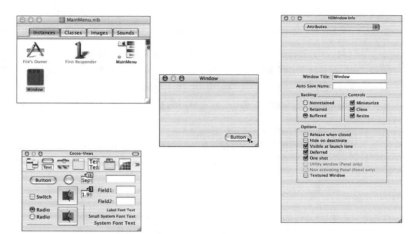

In the upper left of Figure 14.6 is the nib file itself. This will be described further in the other hours in Part III of this book. For now, simply note that a window in the nib file has been created automatically; that will be your application's window. It may be shown; if not, double-click to open it. The application window is shown in the center of Figure 14.6.

At the right of Figure 14.6 is the Interface Builder Info window. It shows information about whatever the currently selected object is. Here, the application window is selected, and the Info window reflects its information. You'll use the Info window a lot as you work with Interface Builder. If it's not visible, you can open it using the Show Info command from the Interface Builder Tools menu (Shift+Command+i).

In the lower left is the Interface Builder palette window. It contains a variety of interface elements. They are grouped into categories; you choose the category you want from the toolbar at the top of the palette, and then you drag the interface element you want into the appropriate window. You can drag text fields, buttons, check boxes, radio buttons, labels, and more to your window and place them wherever you want. You'll find step-by-step procedures in the following hour.

To continue with creating the basic application, drag a button from the palette into the window as shown in Figure 14.6.

14

As you move interface elements around in a window, guides will appear. These guides help you position the interface elements in an organized manner, adhering to the Aqua interface guidelines.

You can switch back and forth between Project Builder and Interface Builder. If you've added a button to the window as shown here, you can build and run the application. Even if you have not made any modifications, it's a good idea to build and run it at this point.

Most templates will build and run successfully: If they don't, things are likely to go from bad to worse. To build and run the project, click the third icon from the left in the toolbar shown in Figure 14.5. (You'll be prompted to save unsaved files before continuing.) After building and running the application, you should see the window displayed in Figure 14.7.

FIGURE 14.7
Build and run the application.

If this doesn't work, check the installation of the developer tools: Things won't get better by themselves.

Looking at Interface Builder

Creating sophisticated interfaces such as these is easy in Interface Builder. Here's the sort of work that you'll do to implement this interface. This is the quick overview; the details are provided in the later hours of this part.

Designing the Table View

In Interface Builder, you can drag interface elements from a palette into your window. Figure 14.8 shows a table view being dragged from the palette (on the right) into the window (on the left). The table view comes packaged with all of the functionality including a scroll view, which contains the table view and provides scrolling if needed. The table view is one of the Data elements in the palette. You select the Data elements using the Data elements icon—the fifth from the left in the toolbar of Figure 14.8. (It has the word TEXT in it twice.)

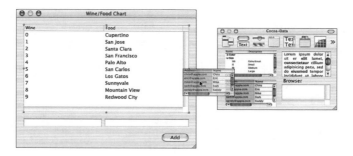

The table view that is inserted into your window contains dummy data. In addition, if you look closely, you'll see that its outline contains small resizing buttons that you can use to resize and reshape it. And, of course, you can drag it anywhere you want within the window.

The Info window in Interface Builder is where you enter settings for windows, views, and controls such as buttons, text fields, and table views. You can build an interface easily by dragging elements from the palette into your window and rearranging them, but in order to use AppleScript Studio effectively, you almost always need to use the Info window. Its two most frequent uses with AppleScript Studio are

- Naming interface elements
- Associating AppleScript handlers with interface elements

The Info window shows information for whatever interface element is selected. Thus, if you click in the title bar or background of your window in Interface Builder, you'll be able to set the attributes for that window as shown in Figure 14.9.

As you can see here, you can specify the button controls at the left of the title bar as well as other attributes. Perhaps most important is the window title, which you can enter in the first data entry field.

The Info window reflects whatever the current selection is, and its title shows you the Cocoa class name of that selection. Note in Figure 14.9 that the Info window's title is NSWindow Info—NSWindow is the formal class name for windows in Cocoa. If you have any doubt about what object is selected in the Interface Builder design window, or if you're not sure what its formal name is, this is an easy way to find out.

14

FIGURE 14.9

Use the Info window to enter control settings.

When you click an interface element to select it, its information is shown in the Info window. Sometimes, there are nested interface elements. For example, the table view is contained within a scroll view. If you notice that the Info window's title reflects a container (such as the scroll view), double-click the object to open its inner object—the table view in this case. Figure 14.10 shows the attributes for the table view. Note the Allows Reordering check box, which lets you rearrange columns as shown previously in Figure 14.2.

You can drill down further into the data display by double-clicking the table view. Doing so selects a column, as shown in Figure 14.11.

Figure 14.11 demonstrates an important functionality of Interface Builder. You can set two different identifiers for each column. The Column Title field lets you enter the title that the user sees. In this case, it is "Wine." At the bottom of the attributes, you can set an identifier for the column. Here it is "FirstColumn." Note that the column title can be localized easily. Your AppleScript code that will need to refer to the column can use the identifier, which will not be localized. You'll see how this works shortly. You can also set other attributes for the columns, such as alignment, using the Info window.

FIGURE 14.10

Set attributes for a table view.

FIGURE 14.11

Attributes for a column view.

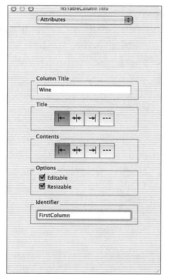

In addition to using the Info window to name objects such as a column, you can use it to set AppleScript-specific information. You do that by choosing the AppleScript pane in the pop-up menu at the top of the Info window. Figure 14.12 shows the AppleScript settings for the table view.

14

FIGURE **14.12**

AppleScript settings for the table view.

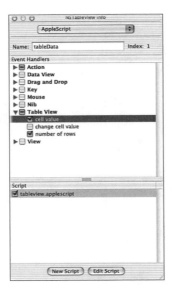

At the top, you can provide an AppleScript name for the object. This can be the same as an identifier you provided in the attributes pane, or it can be different. In this section, each type of identifier—AppleScript identifier, name, attribute identifier, and so forth—is given a different value. In that way, you won't be confused when you look at the code because each value is unique. In your own application, making a distinction between `FirstColumn` and `column1` may be more complexity than you want to deal with. It does, however, frequently help with debugging.

The Apple events that the selected object can handle are displayed in the central portion of the AppleScript pane. They are grouped into categories, as you can see in Figure 14.12. The table view object supports three Apple events. (You use the disclosure triangles to open each set of Apple events.) You need to implement handlers for at least two of them: `cell value` and `number of rows`.

> Appendix B, "Operators," provides a complete list of interface handlers. This section provides the overview that you'll need to put the rest in context.

Adding Other Interface Elements

You can add other interface elements from the palette. (There's more on this in the next hour.) If you drag a text field into the bottom of the window, the Info window will reflect its attributes, as shown in Figure 14.13. You can set a title for the text field; if you do, it will be shown as the initial value of that field. Here, it is blank.

FIGURE **14.13**
Add a text field.

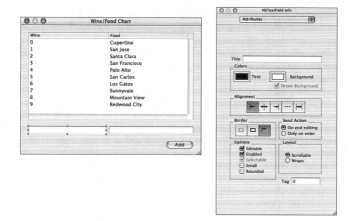

You will need a name for the text field for use in your AppleScript code. To enter a name, use the pop-up menu at the top of the Info window to go to the AppleScript attributes and set the field's name as shown in Figure 14.14.

FIGURE 14.14
Setting an AppleScript field name.

14

When you add a button to the window, you can set its attributes as well. Here, you do want to set a title for the button: the text that will appear in it. Note that you can set a keyboard equivalent. (You can use the pop-up menu to choose a standard keyboard equivalent; the other information will be automatically filled in for you.) Here, the Return key is used, and the button becomes the default button. Interface Builder will take care of making it throb in accordance with the interface guidelines.

As before, you need to set AppleScript attributes for the button; to do so, you use the pop-up menu at the top of the Info window as shown in Figure 14.15.

FIGURE 14.15

AppleScript settings for the button.

You want to make certain that the button responds to the `clicked` Apple event, and you do so with the `clicked` check box shown in Figure 14.16. (You may have to use the disclosure triangle to open the Action group.)

At the bottom of this window, you'll see a list of your AppleScript files (by default, there is one). Click the check box next to the file in which you want to place the code. Then, when you click Edit Script, you'll see that a dummy `clicked` handler has been created in the AppleScript file (see Figure 14.17).

Working with Handlers

When you check a handler, a dummy handler will be created automatically for you in a script file. The handler will look something like this:

```
on clicked theObject
  (*Add your script here.*)
end clicked
```

FIGURE 14.16
Add a clicked *handler for a button in Interface Builder.*

FIGURE 14.17
Write the code for your clicked *handler.*

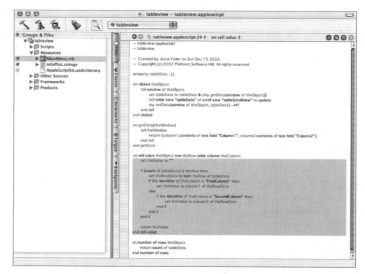

This section shows you how to write the necessary handlers for the AppleScript Studio application described in this hour. There are only four of them:

- You need a clicked handler to move the data from the two text fields into the table view.

- You need a number of rows handler to let you know how many rows are in the table.

14

- You need a `cell value` handler to provide the data for an individual table cell.
- You need a `getData` handler to move the data from the text fields into a record to append to the table view. (It is called by the `clicked` handler; it could have been incorporated into that handler.)

 Each interface element comes with its own set of handlers that you can implement if you want to. Some—such as the ones described here—are required. As you proceed through this part of the book, you'll become familiar with the handlers that go with each interface element. Table views, which are among the most complex elements, require only four handlers—a tribute to the power of AppleScript Studio.

The required table view handler `number of rows` provides an example of how you implement a handler. Here is the code you'll need to write:

```
on number of rows theObject
   return count of tableData
end number of rows
```

As you can see, it's just one line of code to be added to the dummy handler that was created for you automatically. How does it work? Refer to Figure 14.12 and note that the table view was given an AppleScript name of `tableData`; that lets AppleScript identify the object you want to query. As long as you've identified the object, this line of code will work.

The other required handler provides the data for the table view. It is a handler that is called with a specific row and column: Your job is to figure out what data should be displayed. Here's the dummy handler:

```
on cell value theObject row theRow table column tableColumn
   (*Add your script here.*)
end cell value
```

There are three parameters to this handler. The first, which you saw in the previous example and which is common to most AppleScript Studio handlers, identifies the object that is sending the message: the button that is clicked or the table view that is requesting data. Sometimes it's important to use that parameter; other times (such as these) it doesn't matter. The second and third parameter in this handler identify the row and column for which you must provide data. The code here is slightly more complex, but it is still not particularly daunting. Here it is:

```
on cell value theObject row theRow table column tableColumn
  set theValue to ""

  if (count of tableData) ≤ theRow then
    set theRowData to item theRow of tableData
    if the identifier of tableColumn is "FirstColumn" then
      set theValue to column1 of theRowData
    else
      if the identifier of tableColumn is "SecondColumn" then
        set theValue to column2 of theRowData
      end if
    end if
  end if

  return theValue
end cell value
```

Much of the code in this handler is routine; you'll use it or a variation over and over again. First, you set the value that you'll return to an empty string; that way there will be something to return, even if it's blank. Next, you check that the row for which you're being asked to provide data is valid. If it is, you set a local variable, theRowData, to the item of tableData that corresponds to the row requested in theRow.

Next, you need to determine which column you need to return. The parameter theColumn is a column (not the number of a column). As an AppleScript syntax element, it has properties—including an identifier (which you set as shown previously in Figure 14.11). You can test whether it is FirstColumn or SecondColumn that you need to return.

So far, you've seen how to identify interface elements using their names in the AppleScript settings or the identifier in the attributes of the Info window. (All interface elements can have AppleScript names; some, such as columns, can also have identifiers in the attributes pane.) But there are two lines of code in this handler that use yet another pair of identifiers: column1 and column2. Those are set as you enter data. Here are the final two handlers.

When you click the Add button, you'll need a clicked handler to process the data. Here's where those labels column1 and column2 come into play. In addition, you'll see how a frequently occurring case of identification is resolved.

The button itself is located inside the window. It knows about itself and its window, but it has no information about other elements in the window. In order to move the data from the text fields into the table view, the button needs to find some way of referencing them. A very common snippet of code follows. Because the first parameter of the handler (theObject) identifies the object sending the message—the button in this case—you can ask that object to identify its window. Thus, this tell block sends AppleScript commands to the window in which the button is located:

14

```
tell window of theObject
end tell
```

If you have assigned AppleScript names to the interface elements in the window, you can then access them. Here's the full handler to a click in the button:

```
on clicked theObject
  tell window of theObject
    set tableData to tableData & {my getData(window of theObject)}
    tell table view "tableData" of scroll view "tableScrollView" to update
  end tell
end clicked
```

You ask the window to set the table view (tableData) to itself with the addition of another record, which your own handler getData retrieves from the text fields. You then ask the table view to update itself.

```
on getData(theWindow)
  tell theWindow
    return {column1:contents of text field "Field1", ¬
      column2:contents of text field "Field2"}
  end tell
end getData
```

Notice how the window (referred to as window of theObject) in the clicked handler is passed in here: You need it again so that you can get to the two text fields. And here you'll see where the labels column1 and column2 come into play: You identify the data in the record that you return from getData, and those labels carry through and can be used in the cell value handler.

This may seem like a lot to do, but in fact, it's quite simple, and it relies on the two basic steps identified previously:

- Identify interface elements in the Info window.
- Provide handlers for them to manipulate data.

So much functionality is provided in Cocoa, Interface Builder, and AppleScript that the code you have to write is quite limited. You don't have to implement anything involving scrolling, column rearrangement, or the like. You just need to pick up the data from the text fields, put it into a record, and store it at the end of the table view. After that, it's just a matter of retrieving whatever cell is requested.

This overview will be repeated throughout Part III of this book in different permutations, but rest assured that everything you see is a variation on this simple paradigm.

There is only one other basic issue that you should be aware of. All variables within a single AppleScript file obey the rules of scoping described previously. Because you need to refer to `tableData` repeatedly, it is declared as a property at the top of the file as follows:

```
property tableData : {}
```

As you can see from the Info window's AppleScript pane, you can have multiple script files. In simple cases, all handlers can go into one file. However, only one handler of each type can exist in a single file. If you have several buttons, you have only one `clicked` handler. You can query the name of the button in that handler to see which one was clicked. However, if you have many different types of tasks to complete, you might want to set up separate AppleScript files, each with its own `clicked` (or whatever) handler to keep the operations separate and easier to follow.

Summary

This hour has provided you with an introduction to AppleScript Studio. It consists of a variety of features that have been added to the Cocoa framework and that are available through Project Builder and Interface Builder. With AppleScript Studio, you actually build Cocoa applications with all of the features that they can support. You may only use AppleScript, but everything available to Mac OS X developers is at your disposal.

Q&A

Q Why is AppleScript Studio so important?

A With AppleScript Studio, Apple has made AppleScript itself a development language on par with C, C++, and Objective-C. Interface Builder itself is the tool that is used to implement many of Apple's applications such as iPhoto and iCal: Anything you can do there you can do in AppleScript Studio.

Q Should I use AppleScript Studio instead of Script Editor?

A The two have very different roles to play. If you want a full-featured Aqua interface, AppleScript Studio is the way to go. If you simply want to write a script—perhaps one that has no interface at all, but just automates a task for you—Script Editor may be all you need. In general, if you're writing an application that will be used by many people over a period of time, AppleScript Studio will work out better.

Q Do I have to learn all of Cocoa to use AppleScript Studio?

A No. If you do know Cocoa, you'll be able to see how a number of features are implemented behind the scenes, but you can follow the steps in this part of the book and achieve very impressive results without knowing what goes on behind the scenes.

14

Workshop

The workshop contains quiz questions and activities to help you solidify your knowledge of the material in this hour. Try to answer all of the questions before looking at the quiz answers that follow.

Quiz

1. What are nib files?
2. When do you use properties in a file?
3. What do you use the Info window for?

Quiz Answers

1. Nib files contain language-specific resources for your application. They include windows, menus, and other interface elements. They may also contain images, but more often contain references to image files that are stored elsewhere.
2. Properties let you declare variables that can be referenced by several handlers within a file.
3. The Info window is used to enter settings for a selected interface element. Its panes include Attributes (for names, alignment of text fields, and so forth), Help (to enter help tags), AppleScript (to work with handlers and AppleScript names), Connections (to connect interface elements), and Size (to determine the size of objects and how they respond to the resizing of their containing view).

Activities

Create a new AppleScript Studio application from the template. Experiment with adding elements from the Interface Builder palette to the window. Change their settings in the Info window to see how they work. Use the Interface Builder Test Interface command in the File menu to run the interface.

Try developing an interface for a common task or routine that you do. What data will need to be entered? If you're used to Script Editor, you're used to using several dialogs to accumulate data that will be needed. With Script Editor, you can get all the data at once. Experiment with arrangements of fields in your window to gain an understanding of what looks good and what makes sense. Remember that organizing fields into groups can simplify the interface.

HOUR 15

Building a Graphical AppleScript Studio Application

In the preceding hour, you saw an overview of what you can do with AppleScript Studio and its sophisticated interface elements. This hour starts with a very simple AppleScript Studio application that walks you through every step of the way.

Then, you find a little programming background to put things into perspective (not much, don't worry). After that, you'll see how to use menus in your AppleScript Studio applications. Together with buttons and the Aqua interface elements, you'll have all the tools necessary to build sophisticated and good-looking applications.

In This Hour

- Writing a Simple AppleScript Studio Application—This is a simple and expandable application that you can use to start experimenting with AppleScript Studio.
- A (Very) Little Programming Background—A few concepts that you've seen in action are now described in more detail.
- Using Menus—One of the big advantages AppleScript Studio has over Script Editor is that you can use commands in the menu bar.

Writing a Simple AppleScript Studio Application

This application will provide a shell that you can play with as you experiment with the interface elements. It will contain two text fields; one will allow input, and the other will only display data. You'll add a button that moves data from the input field and displays it in the output field. You'll use the same techniques that were described in the overview in the preceding hour.

The main example for this hour is located on this book's Web site, `http://www.samspublishing.com`, in the folder called Hour 15. You'll find the project inside that folder in its own folder called SimpleApp Project. The SimpleApp application is also in the Hour 15 project; you can run it by double-clicking it.

Create the Project

Start by creating a new project in Project Builder. (Choose New Project from the File menu, select AppleScript Application, and title your project—SimpleApp is a good name.) Continue with the same basic steps that you saw in the last hour—and that you'll use in each AppleScript Studio application that you work on. Open the Resources group using the disclosure triangle, and double-click MainMenu.nib to open the nib file in Interface Builder.

As pointed out previously, what is now Cocoa and one of the components of AppleScript Studio used to be OpenStep and before that NeXTSTEP. Nib files began life as *NeXT interface bundles*. Applications on Mac OS X are typically collections of files—executable code, nib files with interface elements, and the like. You see a single application icon, but if you Control-click that icon, a contextual menu will appear that allows you to open the package and access individual files. Nib files are localized for different languages; Mac OS X takes care of loading the proper file.

Set Up Interface Builder

With your nib file open in Interface Builder, make sure that the palette is visible. If it is not, open it using the Show Palettes command in the Palettes submenu of the Tools menu. Likewise, make sure that the Info window is visible; if it is not, open it with the Show Info command in the Tools menu.

Your nib file will be visible as shown in Figure 15.1. Make certain that the Instances tab is clicked; of the icons in the tab, all you care about now are two that have been created for you automatically in the AppleScript Application template: Window and MainMenu.

FIGURE 15.1
View the
MainMenu.nib file.

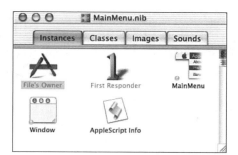

Design the Window

Double-click the Window icon to show the window that has been created for you auto-matically. (It may already be open.) On the palette, select the Views interface elements by clicking the Views icon in the toolbar. In Figure 15.2, it's the third icon from the left; you can see the Views elements in the main portion of the window in that figure. (If the palette isn't open, open it with the Show Palettes command in the Palettes submenu of the Tools menu in Interface Builder.)

As described in the preceding hour, drag elements from the Views palette into your win-dow. You can recognize the elements by their appearance. If you're in doubt, a small help tag will appear as you hold the pointer over an interface element: It will contain the formal name of that object. The text field, for example, is the unadorned rectangle in the upper right of the Views palette. The help tag that appears identifies it as an NSTextField.

FIGURE 15.2

Select the Views interface elements.

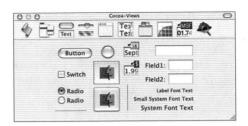

Drag four elements into the window, as follows, to build the window shown in Figure 15.3:

- A text field into which you can type information.
- A field with uneditable text to use as a label for the text field; choose the Label Font Text in the lower right of the Views palette.
- A field with slightly larger text—Small System Font Text—which you'll use to display the text entered into the text field.
- Finally, you'll need a button to start everything in motion.

As you drag the elements into your window, the guides will appear to help you align elements. You can add your own guides and even disable the Aqua guides using the Guides submenu in the Interface Builder Layout menu. The window should look like the one shown in Figure 15.3.

FIGURE 15.3

Begin building the window for SimpleApp.

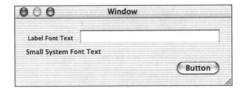

Identify Window Elements

Your AppleScript code needs to be able to refer to the window's graphical elements by name. You'll use the Info window to make various modifications to them as shown here.

Start by selecting the Label Font Text field that you dragged into the window. You don't need that text there; you can double-click it in the window and type new text, or you can use the Attributes pane of the Info window to type new text. Perhaps "Enter Text Here" will do. Figure 15.4 shows the Attributes pane for this object.

Next, you'll need to provide an AppleScript name for the text field into which you'll type information. Select it, use the pop-up menu to show the AppleScript pane, and give it a name such as `entryField1` as shown in Figure 15.5.

FIGURE 15.4
Set the attributes for a text field.

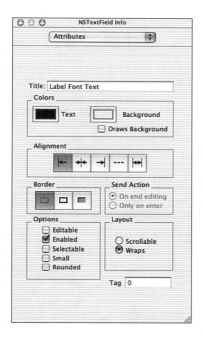

FIGURE 15.5
Name the entry field.

In addition to the names that you provide on the AppleScript pane, Interface Builder automatically provides index numbers for the elements you create. You can use these index numbers instead of names in your scripts; however, because you do not control the assignment of the index numbers, they will vary depending on the sequence in which you create interface elements, whether you delete some along the way, and so forth. In fact, the index numbers of your interface elements may differ from those shown here. Don't worry: You'll be using the names that you assign.

In a similar way, name the Small System Font field `resultField`. Neither field will respond to Apple events, so you don't need to check any of the check boxes. However, the button will need to respond to a mouse click: Select the button in the window, and then add a clicked handler as shown in Figure 15.6 by checking the `clicked` check box. Use the Attributes pane to make this a default button with a keyboard equivalent of the Return key; also use that pane to change its title to Move Data. If you've forgotten, refer to the preceding hour where this technique was described.

FIGURE 15.6

Set up the button.

Write the Handler

The `clicked` handler has the same style as the one described in the preceding hour: You tell the button's window to get the contents of one field and put them in another. Here is the entire code:

```
on clicked theObject
  tell window of theObject
    set the contents of text field "resultField" to ¬
      the contents of text field "entryField1"
  end tell
end clicked
```

When you have clicked the check box for the `clicked` Action, enter this code by clicking the check box at the bottom next to SimpleApp.applescript and then clicking the Edit Script button. A dummy handler will have been created for you, and you just add this code within it.

> Because Project Builder uses a different text-editing mechanism than does Script Editor, you can let it wrap the lines of text as needed. The continuation character shown in this and other code snippets is used to let you know that you type this on a single line.

Run the Application

Now you're ready to test your handiwork. Build and run the application using the icon described in the past hour, the Build and Run command from the Build menu in Project Builder, or the Command+R keyboard equivalent in Project Builder. After you've typed in some data, you can click the button to move it to the static text field.

A (Very) Little Programming Background

It's time for a brief look at what's actually going on here. Don't worry: The concepts are simple and, in fact, they've already been described previously in this book.

The interface elements that you're using in AppleScript Studio are scriptable; that scripting is built into them in the Cocoa framework of which they are a part. This scripting is separate from an application's dictionary. An application supports AppleScript through its dictionary of commands and classes; Cocoa interface elements automatically have scripting capabilities that you use in AppleScript Studio.

In Hour 8, "Introducing Script Editor," you saw how dictionaries are laid out. There are suites of related syntax elements in an application. Within those suites you find commands (the verbs) and classes (the nouns). Commands may have parameters that provide details about how they are to be carried out (the number of copies to be printed, for example). Classes may have properties (such as names or the position of a window); they may also have elements (items contained within them such as files within folders). In AppleScript Studio, you will find these same concepts along with one additional one, that of events and handlers. Here is how to find out more about the AppleScript Studio syntax.

In Project Builder, choose AppleScript Studio Help from the Help menu. This will provide you with the details of the syntax. The first window you see will look something like Figure 15.7. Choose AppleScript Studio Terminology Reference to look at the syntax. (It is provided in a PDF version if you want to print it out.)

FIGURE 15.7
Project Builder shows you an overview of AppleScript Studio Help.

In Figure 15.8, you can see the suites that are described in AppleScript Studio Terminology Reference. These are the same sorts of suites you find in dictionaries in Script Editor. Most of the interface elements that you deal with in Interface Builder are described in the Control View suite, which is shown in Figure 15.8. You can use the links at the left to view individual controls. Note that Next and Previous buttons on the detail page (at the right) let you navigate through the documentation. At the top left of the window, next and previous arrow buttons let you navigate through your own trail. In other words, the Next and Previous buttons at the top right of the window are Next and Previous relative to the documentation itself; the next and previous arrows are whatever pages you have viewed.

FIGURE 15.8

Use AppleScript Studio Terminology Reference to find out about AppleScript Studio.

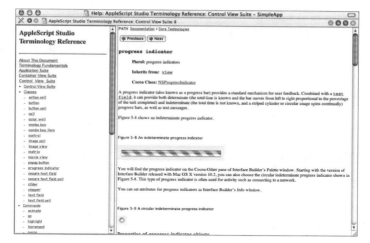

Within the suite, you'll find various classes, such as the progress indicator class shown in Figure 15.8. In the standard format of the documentation, you'll see the class from which it inherits (if any). This is the same as in a Script Editor dictionary.

There's one new feature here: You'll see the actual Cocoa class that is involved. Unless you're writing code, you won't need to worry about this, but it's here for that purpose.

Properties

After a description of the object, you'll find a list of its properties as shown in Figure 15.9.

FIGURE 15.9

View the list of object properties.

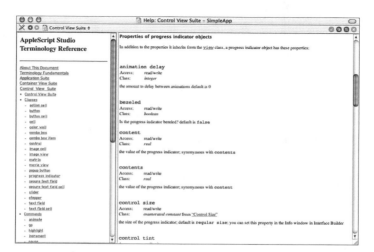

Exactly as in a Script Editor dictionary, you'll see the type of each property (integer, for example), and its type of access (read-only, for example). You access these properties with AppleScript just as you always do. For example, the progress indicator object contains a content property, as shown in Figure 15.9. You can thus write the following line of code:

```
tell progress indicator "myStatus"
  set the content to 14.5
end tell
```

Or you can write

```
set the content of progress indicator "myStatus" to 14.5
```

Elements

Some interface objects contain elements. If they do, the elements are noted in the reference for the object. The object that most frequently contains elements is the view object itself. All interface elements are ultimately descendants of view objects, so all interface objects can contain these basic elements. They are described in the documentation for the view object itself, and are not repeated for each one. Although theoretically they can be contained in all views, in some cases there is no way to do so: You cannot place a button inside a text field.

Some types of interface elements are designed primarily as containers: They are defined in the Container View suite. They include boxes, clip views (used by scroll views to display data), drawers, scroll views, split views, tab views, tab view items, and views themselves.

Here are the elements that can be contained in views:

- Boxes
- Browsers
- Buttons
- Clip views
- Color wells
- Combo boxes
- Controls
- Image views
- Matrixes
- Movie views
- Outline views

15

- Pop-up buttons
- Progress indicators
- Scroll views
- Secure text fields
- Sliders
- Split views
- Steppers
- Tab views
- Table header views
- Table views
- Text fields
- Text views
- Views

You have already seen in the preceding hour how to reference elements within views by name. You use syntax such as

```
tell table view "tableData" of scroll view "tableScrollView" to update
```

You can now see that the table view is an element of the scroll view.

There are other ways of referencing elements. AppleScript Studio and Cocoa combine to let you use a number of standard key forms in addition to names. Those key forms are

- Numeric index or absolute position—Window 1 or view 3 of window 1
- Relative position—View in front of last view
- Range—Name of views 1 through 5
- Id—Id of view 3
- Satisfying a test—First view for which `visible = true`

In most cases, using a view's name is the simplest and least ambiguous way of identifying it.

> The Container View and Control View suites described in this hour are not the only suites in AppleScript Studio. The other suites—Application, Document, Drag and Drop, Menu, Panel, and Text View—are described later in this part of the book. (Menu and Text View are in this hour.) Rest assured that all of the suites have similar structure and syntax.

Commands

Further down the description of a class, you'll find the commands to which it responds as shown in Figure 15.10.

FIGURE 15.10

View commands for a class.

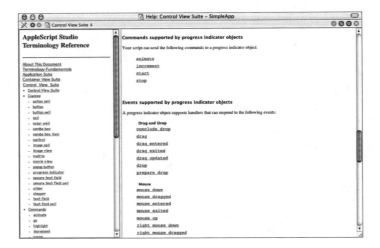

Commands are exactly the same as the commands you find in dictionaries in Script Editor. For example, you can write this code in Script Editor using the `count` command:

```
tell application "Finder"
  count windows
end tell
```

You can write the following code to start a progress indicator:

```
tell progress indicator "PI"
  start
end tell
```

The semantics are different (counting is not starting), but the syntactic structure is identical.

Events

Finally, you come to the one syntax element in AppleScript Studio that is not present in dictionaries: events. Events for a class are shown at the bottom of Figure 15.10. These are the events that you select in the AppleScript pane of the Info window and for which dummy handlers are created for you automatically by Project Builder and Interface Builder.

Summing Up the Programming Details

Although Script Editor's interface is a far cry from Project Builder and Interface Builder, and although AppleScript Studio is much more sophisticated than AppleScript alone, what you're working with is exactly the same: suites that contain commands and classes—with the classes containing properties and elements. The only thing new is events and handlers, which are associated with classes.

With this section, you've now seen the structure of the syntax that has been used previously in this part of the book. You've also seen how to use the Help menu in Project Builder to get additional information about AppleScript Studio.

Using Menus

You can use the Menus palette and the Menu suite to add menu commands to your AppleScript application. The Menus palette is shown in Figure 15.11. You access it using the icon in that is the second from the left in the toolbar in that figure.

15

FIGURE 15.11

Modify menus with the Menus palette.

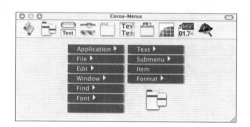

Your application's menu bar is built automatically as part of the AppleScript application template; however, you can modify it. If the menu bar is not shown, double-click the MainMenu icon in the nib window.

- Add a new menu. Drag the Submenu icon from the Menus palette to the menu bar and place it where you would like it to be. This will insert a menu with a single command.

- Name the menu. Double-click the command name to edit it. You can call it Demo. (If you're adding a command to an existing menu, you can skip this step.)

- Add a new command. If you added a new menu, you have a single command ready for you, and you can proceed to the next step. If you want to add one or more commands to this or any other menu, drag the Submenu item to the position in the menu where you want to add the new command.

- Name the command. You can double-click the command name to enter your own text.

Figure 15.12 shows the new menu named Demo and the command named Move Data.

FIGURE 15.12

Add a new menu.

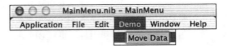

If you want to add additional menu commands, you can drag the Item icon to the menu and rename it in a similar manner.

Implementing a Menu Command

You can build on the SimpleApp application built earlier in this hour so that the menu command acts as the Move Data button did. To do this, select the Move Data command that you've just added and select the AppleScript pane in the Info window. You'll see the two events that the Menu class handles; click choose menu item to add a handler that responds to that command.

As you have seen several times, a dummy handler will be added to your AppleScript file, and you can add code to it. Be sure to click the check box next to the script filename and then click Edit Script to edit it. Here's the dummy handler:

```
on choose menu item theObject
  (*Add your script here.*)
end choose menu item
```

What you want to do is exactly what you did in the clicked handler: Move data from entryField1 to staticField. There's only one problem; you can't reuse the code. For reference, here's the clicked handler:

```
on clicked theObject
  tell window of theObject
    set the contents of text field "resultField" to ¬
      the contents of text field "entryField1"
  end tell
end clicked
```

When the clicked handler is called, the parameter theObject is the object that was clicked: the button. You can use it to get a reference to the window, and you can then tell the window to act on the two text fields in question. The menu command has no relationship with the window, and so you can't use it to get a reference to the window. Somehow or other, you'll need that reference in order to get to the text fields.

This is a common problem, and the solution is one you'll use over and over. You can create a property in your script and set it to the window. Because the property is available to all handlers in the script, you'll have the reference to the window available. The only problem is how to actually set that property.

Click on the window in Interface Builder (either its background or its menu bar), and then look at the AppleScript pane in the Info window to see the events to which the window responds. Among the events is opened: If there's any doubt in your mind what that event is, you can use AppleScript Studio Help in Project Builder to look at the window class and review the meaning of the opened command. (The window class is inside the Application suite; there are some occasions in which a particular class could logically be in one of several suites, and in that case, it's easy enough to use the interactive documentation to check out the contents of the various suites.)

You'll see that the opened event occurs after the window or other interface element has been opened. That is, it has been created—instantiated and materialized, to use more technical and specific terms; all of its controls and subviews are present. (Some events occur earlier in the process. For example, windows respond to a will close event, which is called *before* the action occurs.)

You can use the opened event to attach the window to a property in your script. Like the clicked event, the opened event has a parameter that contains the object that has triggered the event—the window, in this case. Thus, you can declare a property in your script and implement an opened handler as follows:

```
property myWindow : null

on opened theObject
  set myWindow to theObject
end opened
```

The property declares myWindow and sets it to null; the first time the window is opened, myWindow is set to the window. You can then use myWindow throughout your script. This means that your choose menu item handler can look like this:

```
on choose menu item theObject
  tell myWindow
    set the contents of text field "staticField" to the ¬
      contents of text field "entryField1"
  end tell
end choose menu item
```

Factoring Your Application

This has the same result as the clicked handler. But there's a further step you can take, and in doing so, you'll see how to structure your AppleScript Studio applications most effectively. Both the clicked and choose menu item handlers need to have the same effect. You can guarantee this by writing a handler of your own—call it moveData. The moveData handler contains precisely the code just shown in choose menu item:

```
on moveData()
  tell myWindow
```

```
      set the contents of text field "staticField" to the ¬
        contents of text field "entryField1"
  end tell
end moveData
```

Now rewrite the `clicked` and `choose menu item` handlers to call your new handler as follows:

```
on clicked theObject
  my moveData()
end clicked

on choose menu item theObject
  my moveData()
end choose menu item
```

Because you're calling the same handler, the results of the button and the menu command must be the same. What you have just done is to *factor* your application: You have separated the interface (the button and the menu command) from the functionality. (The `moveData` handler directly accesses two fields in the interface, so it could be factored even further, but that's a fine point.) Factoring an application in this way means that you can change the functionality without changing the interface (perhaps in addition to moving data, you want to capitalize the text). On the other hand, you can add additional interface features (perhaps an AppleScript command to make your application scriptable), and the functionality will be available to the command.

It is generally a good idea to write handlers in this way so that they can be called from buttons, menu commands, and scripts. You need only remember two important points:

- Your own handlers have a slightly different syntax than the built-in event handlers—note the parentheses.
- Within your script, you must preface your handler names with `my`.

Catching Errors

Whenever code might fail, you should enclose it in a `try` block so that users do not encounter error messages. Here is the modified code:

```
on moveData()
  try
    tell myWindow
      set the contents of text field "resultfield" to
        the contents of text field "entryField1"
    end tell
  end try
end moveData
```

15

This will not explain what has gone wrong, but it will prevent an error. It is always a good idea to use a `try` block to surround any code that could fail for any reason.

Enabling Menus

There is a glaring fault in this code. The `try` block will actually catch the glaring fault, but it is not the best way to do so. The problem occurs if you close the window. The defaults are set to display the window when the application is launched as well as to have a Close button. That combination allows someone to launch the application, close the window, and then use the Move Data menu command to attempt to manipulate fields in a window that no longer exists. With the `try` block in place, you won't get an error, but it's part of your job to prevent this illogical situation from occurring (using a command on a window that doesn't exist).

This is a common situation, and its solution demonstrates how easy it is to use the AppleScript Studio handlers to gain control over your interface. Two steps are involved. Remember that the `myWindow` property is set when the window is first opened. Because the window is opened automatically when the application is launched, `myWindow` will always be set to some value other than null. Select the window in Interface Builder and go to the AppleScript pane of the Info window: You'll find a `will close` handler. Create a handler and use it to reset `myWindow` to null when the window is closed:

```
on will close theObject
  set myWindow to null
end will close
```

A naming convention in the events is shown here. Events such as `will close` are triggered just before something will happen. Companion events such as `should close` are triggered when the possibility of an event occurs. The `will close` event enables you to do something that must be done when the event occurs; the `should close` event enables you to return a true or false value determining whether or not you will allow the event to transpire. Returning false to a `should close` handler will prevent a window from closing.

Now select your Move Data menu command (not the menu, but the command itself). Once again, in the AppleScript pane of the Info window, examine your handlers. You'll find one called `update menu item`. It updates the status of the menu command to enabled or disabled depending on whether the value returned from the handler is true or false. Implement that handler with one line of code:

```
on update menu item theObject
  return (myWindow is not null)
end update menu item
```

When the window is not null (that is, it is opened), the command will be enabled. As soon as the window is closed, myWindow will be null, and the menu command will be disabled. Whenever you implement a menu command, you should consider the circumstances under which it should be enabled and use update menu item to set it appropriately. As you can see, it's usually very easy to determine the circumstances: Some variation on the code described here will do the trick in most cases.

Summary

This hour has provided you with a step-by-step walk-through of building an AppleScript Studio application. It's very basic, but it contains the elements you'll need for many far more complex applications. You've seen how to allow users to enter text and how to use a button to retrieve that information. At that point, you can do any processing that you want.

You've learned about some basic programming concepts that are important in AppleScript Studio, and you've seen how to manage the enabling and disabling of menu commands.

In the next hour, you'll move into more sophisticated interface elements and see how to build on these basics.

Q&A

Q How important is it to memorize the different interface elements and their properties?

A It's not important at all. In this part of the book, you'll see many interface elements (such as text fields) used over and over. Along with buttons, these are perhaps the most commonly used, and you'll get used to their features. With AppleScript Studio, the similarity of interface controls means that you can work with one you've never used before and probably guess correctly how to use it. If all else fails, the integrated help in Project Builder will assist you.

Q I know this is a graphical user interface for interface development, but how can I get a listing of all the interface elements in my window?

A There are times when you want to see an organized hierarchical listing based on text. In the Instances pane of the nib window, click the Outline view button (just above the vertical scroll bar at the right) to do so.

Q How important is it to provide names in the AppleScript pane and identifiers in the Attributes pane of the Info window?

A Your applications will run properly with blank or identical names in many cases, but over the long run, it's easier to get into the habit of naming interface elements as soon as you create them.

Workshop

The workshop contains quiz questions and activities to help you solidify your knowledge of the material in this hour. Try to answer all of the questions before looking at the quiz answers that follow.

Quiz

1. Which part of an AppleScript suite is only present in AppleScript Studio—classes, events, properties, or commands?

2. What does "factoring an application" mean?

3. In the menu-enabling example given in this hour, why is it important to implement a `will close` handler for the window?

Quiz Answers

1. Events are unique to AppleScript Studio.

2. This refers to separating the interface of an application from its functionality. The separation makes it easier to maintain the application and simplifies tasks such as translation.

3. The handler that enables the menu command checks a property in the script that contains a reference to the window. If the window is closed, you need to set that reference to null so that the menu command check doesn't fail with an invalid reference.

Activities

Enhance the basic application described here to allow entry of first and last names in two separate fields. Display the full name in a static text field. (Hint: Remember the & concatenation operator in AppleScript.)

Further enhance the application by adding another window into which you can type an address. Add a third window that displays the first and last name along with the address. (Hint: Properties in your AppleScript file enable you to share information among windows.)

Hour 16

Writing Code for AppleScript Studio

This hour builds on the preceding hour and the simple application created there. Here you'll find a wide variety of the interface elements in action. You'll see how to write code to manipulate them; and, more important, you'll see how often you don't have to do anything at all to use them.

As you go through this hour, you'll see that most of the interface elements that you use have a common set of properties and event handlers; all have a few basics in common. And, in most cases, each one has a few special tricks up its own sleeve.

The main example for this hour is located on this book's Web site, http://www.samspublishing.com, in the folder called Hour 16. You'll find the project inside that folder in its own folder called More Complex App Project. The More Complex App application is also in the Hour 16 project; you can run it by double-clicking it.

In This Hour

- Working with Tab Views—A great space-saving interface element; you'll see how to use tab views with very little effort.

- Using Pop-up Menus and Combination (Combo) Boxes—Instead of tabs, you can switch from one view to another with pop-up menus.

- Finding Out About Events—This section recaps the event-handling code that you have used—and will continue to use—throughout your AppleScript Studio applications.

- Using Sliders—These interface elements are the best way to handle variable data particularly when specific values don't matter.

- Using the Color Well and Image Views—Use these tools to integrate images and color to your interface.

- Using Progress Indicators—A cardinal rule of good interface design is to keep the user updated about what's going on. Progress indicators are a good way to do so.

- Using Formatters—These tools enable you to automatically format dates and numbers.

Working with Tab Views

Figure 16.1 shows the More Complex App application that will be built in this hour. It features a tab view with five tabs; each of them displays a set of interface elements and demonstrates how to use them.

FIGURE 16.1

Tab views save space in views and organize information for the user.

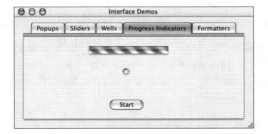

Tab views are an effective way of organizing information in your interface. They work well when logically related information can be split into sections that stand on their own. If people need to constantly switch among different tabs, they may find it annoying. (System Preferences uses tab views extensively, and you can see how related settings—such as Network preferences—can be split into these different sections.)

Tab views need not have tabs at all. You can control the elements in a tabless tab view using a pop-up menu as shown in Figure 16.2.

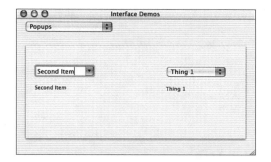

The code provided on the Web site implements both a pop-up menu and tabs in the tab view, so you have both sets of code. For the sake of clarity, the figures in this chapter (except for this one) only show the tabbed version. You can refer to the code on the Web site as you work through this hour. Alternatively, you can create a new AppleScript application—call it More Complex App and work with it. If that's what you're doing, drag a tab view into the window and set it up as described in the following section to match the tabs in Figure 16.1. You should name it `tabView`.

Setting Up a Tab View

Tab views are objects in the Container View suite. You add them to a window by dragging them from the Containers section of the palette, as shown in Figure 16.3. (You show the Containers section using the small tab view icon in the toolbar—seventh from the left in Figure 16.3.)

FIGURE 16.3

The Container Views palette provides tab views.

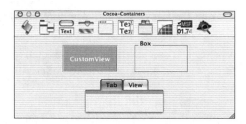

You can resize the tab view in your window. Use the Attributes tab of the Info window to set the number of tabs, as well as the style of the tab view as shown in Figure 16.4.

FIGURE **16.4**

Set tab view attributes.

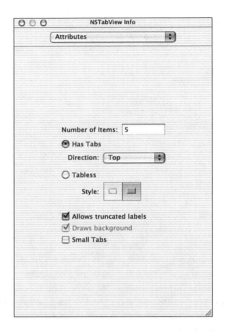

You can set the labels for the tabs just by double-clicking them and typing. As you saw in the preceding hour with the scroll view, table view, and columns, you can drill down into your interface using Interface Builder. Watch the title of the Info window to see what you have selected—a tab view or a tab view item.

When you set up tab view items, it's important to set up appropriate identifiers for them. You can set three types of identifiers using the Info window:

- In the Attributes pane, you can set the *label* for the tab view item. This is the text the user sees on the tab.

- Also in the Attributes pane, you can set an internal *identifier* that Cocoa programmers can use in accessing the tab view item. You don't need to set this for use with AppleScript Studio.

- On the AppleScript pane, you can set the *name* of the tab view item. This is the name you'll need to use to manipulate it with AppleScript.

Rather than being a complication, this system of multiple names is a simplification that aids in localization of code for different languages. Because you write your AppleScript code using the name and your Cocoa code (if any) using the identifier, you can change the label—the text the user sees—

without modifying your code. Thus, when you change the label from German to Portuguese (for example), your code needs no modifications at all.

Using a Pop-up Menu to Control a Tab View

The behavior of a tab view with tabs is very simple: The user just clicks the appropriate tab, and the interface elements that you've placed in that tab appear. The behavior of a tabless tab view managed by a pop-up menu is different, and it is described here.

Start by dragging a pop-up menu from the Other Views palette items into your window. The Other Views palette items are shown in Figure 16.5. Name it tabPopup.

FIGURE 16.5

Other Views palette items include pop-up menus.

You'll see some terminology inconsistencies that reflect the fact that Cocoa, AppleScript Studio, and the Mac OS X interface combine elements from the original Macintosh operating system, from NeXTSTEP and OpenStep, and from other sources. Pop-up menus are one of these. User documentation that follows Apple's human interface style guidelines refers to *pop-up menus*. The actual Cocoa class that implements pop-up menus is the NSPopUpButton class; and AppleScript Studio code refers to the items as *popup buttons*. A similar inconsistency exists with regard to the *clipboard,* which NeXTSTEP and OpenStep programmers refer to as the *pasteboard* and Macintosh programmers refer to as the *scrap*. This book normally uses the interface names in text and the technical class names in its code snippets.

The pop-up menu from the palette initially contains three items. You can click on the pop-up menu to display its items and then select an item; after that, you can double-click its text to modify it. To add additional items to a pop-up menu, open it by clicking on it to reveal the menu items. Then, drag an Item icon from the Menu palette items into the pop-up menu and place it at the position you want. Double-click its default name and type in the name that you want.

As with tab views and other container views, clicking once on a pop-up menu will select it. You can set its attributes in the Info window. Opening the pop-up menu will display the items, and you can click each one to modify it in the Info window. As with tab view items, you can assign several identifying values to each menu item:

- The *title,* which is set on the Attributes pane, is what the user sees in the pop-up menu.
- The *name,* which is set on the AppleScript pane, is what you use to manipulate it with AppleScript.

In order to control the tab view with the pop-up menu, you need to assign unique AppleScript names to each of the tab view items. Remember that these names are distinct from the text that users see on the tabs. Similarly, assign AppleScript names to the pop-up menu items; these, too, are distinct from the names the user sees in the pop-up menu. There's just one trick involved: Use the same AppleScript names on the pop-up menu items and on the tab view items.

Select the pop-up menu and go to the AppleScript pane of the Info window. An `action` handler is visible; click the check box to create your own handler. Click the check box at the bottom of the window next to the AppleScript file, and then click Edit Script.

Similar to the code you wrote for the `clicked` handler for the button in the last hour, create the code for this handler. Common handlers such as `clicked` and `action` often are used for multiple interface elements, so it's important to check the AppleScript name of the object that has triggered the handler's action.

Then, use the same style of code to tell the window containing the object to take action. In this handler, you have two steps to take:

- You need to get the name of the current pop-up menu item. Remember, this is the AppleScript name. You can tell the window to do this for you.
- You need to set the current tab view to the name of the pop-up menu item. For this step, you need to tell the tab view to set its current tab view. Because you have made the AppleScript names of the tab view items and the pop-up menu items the same, that's all you need to do.

Here is the code:

```
on action theObject
  if the name of theObject is "tabPopup" then
    tell window of theObject
      set choice to the name of current menu item of popup button "tabPopup"
      tell tab view "tabView"
        set the current tab view item to tab view item choice
```

```
        end tell
      end tell
    end if
end action
```

The only things that you have to remember to control a tab view from a pop-up menu are

- Use the same AppleScript names for tab view items and for pop-up menu items.
- Ask the window itself to access the pop-up menu.
- Ask the tab view within the window to access its tab view items.

Now that you've seen how to set up a tab view, you can explore the various tabs that demonstrate interface elements.

16

Using Pop-up Menus and Combination (Combo) Boxes

The first tab is shown in Figure 16.6. It demonstrates the use of a combination (combo) box on the left and a pop-up menu on the right.

FIGURE 16.6

Use pop-up menus and combo boxes to let users choose among options.

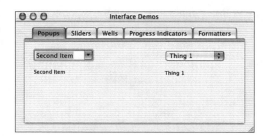

Pop-up menus let you choose from items in the menu. A combo box combines a pop-up menu with a text field into which you can type a value. (Combo boxes are one of the interface elements that can inspire heated discussion. Depending on one's point of view, they are either the niftiest improvement to the graphical user interface ever thought of or the worst transgression of every design standard ever thought of.) Add the pop-up menu and combo box to your project now.

Add two text fields to contain the values of the combo box and the pop-up menu. (You can use the same Small System Font Text fields you used in the preceding chapter.)

Here's how you can place the currently selected value in the text fields. (You'll see two different techniques in use.)

Using Connections to Get Pop-up Menu Values

The Info window has many panes; each provides a set of parameters for the selected item in your design window.

Holding down the Control key, drag a line from the combo box to the text box below it as shown in Figure 16.7.

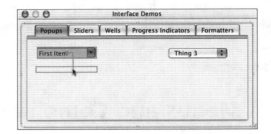

Cocoa and Interface Builder support the idea of *connections* between objects. If you connect a combo box to a text field, you can choose that the connection displays the value of the combo box. When you release the mouse after having drawn the line shown in Figure 16.7, the Info window will automatically display its Connections pane, as shown in Figure 16.8.

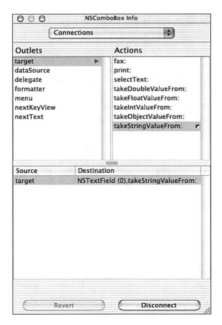

Each interface element has one or more *outlets*: specified objects to which you can connect other objects. One of the most commonly used outlets is a *target*, the object to which information is sent. Outlets are listed in the left-hand column of the Connections pane. If you select the target outlet, you'll see the types of actions that can be triggered in the right-hand column. Without knowing more about how this works, you can infer what to do: Choose the `takeStringValueFrom` action in the right-hand column.

What this does is to make the text field the target of the combo box. (The target is the object to which the line is drawn.) It will call the selected action—`takeStringValueFrom`—as needed. And in that way, the text field will always show the currently selected value of the combo box.

At this point, you can build the application, and you'll see that it does indeed work. Cocoa takes care of when the value in the text field should be changed.

Using AppleScript to Get Pop-up Menu Values

You can also set the value of a text field with AppleScript. The pop-up menu on the right will be used in that way. Select the pop-up menu, go to the AppleScript pane of the Info window, and choose the `action` handler. As you did previously, you'll test to see what has triggered the handler. You already have code to check to see if the name of `theObject` is `tabPopup`; add code to check if the name of `theObject` is `popup`—the AppleScript name for the pop-up menu that you will need to set in the AppleScript pane of the Info window when the pop-up menu is selected.

If it is selected, retrieve the title of the current menu item and set the contents of the text field to that value. Remember that the title is the user-visible string. As before, you need to tell the tab view item to do the work because the text field and the pop-up menu are located within the tab view.

```
on action theObject
  if the name of theObject is "tabPopup" then
    --code from previous example
  else if the name of theObject is "popup" then
    tell tab view item "popupsitem" of tab view "tabView" of window of theObject
      set the contents of text field "popupValue" to
        the title of current menu item of popup button "popup"
    end tell
  end if
end action
```

The code shown here assumes that you have named your interface elements as follows in the AppleScript pane of the Info window:

16

- The tab item named Popups has an AppleScript name of `popupsitem`.
- The pop-up menu is named `popup`.
- The text field to display the pop-up menu value is named `popupValue`.

Combo boxes combine a text field with a pop-up menu; if you look in the AppleScript Studio documentation, you'll see that combo boxes in fact are descendants of text fields and `NSTextField`.

Finding Out About Events

The examples that you've seen so far all follow the same pattern, which you will use over and over in AppleScript Studio:

- Make sure you have assigned proper AppleScript names to interface elements; also assign appropriate titles and identifiers as needed in the Attributes pane.
- When you implement a handler such as `action` or `clicked`, you almost always will need to check to see what the object is that has triggered the handler because many different objects can do so. (If you use multiple AppleScript files, you can have handlers that are only called by a single object, but that almost always creates file structures that are too complex. You'll find out more about working with multiple AppleScript files in Hour 19, "Using Documents and Data Sources with AppleScript Studio.")
- Tell the window of the object to do whatever is necessary. You may needed embedded `tell` blocks to address commands to tab view items or other containers within the window.

As you saw in the preceding hour, you can use the AppleScript Studio documentation to see the class description, properties, handlers, commands, and elements for each interface object. Without looking at the documentation, you can frequently find the right handlers to use. You've already seen some of the common ones; this section provides a roadmap of the others. Depending on the interface element, these handlers may be available or not. The `clicked` handler, for example, is available for buttons but not for pop-up menus.

> This section shows you how to find the handlers available for each interface element in the documentation as well as in the AppleScript pane of the Info window. From now on, handlers are simply referred to by name without adding a description.

Nib Handler

Figure 16.9 shows the AppleScript pane for the tab view item interface element. It's the simplest set of handlers—one.

FIGURE 16.9

The awake from nib *handler is called as soon at an object is loaded.*

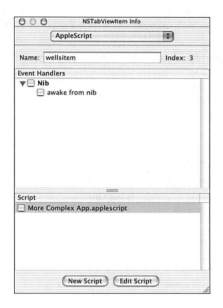

16

Interface elements are stored in nib files, and they are loaded automatically as needed. Every interface element has an awake from nib handler, which is called as the object is unarchived from the nib file. You override the awake from nib handler if you need to do something very early on (such as setting a dynamic value); the handler executes after the object is instantiated and is in a known state. By setting a dynamic value at this time, you can avoid having the object displayed even briefly in a window with an incorrect value; you also avoid the flash of an unwanted update at that time.

Action Handlers

Action handlers respond to actions in the interface element. Among them are clicked, double clicked, and action. Rather than worry about which element responds to which handler, just check the AppleScript pane to see which is available. As you have seen in this hour and the preceding one, handling these events is fairly routine: Check the object that has triggered the event and then tell its window to do something.

Drag-and-Drop Handlers

Drag-and-drop handlers are called at various stages of a drag-and-drop operation from its beginning to end. If you are going to implement one of these handlers, the most likely one is drop: It is called right at the end of the process. You return true from the handler if you want the drop to be completed; otherwise, return false and it will be stopped. AppleScript Studio implements the correct behavior for drag and drop; you don't need to do anything to have an image view object receive dropped images. However, if you need to update other information on completion of the drop, you can do so by overriding this handler.

Editing Handlers

Editing handlers let you know when editing of a text field has begun or ended. Again, you need not override them for proper functionality, but you can override them if you need to keep track of additional information (the number of edits, for example, or to store the previous data in a log file before accepting the edited data).

Key Handlers

Key handlers notify you of key down and up events.

Mouse Handlers

Mouse handlers are called in response to mouse events including movement, entering or exiting an object, and pressing or releasing a mouse button. (Two-button mice are supported.)

View Handler

The bounds changed handler is available for all views that can be resized. Overriding this handler lets you reposition objects if necessary when a view has been resized.

Special Handlers

Many interface elements have their own specific handlers. The handlers for a tab view are shown in Figure 16.10.

FIGURE **16.10**

Tab view handlers.

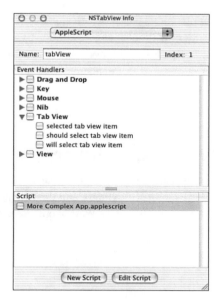

Using Sliders

The Sliders tab of the tab view demonstrates how the four types of sliders work and how they can be connected to a text field. It is shown in Figure 16.11.

FIGURE **16.11**

Connect sliders in the Sliders tab.

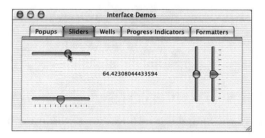

A text field has been placed in the center of the window, and connections are drawn from each slide to that field. Follow the same process previously shown with the combo box: Control-draw a line from a slider to the text field. Select the target outlet in the left-hand column of the Connections pane of the Info window. Then, for the two sliders without scales, choose the `takeFloatValueFrom` action; for the two sliders with scales, choose the `takeIntValueFrom` action.

When you build and run the application, you'll notice a difference in behavior between the two types of sliders. The sliders without scales continuously update the text field as you move the slider. For those with a text field, nothing happens until you release the mouse button. Then, the slider is adjusted to the nearest scale gradation, and its value is sent to the text field.

As you can see, you can attach multiple objects to a single target.

Using the Color Well and Image Views

Figure 16.12 shows the Color Well and the image view object. (Both are located in the Other Views section of the palette along with sliders and the like.) Default behavior here is usually appropriate. Double-clicking the Color Well opens the Color Picker.

FIGURE 16.12

Open the Color Picker by double-clicking a Color Well.

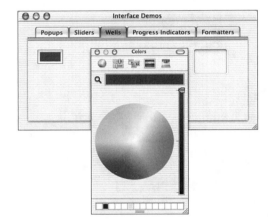

Using Progress Indicators

Progress indicators are shown in Figure 16.13. You can start them with a button as shown in the code that follows:

```
on clicked theObject
  if the name of theObject is "start" then
    tell current tab view item of tab view "tabView" of window of theObject
      tell progress indicator "PIwheel" to start
      tell progress indicator "PIbar" to start
    end tell
  end if
end clicked
```

FIGURE 16.13

Progress indicators provide feedback for users.

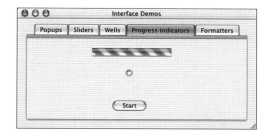

Rather than starting a progress indicator with a button, you may want to start one automatically when a lengthy process begins. For example, you might have a tab view with a tab that involves connecting to a remote database. You can use the following code to set a field in that tab view item to a message and to start a progress indicator. Here is what you might write using the tab view handlers shown previously:

```
on will select tab view item theObject
  tell current tab view item of tab view "tabView" of window of theObject
    tell progress indicator "PIwheel" to start
    set the contents of text field "status" to "Connecting to database"
  end tell
end will select tab view
```

Using Formatters

Formatters are an extremely powerful part of Interface Builder's text support. You will find the formatters in the Views palette, as shown in Figure 16.14.

FIGURE 16.14

Formatters in the Views palette help format numbers and dates.

Formatters provide a fine level of control over formatting and data entry. For example, with formatters attached to the two fields shown in Figure 16.15, you can specify how the data will be shown. Figure 16.15 shows the data as entered in the currency field.

Note the insertion point at the end of the data in the second field; the user has not yet clicked out of the field. When the user does click out of the field, a formatter comes into play and modifies the entered data, as shown in Figure 16.16.

FIGURE **16.15**

Data is entered before formatting.

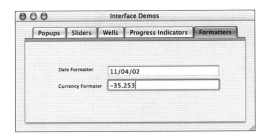

FIGURE **16.16**

Formatted data is set when you leave the field.

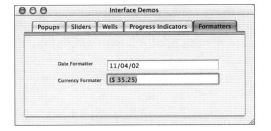

As you can see, you can insert currency symbols, specify the number of decimal places, and determine formatting for negative numbers.

To use a formatter, drag it onto a text field. When you select the text field, you now will see a Formatter pane in the pop-up menu at the top of the Info window. The Date formatter is shown in Figure 16.17.

The Allows Natural Language check box at the bottom of the pane is an important feature. It will allow your users to enter data in a way that is natural to them but that does not adhere to the format. The formatter will then reformat it as needed. It will also make a number of assumptions: If month and year are not entered, for example, it will supply the current month and year. If you do not allow natural-language entry, users must enter the date in exactly the way you have specified. The formatter will enforce this before allowing the user to exit the field; the enforcement consists of a beep, and, as you'll see with the currency formatter, you should be prepared for formatting errors.

Currency formatters format currency and, in fact, any number. The Currency formatter pane of the Info window is shown in Figure 16.18.

You can use any of the supplied formats, or you can create one for yourself using the data entry fields at the bottom of the window. Note that you can supply a minimum or maximum value (or both) for the field.

FIGURE **16.17**
Date formatters format dates and times.

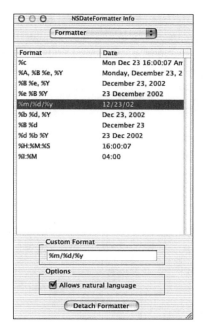

FIGURE **16.18**
Currency formatters are used for currency and numbers.

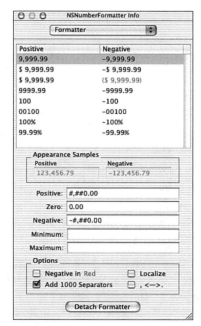

16

As with the date field, you need to prepare your users for having their input rejected with a beep. When you attach a formatter to a field and set it so that data could be rejected, make certain that your interface contains information to guide the user. If a date must be entered in a specific format, provide a sample of that format. If a numeric value has minimum or maximum values, that, too, should be shown in the interface. Otherwise your users will not understand why they are trapped and unable to leave the field.

Summary

In this hour, you've seen how to use a variety of interface elements to let users enter and display data as well as to control the appearance of their windows with tab views and pop-up menus.

If you are running More Complex App, look at it—and then look at the amount of AppleScript code that is needed to implement all of this! There's very little for you to do.

You can use your time most effectively if you plan in advance what you'll be doing. That, together with the built-in debugging tools of AppleScript Studio, will make you more productive than ever. In the next hour, you'll look at planning and the debugging tools.

Q&A

Q How do I change the look of interface elements such as progress indicators?

A Certain types of customization are available in the Attributes pane of the Info window. You can further modify the appearance of interface elements using Cocoa. However, the more you stray from the basics, the more confusing your application is apt to be to users.

Q How do I automatically select a new tab view?

A In general, let users select tab views using tabs or other interface elements such as pop-up menus. If you automatically whisk them off to another tab view without their taking action, it may confuse or annoy them.

Q I have an existing AppleScript application built using Script Editor. Is there an easy way to convert its dialogs to AppleScript Studio?

A Traditional dialogs still work, so you don't have to do anything. What you might want to do is to rethink any series of dialogs that collects information to be acted on all at once. They are prime candidates for consolidation into an AppleScript Studio window with a number of entry fields. You can do this over time, mixing and matching dialogs and AppleScript Studio windows.

Workshop

The workshop contains quiz questions and activities to help you solidify your knowledge of the material in this hour. Try to answer all of the questions before looking at the quiz answers that follow.

Quiz

1. How do you set the error message for incorrectly entered data in a formatter?

2. Why is the behavior of gradated sliders different from that of nongradated sliders when updating a connected text field?

3. How do I add items to a pop-up menu?

Quiz Answers

1. There is no error message. That's why it's so important to let the user know what format is expected (or to use the natural-language option for dates).

2. Gradated sliders aren't updated until you release the mouse button and the actual value is pinned to a valid gradation. That's why there's no live updating of a connected text field.

3. Drag the Item icon from the Menus pane of the Interface Builder palette into your pop-up menu wherever you want it. Double-click to edit the item name.

Activities

You saw how to use a pop-up menu to control a tab view. In a similar way, a set of radio buttons can be used. The radio buttons are in the View pane of the Interface Builder palette, and they haven't been discussed yet in this book. Drag them to a window and use them to control a tab view.

Implement a tab view to combine all of the example scripts that you've created so far in this book.

Hour 17

Planning and Debugging AppleScript Studio Applications

You've barely scratched the surface of Project Builder in this part of the book. It has a variety of tools that you can use to manage your projects—everything from customizing your application icons to debugging your applications and even tracking your source code through multiple versions.

This hour shows you some of the features that you can use to plan and debug your applications. You don't have to plan and you don't have to debug: You may be one of those people who can always just write a perfect application without thinking about it, and your code may never fail. But for those few times when you do get stuck or when things don't work the way you think they should, this hour's tips should help you get back on track.

In This Hour

- Project Builder Preferences—The Project Builder preferences enable you to customize your development environment. Particularly if you're spending a lot of time developing AppleScript Studio applications, you should make your workspace suitable to the way you work.

- Project Builder Targets—Targets enable you to adjust settings such as the icon for your AppleScript Studio application and the types of documents (if any) that will launch your application when they're double-clicked. For professional-looking applications, these settings are essential.

- Project Builder Styles—Use styles to switch between development and deployment versions of your application.

- Debugging with Script Editor—Script Editor enables you to isolate AppleScript code and test it on its own.

- Debugging with Project Builder—Using Project Builder, you can experiment and test hypotheses about problems in your application.

- Debugging with Project Builder's Debugger—Finally, the debugger built into Project Builder enables you to closely monitor the progress of your application as you track down bugs.

Project Builder Preferences

Project Builder is enormously customizable. (Perhaps that's in part because it's Apple's primary software development tool; as a result, the engineers working on developing Apple software have direct physical access to the engineers working on developing Project Builder.) Because of the degree of customization possible with Project Builder, the displays can vary widely. You can customize Project Builder yourself using Preferences from the Project Builder application menu.

One of the most important customizations regards the use of windows in Project Builder. The Task Templates tab of Preferences lets you choose from several predefined window templates or create your own as shown in Figure 17.1.

Two of the most commonly used templates are the Single Window template in which everything fits into resizable panes in a single window, and the Some Windows template in which a limited number of windows are used. The Single Window template is shown in action in Figure 17.2.

FIGURE 17.1

Customize your window layout.

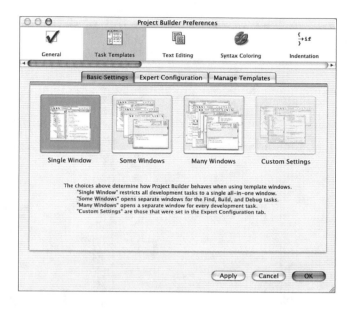

FIGURE 17.2

Use the Single Window template to keep everything together.

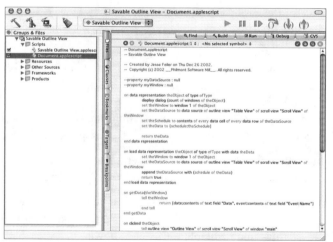

Project Builder Targets

So far, you've looked primarily at the Files tab of Project Builder. In this tab, you can see the files and groups in your project. You click editable files to edit them in Project Builder, and you double-click nib files to open them and edit them in Interface Builder. It's time to explore the Targets tab because that's how you create projects that are finished in the sense of having custom icons, stripping out debugging code, and so forth.

The Targets tab is shown in action in Figure 17.3, which is displayed in Some Windows view (as are the other screen shots in this chapter).

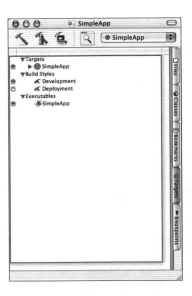

You can use a single Project Builder project to build several different targets. In the examples in this book, only a single target is used, and that is likely to be the case for most of your work. In addition to using the Targets tab to distinguish between separate products to be built, you use it to customize settings for your application, such as its own icon and document types. Those settings are set by default, but customizing them makes your AppleScript Studio application more professional looking.

Within a single target, you can have several build *styles*; the most common are deployment and debugging. They are described in the following section.

If you double-click a target, you can view and change its various settings. The settings are grouped into sections with disclosure triangles in a scrolling list at the left; at the right the settings in an editable format are shown.

Summary Settings

The Summary settings are shown in Figure 17.4.

You use this area to specify the name of your application. It may be the same as your project name, but often in complex projects it is different. (You also may use an internal code for your project and want users to see the final name—which might not be known when you create the project.) You can provide a comment, too, if you want.

FIGURE 17.4
Set Target Summary settings.

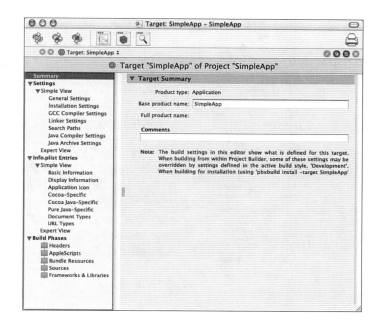

17

You can run Project Builder from the command line in Terminal using the `pbxbuild` command. If you do, you can have it automatically install your application in an appropriate location. Basic instructions are provided in the Summary Settings pane as shown here; further information is provided in the `man pbxbuild` page in Terminal and in the Project Builder documentation. If you don't want to worry about this, you can simply drag your completed application from the Build folder within your project to wherever you want to put it. (As noted previously, the Build folder is contained within your project and is maintained by Project Builder. It contains the built application as well as internal index files.)

Settings

The Settings section lets you control a host of settings with regard to compilers, linkers, and Java, as you can see in Figure 17.5. Select these more detailed settings from the list at the left of the window or by using the disclosure triangles in this window. Here, too, you can change the name of the application (any changes will be redisplayed in the Summary settings discussed in the preceding section). Note also that you can choose to have the built application installed.

Figure 17.5

Set further settings for your target.

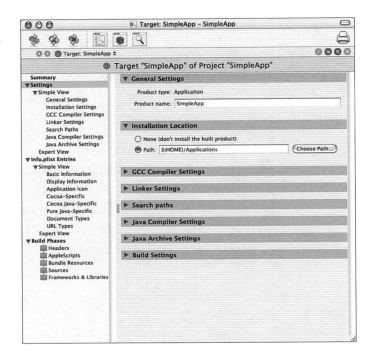

Info.plist

Each application has an Info property list (plist). This is a text- or XML-based list of settings and properties that determine how the application is handled by the Finder and operating system. To create an application that really looks like an application, you need to adjust a few items in the plist. Fortunately, that's very easy.

The beginning of the Info.plist entry section is shown in Figure 17.6. As you can see, the first sections are devoted to Finder information about your application: name, the name for Get-Info, and so forth.

This is the section where you can provide an icon for your application. You specify a file that contains your icons here. An icon file contains more than one image: Icons need to be shown in several sizes in selected and unselected styles, and so forth. Developing good Mac OS X icons can be a challenge—but a very rewarding one. For more information on developing icons, see the User Experience page on the Apple Developer Connection Web site: http://developer.apple.com/ue.

FIGURE 17.6
Use Info.plist settings to set the application icon.

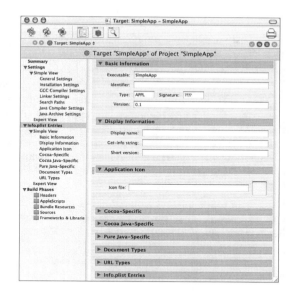

Types, Signatures, and Extensions

In the Info.plist settings, you'll see places where you can specify the type and signature for the application as well as the extension for your document files. There's quite a background to this.

One of the challenges for an operating system is determining how to open a file. When you double-click an icon, what should happen? If it's an application, the operating system itself starts to read the file and execute its code. If it's a document, the operating system launches the appropriate application and asks it to read the file.

How does the system know which application is appropriate?

On Mac OS 9 and earlier, a four-character signature was assigned to each application. Similarly, a four-character type was assigned to each file type. In addition, documents also contained a four-character creator code that matched an application signature.

The general behavior was that if you double-clicked a document, it was opened by the application whose signature matched the creator code in the document if possible. If the application could not be found, another application that could handle that file type would be launched.

This was a good way of working in most cases, but there were several problems with this approach. One problem centered on the fact that the creator and file type information was stored in a part of the document file (called the resource fork) that existed only on the Macintosh. In other words, if you

17

sent a file to a colleague using Linux or Windows, the type and creator code disappeared.

On other platforms, an extension—usually a three-character code—was used to handle the problem of knowing what application to launch. You've probably seen JPEG files with the .jpg extension or Microsoft Word files with the .doc extension. Because filenames can normally survive transfer from one operating system to another, using the extension to decide what application to launch can be a more robust mechanism. Of course, the disadvantage is that all files with a given extension are usually opened by a given application. The flexibility of having a Photoshop JPEG file continually opened by Photoshop whereas an Illustrator JPEG file is opened by Illustrator is lost.

Just to add to the mix, the original native disk format for Mac OS X did not support the concept of resource forks, so the problem had to be resolved in the first releases of Mac OS X. It has been resolved, and the answer is "yes."

Mac OS X now supports extensions as well as signature, types, and creator codes to determine how to open files. You can find documentation on the Apple Developer Connection Web site regarding the specific sequence of rules that are invoked to try to determine the single application to use in opening a file.

Document Types

Further down the Info.plist settings, you'll find the Document Type settings. You need to adjust these for any document-based AppleScript Studio applications as shown in Figure 17.7. If your application isn't document based—that is, it doesn't read and write data to its own documents—you can skip this step. Applications that interact only with databases, networks, and users are normally not document based.

At the top of this pane, you find a summary of all of the document types that your application can handle. Use the + and – icons to add or delete them; use the lower portion of the window to provide the details.

What is shown in Figure 17.7 is the default document type created in the AppleScript Studio document-based application template. It provides a generic document.

Apple's Developer site (`http://developer.apple.com`) provides more information on document extensions and types. You can also get a sense for how these elements interact by examining an application that is well written. Open the application's package by holding down the Control key while clicking on the application. A contextual menu will open; choose Show Package Contents. In the Finder window, open the Contents folder and then double-click Info.plist (or drag Info.plist to Project Builder to open it there). In iDVD3, for example, you'll find that there are three document types:

FIGURE 17.7

Set Document Type settings.

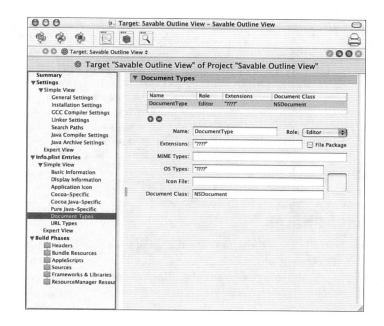

17

- Projects use the dvdproj extension. All your iDVD projects have filenames such as myproject.dvdproj (although you may choose not to show the extension in the Finder). The file's kind as shown in the Finder and as set in the Info.plist is iDVD 3 Project.

- You can save iDVD themes. They all have the extension theme, and their name is iDVD 3 Theme.

- If you save iDVD favorites, they have the extension favorite and the name iDVD 3 Favorite.

All of these files have the same four-character OS Type—iDVD. The combination of extension and OS Type lets the Finder correctly open each file.

If you are writing Cocoa code, you may be overriding the NSDocument class: You will change the class name here if that is the case. You also can provide extensions, types, and icons for each of your document types. For most AppleScript Studio applications—even those that use documents—you should stick to the basic NSDocument class.

If you don't provide icons for your documents, they will have a generic document icon. If you don't provide extensions and/or types for your documents, they won't be automatically launched in the appropriate application when the user double-clicks on them. Things will work, but they won't look right. It's worth the time to take a few hours to study the documentation on the User Experience Web site as well as the Project Builder documentation. When you learn how to set up your documents and applications, you'll be able to reapply the knowledge in all of the applications you build with Project Builder—whether they are written in AppleScript, Java, Cocoa, or Carbon.

Build Phases

The Build Phases settings are shown in Figure 17.8. You rarely need to modify these settings. If you have added files to your project using the Add Files command in the Project menu (or by dragging them into the Files tab), they will automatically be added to this list.

FIGURE 17.8

The Build Phases window shows your files.

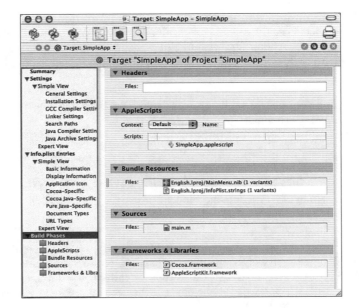

This window does provide a good summary of all the files that go into your project, including the localized files for various languages (in the Bundle Resources section). Figure 17.9 shows these files as they appear in the Files tab itself. The Credits.rtf file is selected and shown at the right; another step in finishing your project is providing this information. It's just a matter of typing it into this file, and it will appear in the right place.

FIGURE 17.9

Supply credit information in Project Builder.

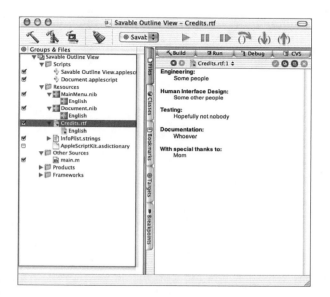

Project Builder Styles

In the Targets tab, you'll find build styles listed below your targets. The two most common styles are development and deployment. You can double-click them to change their settings, but you usually don't worry about that. What you do care about is using the small radio button to the left of the Build styles to select which style you are using as shown in Figure 17.10.

FIGURE **17.10**
Select a Build style.

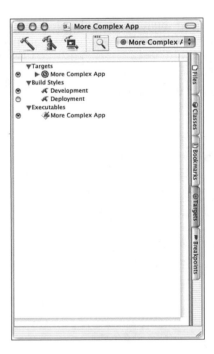

Debugging Overview

This hour has shown you how to set up your project in Project Builder. Now the focus
turns to debugging. There's more to debugging than meets the eye. Most problems in
code don't result in catastrophic crashes; rather, they result in errors or even inconve-
niences. It may seem strange, but knowing when a problem has occurred is a major part
of debugging. (You'll see in the next part of the book how to integrate Web services with
AppleScript. You can use Web services to get real-time information such as stock quotes,
exchange rates, and the weather. If you retrieve weather data that appears to be reason-
able, how can you test to make certain that you indeed got the most recent data? Would
you notice? Would anyone?)

You'll find some information in the sections that follow that should help you to debug
AppleScript Studio applications as well as many other types of applications. Debugging
is a standard part of quality control: It's not some kind of admission of failure. In fact, an
application that hasn't been rigorously debugged can't be relied on in a serious produc-
tion environment.

Who Should Debug Applications?

Ideally, everyone involved with a project should work on debugging. Programmers should check their code; integrators should check that everything works together; and users should check that their expectations have been met. The cost of ensuring that applications do what they should do is a normal part of development. Unfortunately, many people don't realize this.

With AppleScript Studio, you can move into the big leagues, and the casual debugging (if any) of small scripts isn't sufficient in many cases. However, a problem arises with a tool as powerful as AppleScript Studio: Large projects can be created by a single person, and it's hard for one person to do all of the tasks. If it's at all possible, a second person should do the testing and debugging.

When Do You Debug Applications?

Debugging isn't the cherry on top of the ice cream; it's a process that should be done on an ongoing basis. It's much easier to debug small sections of code and verify that they work properly than to take an entire application and have to validate the entire process.

Debugging with Script Editor

Script Editor is an invaluable debugging tool for AppleScript code. Its Result and Event Log windows let you monitor exactly what's happening (refer to Hour 8, "Introducing Script Editor," for more on Script Editor and these tools).

You can't use Script Editor to debug anything in your AppleScript Studio application's interface: It doesn't know about buttons, outline views, windows, and the like. However, you can use it to verify that your application-related AppleScript code is correct.

Write the `tell` blocks that communicate with applications and verify that they're working properly in Script Editor. Then you can copy and paste that code directly into a handler in AppleScript Studio and it should function properly.

Debugging with Project Builder

You can use Project Builder in a variety of ways to do simple debugging. One of the simplest debugging techniques is to add dummy fields to your application's windows in which you place intermediate results. You can then review every step of the process to see where things go wrong (or to verify that things have gone right).

17

Also, remember that the standard `display dialog` command in AppleScript still works in AppleScript Studio. You can display results at any step of the way alongside your AppleScript Studio interface.

> When you are examining intermediate results and checking to see how your script is executing, be very careful that your diagnostics do not introduce problems of their own. Often the simplest display of data is the best because in formatting it, you can inadvertently change values.

Debugging with Project Builder's Debugger

Displaying results in AppleScript dialogs is fine for limited debugging, but if you really want to debug your application, nothing beats Project Builder's built-in debugger. It's not hard to use, and when you've learned the basics, you'll know how to use it for any Project Builder application.

You start by building and debugging your application with the icon shown in Figure 17.11.

FIGURE 17.11

Build and debug your application.

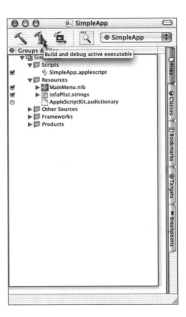

Using Breakpoints

The debugger uses *breakpoints* to halt the program at specified locations. You can add a breakpoint any place you want to in your AppleScript code. Figure 17.12 shows a script. As you can see, it starts with a `clicked` handler.

To add a breakpoint, click in the *breakpoint well*—the column to the left of the window. In Figure 17.13, a breakpoint has been added on the first `if` statement.

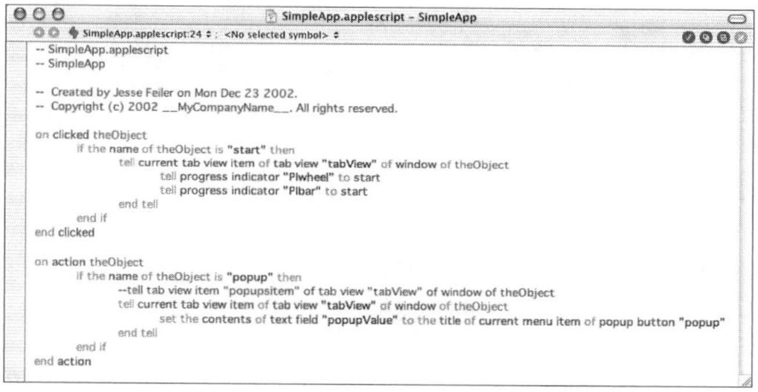

FIGURE 17.12

Start with a script without a breakpoint.

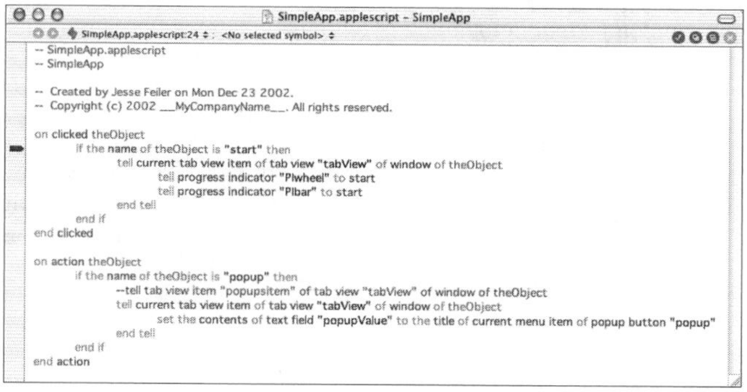

FIGURE 17.13

Add a breakpoint.

When you run your application in Debug mode, it will stop at the first breakpoint it encounters just before it executes that statement. Figure 17.14 shows what happens after you click the button in the window and the breakpoint is encountered.

At the bottom of the window you can see your script. The line at which the application has stopped is highlighted. In the upper right, you can see your application's data. At the top are AppleScript globals. Next come your script's properties and then its variables. Rather than using dialogs to display individual values, you can look at all of them at once.

FIGURE 17.14

Stop at a breakpoint.

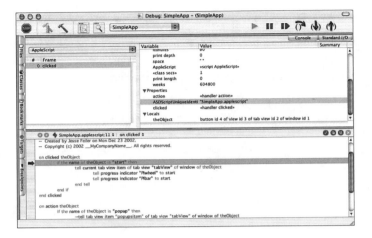

You can track what's happening using the controls at the top right of the debugging window. The most commonly used are the Continue button (right-pointing arrow, fourth from the right) and the Step Over button (third from the right). The Continue button causes the application to run normally until the next breakpoint (if any) is encountered. The Step Over button goes to the next line of code; you can watch as variables change to find where problems occur.

The debugger has a lot to do when it encounters a breakpoint. Even on the fastest computers, there is a noticeable pause as a breakpoint—particularly the first breakpoint—is encountered. If your screen appears to freeze as you hit a breakpoint, wait a few seconds and you'll almost always be rewarded with the debugger window in all of its glory.

To disable a breakpoint, drag its breakpoint out of the breakpoint well. You can review, enable, and disable breakpoints from the Breakpoints tab of the project window as shown in Figure 17.15.

A Debugging Case Study

Here's an example of how to use the debugger to track down a particularly common type of bug. (If you want to try this for yourself, start from a copy of More Complex App from the preceding hour. Don't introduce the bug shown here into a version that's running well.)

FIGURE 17.15

Manage breakpoints in the project window.

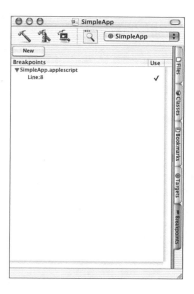

In More Complex App, the on clicked handler tests to see if the name of the clicked object is start (that's the name of the button in the Progress Indicators view of the tab view). What happens if you mistype the name of the button? You can demonstrate what happens by changing this line of the on clicked handler:

```
if the name of theObject is "start" then
```

to this:

```
if the name of theObject is "XXX" then
```

The if statement will fail because the name of the button is mistyped. If you run the application, you can click all you want but the progress indicators won't start.

If you set a breakpoint at that line of code, you can see the program stop here; continuing will jump past the if statement. (You can set breakpoints within it; they will never be reached.)

Because properties are displayed in the debugger window, you can temporarily add a property—testname—to your code, and place the name of the button in it. If you do so, when the breakpoint on the if statement is reached, you'll be able to see the name of the property testname in the debugger window as shown in Figure 17.16. That name is start, but the name in the code is xxx. That's the problem. Change the code (or the name of the button), remove the temporary property statement, and you'll be on your way.

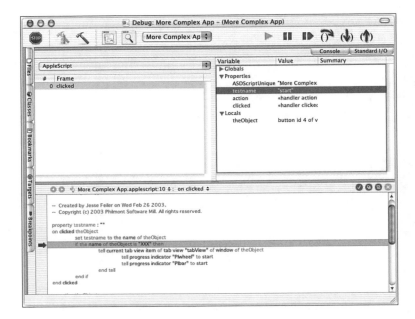

FIGURE 17.16
Use temporary properties to examine values in the debugger.

Debugging Strategies

Project Builder offers a number of strategies to use in debugging applications. Here are a few that are easy to use and yet provide valuable information:

- Breakpoints alone provide significant information. If the logical flow of your application is wrong, you won't stop at a breakpoint that you think should have been called. The way to work around this is to set breakpoints at ever-higher levels until you are certain that one is called. Then you can follow the inner flow to see where things go amiss.

- The debugger window displays the contents of globals, properties, and variables. You may want to temporarily modify your code so that intermediate results are stored in variables that are visible in the window.

- You can double-click the values of variables in the debugger window to change them as the application is running.

- Rather than setting a large number of breakpoints, you can set one at the beginning of a handler and use the Step Over button to step through that handler; it will pause before each executable statement.

Summary

This hour has provided more information about Project Builder. You've seen how to use the Target settings to customize your application's icons and to set up documents so that they can be double-clicked to open them in your application.

You've also seen a number of debugging tools ranging from Script Editor to Project Builder and its built-in debugger. You now have all the tools you need to build your applications.

In the next hour of this part of the book, you'll see how to add help and assistance to your application. Then, you'll move on to more sophisticated data structures and the ability to save data on disk.

Q&A

Q Should AppleScript Studio application icons have any special characteristics?

A No. From a user's point of view, it's of no concern whether an application is written in AppleScript, Java, or one of the C languages.

Q Why does the Step Into button not work in the debugger?

A The Step Into button steps you into a subroutine, handler, or function in which the code is visible. You cannot step into basic system functions, and some AppleScript commands (such as `tell`) fall into that category. You can generally only step into your own code.

Q Is it better to use extensions or file types?

A There is a lot of debate about this. To be absolutely safe, many people think you should use all document identification. If your AppleScript Studio application uses low-level handlers to read and write data (you'll see more on this in Hour 19), your documents can be used on other platforms. If you use the high-level routines, your documents are essentially only usable with your AppleScript Studio application and cross-platform issues disappear.

Workshop

The workshop contains quiz questions and activities to help you solidify your knowledge of the material in this hour. Try to answer all of the questions before looking at the quiz answers that follow.

Quiz

1. What is the difference between Build targets and Build styles?

2. How do you use the `display dialog` AppleScript command from within AppleScript Studio?

3. How do you stop at a line of code if you don't have a breakpoint set on it?

Quiz Answers

1. Build targets are separate deliverables such as applications (you usually have only one unless your project is quite complex). The two standard Build styles are deployment and development.

2. Exactly the same way you always do. You can mix AppleScript Studio's Aqua interface elements with the traditional AppleScript dialog.

3. If you are stopped on a line of code, you can use the Step Over button to step to the next line of code in the subroutine or handler and stop on it.

Activities

Take one of the AppleScript Studio examples, copy it, and then build and debug it. Set a breakpoint at the beginning of each handler and step through it to see what's happening. (Warning: Make certain to make a copy of the example first. The best strategy is to `option`-drag the example to your own Documents folder and out of the Examples folder. This will create a duplicate version.)

HOUR 18

Adding Help to AppleScript Studio

This hour looks at issues involved with providing help and assistance. Although you can write very small AppleScript Studio applications, many AppleScript Studio applications are fairly large and are designed for use by a number of different people. When you're writing code for others to use, help and assistance are more important than if you're writing a one-shot script for your own use.

The first three topics in this hour address the preventive side of help and assistance: making the application's interface clear and intuitive enough so that help isn't needed, catching errors and correcting them without bothering the user, and providing documentation. (If you think that help is only about providing assistance after the problem has occurred, you're missing most of the issue.)

The remaining topics in this hour show you how to provide button-driven help in your windows and how to use Help Viewer.

The button-driven help example shows you how to place an image in a button. In this case, it's just a question mark, but you can use the same technique in many other situations.

In This Hour

- Eliminating the Need for Help with Application Design—If you give some thought to the design of your application and its interface, you can avoid questions and confusion on the part of your user.

- Catching Errors—Mistakes will happen—both in your code and in users' interaction with it. Here's how to catch the errors before they cause serious problems.

- Providing Documentation—No program is so simple that it needs no documentation. Providing documentation in no way suggests that your program is complicated or that your interface design is poor.

- Providing Help Tags—It's easy with AppleScript Studio and Interface Builder to provide help tags for your interface elements, so you might as well do so.

- Providing Button-driven Help—You can add Help buttons to your application to bring up context-sensitive help. With Interface Builder, it's no trouble at all.

- Interacting with Help Viewer—Finally, you can use Help Viewer to present help in a standard way. You can also add your own customized help to Help Viewer's resources.

Eliminating the Need for Help with Application Design

Using AppleScript Studio is programming; designing AppleScript Studio applications involves a great deal of interface design. If you're coming from the world of scripts, this may be new to you. It's not particularly complicated, but there are several issues you should consider.

These issues center on

- Data entry
- Command and menu design

Data Entry

Many errors arise during data entry. Incorrect values or incorrectly formatted data can wreak havoc with your application. If you parse entered data and it's separated by commas rather than the tabs you're expecting and checking for, your parsing code may fail.

The best way to prevent data entry errors is to nip them in the bud. You can do this in a variety of ways. You'll probably choose more than one of these techniques.

Formatters

If you require input data to be in a specific format, use formatters as described in Hour 16, "Writing Code for AppleScript Studio." Users can enter data as they wish and the formatter will clean it up.

Provide Examples

Provide examples of proper input. If you have a text field, you can set its title attribute to provide a sample of the data you expect. Figure 18.1 shows two data entry fields with data filled in.

FIGURE 18.1
Create data entry fields with sample data.

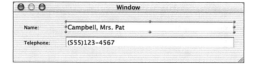

18

Use the Title setting in the Attributes pane of the Info window as shown in Figure 18.2 to set the sample data.

FIGURE 18.2
Set sample data with the Title attribute.

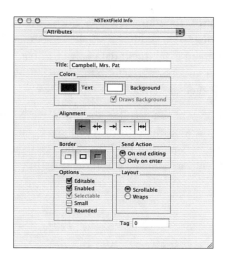

Without any further instruction, many (not all) users will adopt the formatting you have demonstrated. If you use this approach, you should remember that your data entry fields may be nonblank when no data has been entered (your sample data will be there). To avoid making mistakes, override the text field's end editing handler to process the data rather than relying on checking whether a field is empty or not. Because end editing is called after a user has finished editing the field, if there is data there, it is what the user wants. If there is data there and the user has not finished editing—or never edited it in the first place—it's not data you should handle.

Use Multiple Fields

Particularly if you're used to AppleScript dialogs with their single data entry field in each window, you may be used to combining separate data elements. It's easy to create multiple fields using Interface Builder. In doing so, you can control the entry to each one rather than worry about splitting data apart.

For example, if you need a first and last name, you can warn people that you need last-name-first or last-name-comma or some other format; or, you can simply provide two fields: First Name and Last Name.

Other interface elements are available to you to further simplify your life. Take the case of entering dates, as shown in Figure 18.3.

FIGURE 18.3
Enter dates with steppers.

You can use the Stepper control (found in the Other Cocoa Views pane of the Interface Builder palette) to control a text field. In this example, the date is split into three parts (month, day, and year), and there is no direct data entry involved: You can only use the stepper. It is possible to enter an incorrect date in this way, but you can't enter an invalid one (you can't type a month such as "Hune").

In fact, with Interface Builder, you can do all of the work in the interface. Here's how you can set up a stepper for the year field. Select the stepper, and set its minimum and maximum values in the Attributes pane of the Info window as shown in Figure 18.4. Don't worry that decimal points are shown: You'll only use integers to set the year.

FIGURE 18.4

Set minimum and maximum values for the year.

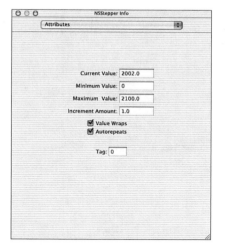

In setting minimum and maximum values, be sure to document what you're doing. There are embedded limits on your application's functionality. In this case, the maximum year allowed is 2100. That may seem far off, but depending on the data involved, it may not be very far off. If your code is reused for another purpose, you may find that the date range that's just fine for retirement calculations doesn't work for kindergarten students. (This is one of the lessons we learned from Y2K.)

Next, connect the stepper to the year text field. Do this by Control-dragging from the stepper to the text field. The Connections pane in the Info window will be visible, as shown in Figure 18.5.

Connect the target (in the left-hand column) to `takeIntValueFrom` (in the right-hand column). (Here is where you'll prevent years such as 2003.4 from appearing—`takeIntValue` only takes integers from the data.) Now, when you use the stepper, the value will automatically be displayed in the year field.

You can combine steppers with data entry fields as shown in Figure 18.6. This provides a simpler interface particularly when the user needs to click from a day such as 3 to a day such as 28 within a single month. However, it does provide the possibility of entering invalid data. As a partial check, the currently generated date can be shown in an uneditable text field at the right so that users can catch errors.

FIGURE 18.5

Connect the stepper to a text field.

FIGURE 18.6

Combine data entry fields with steppers.

Provide Onscreen Clues

Provide labels for your entry fields unless their contents are unambiguous based on the sample data that you provide. Is "Name" the client name or the project name? Is the field next to "Telephone Number" used for fax numbers? This may seem obvious, but it's a common problem with interfaces—particularly those that grow out of one-time scripts where such labeling isn't particularly important.

Command and Menu Design

Another way in which you can forestall problems is to design your menus and commands properly. Use the basic structure provided in Interface Builder (and documented in the Aqua Human Interface Guidelines, available in HTML and PDF on the Web at `http://developer.apple.com/techpubs/macosx/Essentials/AquaHIGuidelines/`).

You can enable and disable menu commands and buttons depending on the state of data entry fields and other interface elements. This is an easy way of preventing clearly invalid data from being entered. For example, you can enable a button when a text field is changed. First, select the text field and turn on the changed handler as shown in Figure 18.7.

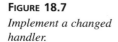

FIGURE 18.7

Implement a changed handler.

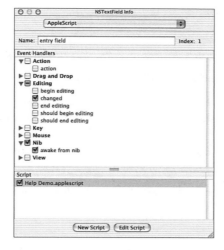

Next, write the code:

```
on changed theObject
  set the enabled of button "Enter button" of window of theObject to true
end changed
```

The only point you must remember is that the button should be disabled at the start. You can do that in Interface Builder using the Attributes pane of the Info window, or you can disable it when it is loaded from the nib as in this code:

```
on awake from nib theObject
  set the enabled of button "Enter button" of window of theObject to false
end awake from nib
```

This technique won't prevent incorrect data from being entered, but it will prevent users from clicking an Enter button when they have entered no data. (Incidentally, it will handle the case of sample data that you've set with the Title attribute. If users don't change that data, the Enter button won't be enabled and they won't be able to transmit it.)

This technique works well when there's a limited amount of data to be entered. If you have a dozen data entry fields on the window and all of them need to be filled in before the Enter button is enabled, users will quickly become frustrated as they hunt for the mystery of what has not been entered.

Catching Errors

The next way to prevent problems is to catch errors in `try` blocks. Anything that conceivably could fail should be caught in this way. In increasing order of usefulness, here is what your `on error` clause should provide:

18

- A report of the error (in natural language, if possible)
- Information on how to correct it
- A suggested correction that the user can approve with an OK button
- An automatic correction that the user never sees

Obviously you have to be careful with the last case, but you can provide effective interfaces with a little planning. If, for example, you ask users to provide a name to be looked up in a database, you can try it last-name-first and, if that fails, try first-name-first without informing the user that you've made this adjustment. Most of the time, if you find data, there will be no problem and the user will thank you.

Hour 20, "Advanced AppleScript Syntax," has more information on `try` blocks and error catching.

Providing Documentation

The last preventive measure is to provide documentation of your AppleScript Studio application and what it does. Use screen shots of the application in process: You can use Grab, which is in the Utilities folder of the Applications folder, to take screen shots easily. If you want more sophisticated screen shot processing (including the ability to capture QuickTime movies), Snapz Pro X from Ambrosia Software (`http://www.AmbrosiaSW.com/`) can be very helpful. It was used to produce most of the screen shots in this book.

Providing Help Tags

You can add help tags to any interface element using Interface Builder. Select the button, field, window, or other control that you want to identify, and then choose the Help pane of the Info window. You can type in your text there.

Cocoa and AppleScript Studio will take care of showing the appropriate help tag when the user holds the mouse stationary over the interface element. Because help tags provide an answer to the implied question, "What does this do?" you can be very concise. Don't write, "This button will…"; the user knows that the information in the help tag pop-up window is about that button. (If your interface elements overlap or cover one another, you may need to rethink your interface.)

In general, help tags should either be identification (such as the help tags in the Interface Builder palette) or a *very* brief phrase. If a button contains a word indicating its function, it may not need a separate help tag.

Providing Button-driven Help

It's easy to add buttons to your windows to provide help. This section shows you how to do so. Commonly, a help button contains a graphic such as a question mark or a lower-case I (for information). If you want to use such a graphic, you start by adding it to your project and then you use it in the button. (This is the standard way to implement such graphic-laden buttons.)

The main example for this hour is located on this book's Web site http:// www.samspublishing.com in the folder called Hour 18. You'll find the project inside that folder in its own folder called Help Demo Project. The Help Demo application is also in the Hour 18 project; you can run it by double-clicking it.

Adding an Image to Your Project

Start by creating the graphic that you'll use in your button. The easiest way is to create a small tiff image containing a question mark or letter I in the font of your choice. Depending on the application program that you use (AppleWorks, Photoshop, or the like), you can add shading, shadows, and other effects until you are satisfied with the image.

It's best to start by selecting the group to which you want to add the file. In the Project window in Project Builder, select Resources. If you don't do this now, you can easily do it later. Then, use the Add File command in the Project menu to open the dialog shown in Figure 18.8. Select your image file. Alternatively, simply drag the file from the Finder into your Project window.

Project Builder lets you add files to various targets of the application. In most cases, you ignore this, and just click Add in the window that opens next (shown in Figure 18.9).

FIGURE **18.8**
Add a file.

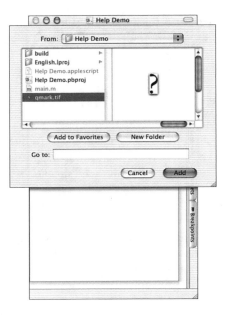

FIGURE **18.9**
Select the file settings.

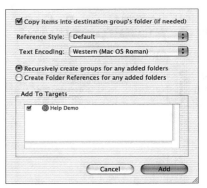

The file will be added to your project as shown in Figure 18.10. If you used the default setting in Figure 18.9 (Copy items...), the file will be copied into your project directory if needed. If you do not use this default setting, your project will contain references to files such as this one, which may be located anywhere on your hard disk or network. You may have problems if you try to move such projects around.

At this point, you can drag your image file to another group if you want to do so. In Interface Builder, the imported image will show up in the Images tab of the MainMenu.nib window as shown in Figure 18.11. Having imported it into your project, you're ready to work with the image.

FIGURE 18.10

Add an image file to your project.

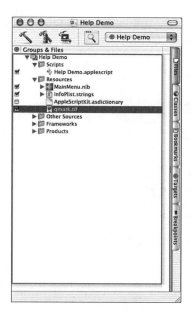

FIGURE 18.11

Import an image into Interface Builder.

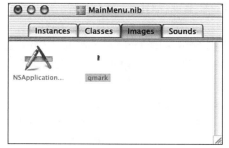

Drag a round button into your window from the palette. By convention, help buttons are in the lower left of windows. The Aqua guidelines that appear in Interface Builder will help you position the button properly. Next, drag the image from the Images tab of the nib window into the button, as shown in Figure 18.12.

FIGURE 18.12

Place the icon in the button.

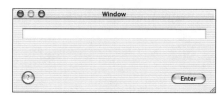

18

Position the image in the center of the button using the Icon Position controls in the lower right of the Attributes pane of the Info window, as shown in Figure 18.13.

FIGURE **18.13**

Set the icon position.

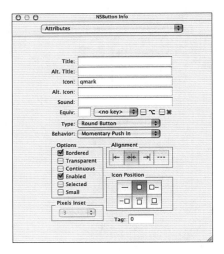

Implementing the Button

Now all you have to do is to create the information to be shown when the button is clicked and connect it to the button. The easiest way to do this is to create a separate window to contain the help information. Do this by dragging the window icon from the palette into your nib file.

Next, provide the help information. You can do this in any way that you want. A common way is to use the text view (shown in Figure 18.14). The text view handles rich text data and can include almost all the formatting capabilities that you want. It comes embedded in a scroll view, so all you have to do is size it to the window and everything will just work.

FIGURE **18.14**

Add a text view.

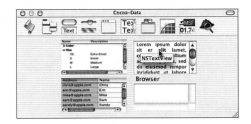

When you add a second window to a nib file, its Visible at Launch Time setting in the Attributes pane of the Info window is normally turned off. Double-check this; otherwise, your help window will appear when the application is launched.

> Text fields are appropriate for handling brief data entry chores: certainly no more than one line. Text views are appropriate for longer data entry tasks.

Enter whatever data you want into the text view, as shown in Figure 18.15.

FIGURE 18.15
Provide help text.

Make sure that your help text is not editable. You may want it to be selectable so that users can copy information out of it and paste it into other documents or e-mail messages. These settings are available in the Attributes pane of the Info window for the text view, as shown in Figure 18.16.

FIGURE 18.16
Make the text view uneditable.

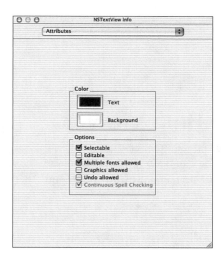

18

To make the button open the window, connect it by Control-drawing a line from the button to the window, as shown in Figure 18.17.

FIGURE 18.17

Connect the button to the window.

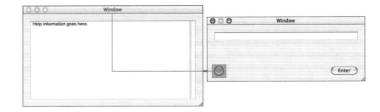

As always when you make a connection in Interface Builder, the Info window opens with the Connections pane visible. To cause the button to open the window, select orderFront from the actions at the right of the window, as shown in Figure 18.18, and then click Connect at the bottom of the window (or simply double-click orderFront).

FIGURE 18.18

Open the window with orderFront.

Interacting with Help Viewer

You can use Help Viewer as an integrated part of your AppleScript Studio application. Help Viewer is scriptable: You can open its dictionary using the Open Dictionary command from Project Builder's File menu, as shown in Figure 18.19.

FIGURE 18.19
Open the Help Viewer dictionary.

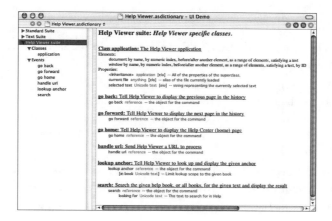

The most commonly used feature of Help Viewer is its search command. You can prepackage a search and attach it to the clicked handler of a help button in your application. Here is such a handler:

```
on clicked theObject
  tell application "Help Viewer"
    search looking for "shared printer"
    activate
  end tell
end clicked
```

Summary

This hour has shown you how to enhance your applications with help and assistance. The bulk of the work (and certainly the most cost-effective part) is the preventive work that you do in creating documentation, designing the interface, and generally preventing the possibility of errors.

You've seen how to display your own help text with buttons as well as how to integrate with Help Viewer, which itself is scriptable.

Q&A

Q When I start adding all this help to my simple script, isn't it starting to get much more complicated? Do I have to do this?

A AppleScript Studio enables you to build very complex applications for yourself, your colleagues, and even standalone products that you can sell or share. There is literally no limit to the complexity of an AppleScript Studio application, so there's no limit to the detail of your help system. You don't have to do it all, but it's there for the asking.

Q Aren't people confused if I enable and disable menu commands? Isn't it better to put up an error message if an incorrect command is chosen?

A A lot of research indicates that enabling and disabling the commands appropriately is what users work with best. It's certainly what they've gotten used to over the last two decades. However, the point is valid. If there is any possibility of confusion, consider renaming or rearranging your menu commands. For example, if no windows are open, a Close command that is disabled makes perfect sense. (What would it close?) If a window is open and you disable a Print command because there is no printer available, the user is unlikely to know what's going on. That's a case in which the command could be disabled (the application knows there's no printer), but it is enabled and the user is presented with a print dialog, which allows further action (such as selecting a printer) that could allow the command to go forward.

Q Should I provide help tags for all interface elements?

A An element with behavior that is unambiguous requires no help tag. An Enter button doesn't need a help tag. Put the information in the most visible manifestation of the object: For a button, that means a label or name within it. The button is visible; the help tag will be visible only after a delay. Furthermore, not everyone knows to use help tags.

Workshop

The workshop contains quiz questions and activities to help you solidify your knowledge of the material in this hour. Try to answer all of the questions before looking at the quiz answers that follow.

Quiz

1. How do I put sample data into a text field?
2. How do I set a title for a text field?
3. How do I have a button open another window?

Quiz Answers

1. Use the Title setting on the Attributes pane of the Info window.
2. Drag the Label Font Text icon from the Views pane of the Interface Builder palette to the window.
3. Control-drag a connection from the button to the window and set the target's action to `orderFront`.

Activities

The best way to learn how to provide effective help is to watch yourself. Try to keep a kind of third eye open whenever you're using the computer: What's confusing? What's easy? What simple technique did you have to learn from someone else because it's hidden?

Go a step further, and watch people using computers. In particular, select one of the demonstration applications you've created and watch someone who has never seen it before use it. Don't teach them: Watch them and watch the mistakes that they make. Then revise the application to make it easier to use.

18

HOUR **19**

Using Documents and Data Sources with AppleScript Studio

This hour focuses on two issues that are "advanced" in the sense that you need them to implement many applications that are more than routine. The concepts are *data sources* and storing data on disk. These topics are also advanced in that they touch on aspects of AppleScript Studio that are normally dealt with only by programmers. Fear not: Most of the work is (as usual) done for you. You have to type a few identifiers and make a few connections, but there's nothing really complicated here.

What might be new to you, though, is the level of abstraction behind these concepts. You need to understand the basics of how these processes work, and then you need to appreciate that all of that will work automatically for you as long as you provide a few necessary hooks for your own processing at specific points in the process.

As in all the hours that deal with AppleScript Studio, lines of code that span two lines on the printed page are presented with the Script Editor continuation character so that you'll know they are a single typed line of text. That character (¬) is not needed in AppleScript Studio itself; it is just to help you if you are retyping the code.

In This Hour

- More on Table and Outline Views—This section shows you some of the additional features of table and outline views beyond those you've seen before.
- Working with Data Sources—Data sources make it even easier to use table and outline views than the technique shown previously in Hour 14.
- Working with Documents: High-level Approach—With these handlers, you can read and write data with almost no effort.
- Working with Files: Low-level Approach—If you need more control, use the low-level handlers shown here.

Working with Table and Outline Views

You saw in Hour 14, "Introducing AppleScript Studio," how to create a table view and modify it with user input. As a refresher, Figure 19.1 shows the table view used in Hour 14.

FIGURE 19.1

Create a table view.

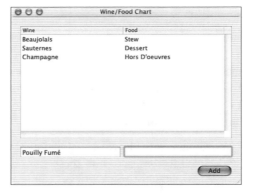

An outline view is a more complex data display; it is implemented as a special type of table view. In an outline view, you can have a hierarchical structure, as shown in Figure 19.2.

FIGURE 19.2
Outline views are hierarchical.

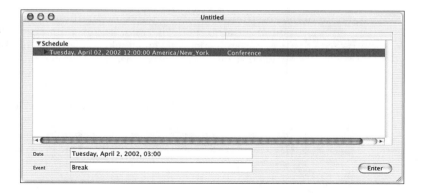

When you click the disclosure triangle, you can see that additional rows in the outline view are placed under (within) a single outline view. In its implementation, a table view contains *data rows*; an outline view contains *data items*, which may contain data rows or data items. In the latter case, this recursion is what creates the outline's hierarchy. (Although the implementation deals with data items that can contain a data row as well as other data items, many people refer to rows of outlines just as they refer to rows of tables.) An expanded row is shown in Figure 19.3.

FIGURE 19.3
Expanded outline view shows more levels.

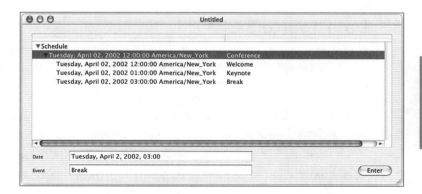

19

With these powerful data presentation tools, you are well on your way to building a functioning application that can become quite sophisticated. The first part of this chapter goes further into the techniques you need, and the second part explores storing and retrieving the data from disk.

The main example for this hour is located on this book's Web site (http://www.samspublishing.com) in the folder called Hour 19. You'll find the project inside that folder in its own folder called Savable Table View Project. The Savable Table View application is also in the Hour 19 project; you can run it by double-clicking it.

Savable Table View is the same application as Table View, used in Hour 14. However, it is reimplemented here to use data sources and to read and write data. Note that it is reimplemented; a new project based on the AppleScript Document-based Application template is used rather than modifying the previous project.

Working with Data Sources

In Hour 14 with Table View, you saw how you can use table views to display data in a structured way with very little effort. The example in that hour implemented the `cell value` handler, which you used to provide the data for a cell located in a given row and column. You can do anything you want in that handler: make up data, retrieve it over the Internet with a Web service, or get it from your own data storage. (The last one is the method used in Hour 14.)

Data Source Basics

Data sources are AppleScript Studio constructs that are designed specifically for the storage and manipulation of data in tabular forms. If you associate a data source with a table or outline view, you don't have to implement cell value handlers. And, when you get around to saving and restoring the data to and from disk, your task will be very simple (think one or two lines of code). Data sources build on Cocoa features that implement tabular views; however, they are implemented using a new Cocoa class—`ASKDataSource` (AppleScript Kit Data Source).

Data sources have one or more of each of the following elements:

- A *data cell* contains the data for one cell as well as its name (which initially is the name of the column in which it is located).

- A *data column* contains the name of the column along with information used in sorting that column. It also contains a backward reference to the data source in which it is located. It contains row and cell elements.

- A *data row* contains a backward reference to the data source as well as column and cell elements.

- A *data item* is a form of data row that is used in outline views. It can contain data items within itself, which is how the nesting feature of outline views is implemented.

In addition, a data source may have a reference to a view with which it is currently associated.

Creating Data Sources

You need to create data sources before using them. The easiest way is to create them when the associated table or outline view is created. You can override your application's launched handler or—more directly—you can override the awake from nib handler for the table or outline view itself. Be careful in Interface Builder: Every object in the nib can respond to the awake from nib event, so be sure that you have selected the proper view.

In the Savable Table View demo, this is done in the awake from nib handler for the table view. The window and its views are constructed in the same way that you saw in Table View in Hour 14. To attach the handler, use the same technique:

- Select the outline view. Use the Info window to make certain you've selected the table view, not its enclosing scroll view. If you have the scroll view selected (you can tell from the Info window's title), double-click to drill down to the table view.

- In the AppleScript pane of the Info window, select the awake from nib check box.

- At the bottom of the window, click the check box next to the file in which you want to write the script, click the Edit Script button, and type away.

In whatever handler you use, you normally write the following code. First, you create a new data source. You can name it whatever you want:

```
set theDataSource to make new data source at end of ¬
    data sources with properties {name:"wineFoodDS"}
```

Next, you create the columns for the data source. Those columns have whatever names you choose for them. They do not appear in the user interface. However, it's important to note that they must match the AppleScript names for the columns in your table. (Use the AppleScript pane in the Info window to set those names for each column as you select it.)

```
tell theDataSource
  make new data column at end of data columns of theDataSource ¬
    with properties {name:"wine"}
  make new data column at end of data columns of theDataSource ¬
    with properties {name:"food"}
end tell
```

19

You can make a column sortable by adding properties to it as in the following code:

```
make new data column at end of data columns with properties {name:"food", ¬
    sort order:ascending, sort type: numerical}
```

The properties for sorting are

- **Sort order**—Ascending or descending
- **Sort case sensitive**—Case sensitive or not case sensitive
- **Sort type**—Alphabetical or numerical

You set up the sorting properties for any column that you want to be able to use to sort the table. To actually use that column, you assign it to the sort column of the data source, as in this example:

```
set sort column of theDataSource to data column "food" of theDataSource
```

In this way, you can intercept a mouse click in a column and use it to sort the table on that column.

At this point, you generally add data to the table or outline; the next two sections discuss two ways of doing this. When your data has been added, you attach the data source to the table or outline view with the following line of code. Note that this line of code assumes that you are calling it from the handler of the table or outline view; if you are calling it from another object, the line of code will not work.

```
set data source of theObject to theDataSource
```

Adding Rows to Data Sources

You can add one or more rows to a data source as your application runs. Typically, you do this as a user enters data and clicks an Add or Enter button.

To add a row to a table view, use a variation on the following code:

```
set theItem to make new data row at end of data rows of theDataSource
```

The row will be added at the end of the data source's rows; its location in the table will depend on what column (if any) the table is sorted by.

In an outline view, you need to specify the parent of the row you are adding. If you are inserting the first item into an outline view, you can use the same code. However, in all other cases, you will need to specify the parent item. You can quickly locate the selected item in an outline view with this code:

```
tell outline view "Outline View" of scroll view "Scroll View" ¬
  of window of theObject
    set parentItem to item for row selected row
end tell
```

Note that this code gets the selection from the view, not the data source (selection has no meaning to the data source). If you are using a `clicked` handler, you can get the window using the common phrase `window of theObject`; otherwise, you will need a window name.

> ## Model-View-Controller
>
> If you're familiar with programming concepts, you may recognize the model-view-controller paradigm in action here. This concept first achieved widespread notice with the SmallTalk programming language in the early 1980s; it has remained an important concept in object-oriented programming. The basic idea of model-view-controller is to separate the display of data (the *view*) from the underlying structure of the data (the *model*) with a third element (the *controller*) having the ability to communicate between the view and the model. Ideally, the model should know nothing about the presentation and the presentation should know nothing about the model. You see a form of model-view-controller in the use of Cocoa and AppleScript views with a data source.
>
> The model-view-controller paradigm doesn't map perfectly to the world of personal computers: Documents, for example, are variously models, views, and controllers in most cases. The recent movement to break the formatting of Web pages away from the content using XML and cascading style sheets is an attempt to address this issue.

When you have the `parentItem`, you can add a new row to it as follows:

```
set childItem to make new data item at end of data items of parentItem
```

This is almost exactly the same as the code for adding a row at the end of a table except that you're adding a row to a parent row of the data source.

In the Savable Table View example, this is done in the `clicked` handler. After checking to make certain that it is the Add button that has been clicked, a reference to the data source is retrieved, and then a new row is added:

```
tell window of theObject
  set thePairs to data source of table view "dataTable" ¬
    of scroll view "dataScrollView"
  set theNewPair to make new data row at end of data rows of thePairs
end tell
```

Populating New Rows with Data

After you have created the row in your table or outline view, you need to insert data into it. The data may come from various sources; a common one (shown in the examples in this hour) is to pick up data from one or more text fields in the window when an Add or Enter button is clicked.

19

A small utility subroutine such as the one that follows is perfect for this task:

```
on getData(theWindow)
  tell theWindow
    set entries to {food:contents of text field "food", ¬
      wine:contents of text field "wine"}
    set the contents of text field "wine" to ""
    set the contents of text field "food" to ""
  end tell
  return entries
end getData
```

This subroutine will return a record with two labeled items. The first, named food, contains the contents of the text field Food; the second, named wine, contains the contents of the text field Wine. You can name the items in the record you return anything, but the names must match the code you use to unload the record.

Following the line of code that makes a new row in the table or a new data item in a parent item in an outline view, you can populate that row by calling your subroutine. First, create a local variable and set it to the result of your subroutine. (Remember to prefix its name with my because it's not a standard handler.)

```
set theEntries to my getData(window of theObject)
```

Then, move the data in the record that you have returned into the data cells of the newly created row.

The names of the fields in the record you return from getData are the names you set there. Here's the actual code to move the two fields into the row of a table or outline view:

```
set contents of data cell "food" of theNewPair to food of theEntries
set contents of data cell "wine" of theNewPair to wine of theEntries
```

Here's a full clicked handler for an outline view:

```
on clicked theObject
  if the name of theObject is "AddButton" then
    tell window of theObject
      set thePairs to data source of table view "dataTable" ¬
          of scroll view "dataScrollView"
      set theNewPair to make new data row at end of data rows of thePairs
    end tell
    set theEntries to my getData(window of theObject)

    set contents of data cell "food" of theNewPair to food of theEntries
    set contents of data cell "wine" of theNewPair to wine of theEntries
  end if
end clicked
```

This section has described how to add rows and their data to outline and table views. You can also edit data and remove selected rows. The AppleScript Studio examples show this process in detail.

Bulk Additions to Data Sources

The technique described in the previous section works perfectly well for adding individual rows to a table or outline view. For bigger additions, use the append command.

The append command takes a list of records and appends them to a data source. Given a list, myData, you can append all of the elements in that list to a data source with

```
append myDataSource with myData
```

You can construct the list manually, naming the elements with the column names. However, this is tedious, and is usually only done in demonstrations. The more common way is to use a list that is automatically constructed from an existing data source, as described in the following section.

Extracting Data from Data Sources

Given a data source, you can extract its data with a single statement:

```
set myData to contents of every data cell of every data row of myDataSource
```

The list that is generated by this statement can be used in an append statement to repopulate a table or outline view. It is the heart of the process of reading and writing data that is discussed in the next section of this hour.

Now you should be able to see how it all can fit together. Create a table or outline view that's empty. Next, allow users to enter data by typing it in and using an Add or Enter button. When the user has finished entering data, extract it into a list.

A list is a data element that can easily be stored using AppleScript Studio. Thus, the list can be saved to disk. When you want to restore the data, you create the table anew (that is, set up its columns); you repopulate it with data using the append command, and users can modify the data as they want. When they're done, the same process is repeated: Extract the data as a list, save it, and then use append to repopulate the table at another time.

All that's needed now is to save the data to disk. The next sections describe that process.

19

Exploring the AppleScript Document Template

Document-based applications are inherently more complex than simple applications that do not read or write data (or that only use databases and Internet capabilities). When you create an AppleScript document-based application in Project Builder, the template for the application is slightly more complex than the AppleScript Application template with which you've been working. This section shows you what has been set up for you. If you want to add custom code to the template, you will need to know a bit about what's underneath the hood. If all you want to do is simply save and restore data using the standard routines, you can skip to the next section.

Figure 19.4 shows the files and groups in the document-based Application template. Note that there are two AppleScript files and two nib files. A nib file and AppleScript file for the document appear in addition to the standard application AppleScript file and the MainMenu.nib file.

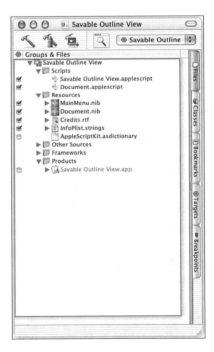

FIGURE 19.4

View the files and groups for an AppleScript document-based application.

In Figure 19.5, you can see the contents of the MainMenu.nib file. It's similar to the other MainMenu.nib files you've seen with one exception: There is no window.

FIGURE 19.5

The MainMenu.nib file for a document-based application has no window.

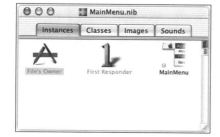

The Document.nib file, shown in Figure 19.6, contains the window along with some other objects that you've seen before, but which haven't been discussed.

FIGURE 19.6

The Document.nib file contains the data window.

The most important object is the File's Owner icon. There was one in the MainMenu.nib file, and there's one here. The File's Owner icon represents the owner of the nib file. For MainMenu.nib, that's the application itself. For Document.nib, that's the document. You can tell that File's Owner is a document by selecting it and then choosing the Custom Class pane of the Info window as shown in Figure 19.7. The NSDocument class is highlighted telling you that the File's Owner in this case is the NSDocument class. (You don't have to do this each time; it's properly set up for you, but these steps are provided here to help you see what's going on behind the scenes.)

The template is set up automatically with connections made between the window and the document. As a result, they can communicate with one another.

19

FIGURE 19.7
The Custom Class pane of the Info window shows you the class name.

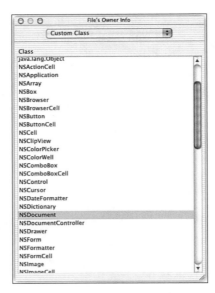

Connections of this sort can only be made in Interface Builder between objects in the same nib file. That is one of the reasons that the window and the document (File's Owner) are in the same nib file. Another reason is that the pair of objects—window and document—may be repeated several times if you have several documents open. For windows of which there is only one in the application (preferences, perhaps), the window would be placed in the application nib file (MainMenu.nib).

To this point, you've looked at the nib file in icon view. You can look at it in outline view; do so by clicking the second button at the top of the vertical scroll bar as shown in Figure 19.8.

FIGURE 19.8
The nib file in outline view gives class information.

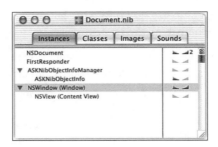

You need not examine the nib file and its objects in the detail provided in this section. If you want to add Cocoa code to your AppleScript Studio application, you will need to be aware of these issues; otherwise, you can skip them.

Here you'll see the objects in the icon view shown in an outline with their class names displayed. Disclosure triangles let you look at the class hierarchy for an individual object. The column at the right shows the connections to and from each object.

In Cocoa, objects have *outlets*—connections to other objects that can be used for communication. (Although outlet implies direction, the communication can be bidirectional, but it is the object that contains the outlet that initiates the communication.) For example, every NSDocument object has a window connection. If it is attached, the document object knows what window its data is being displayed in.

At the right of this column, a left-pointing arrow lets you see the objects with connections that are attached to the one you are viewing. In Figure 19.9 you can see that the NSDocument object is attached to outlets in the ASKNibObjectInfo object (the AppleScript outlet) and in the NSWindow object (the delegate outlet).

FIGURE 19.9

View the outlets to which NSDocument is attached.

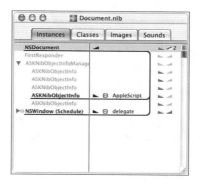

Clicking the right-pointing arrow lets you see the outlets for an object and what is attached to them. In Figure 19.10, you can see that the NSWindow object is attached to the window outlet of the NSDocument object.

Another view of outlets is provided in the Connections pane of the Info window as shown in Figure 19.11. If you select File's Owner (the NSDocument object), you will see that the window outlet is connected to the NSWindow object. At the bottom, the Disconnect button lets you break this connection. You can also use this pane to make connections between objects.

19

FIGURE 19.10

View the outlets in NSDocument *to which other objects are attached.*

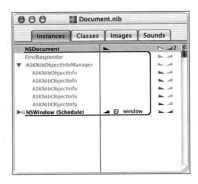

FIGURE 19.11

Make connections in the Connections pane of the Info window.

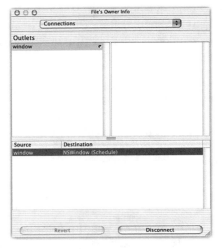

All of this is done for you, and you don't need to modify it (in fact, modifying it may break it). The connections show you how the document and the window can communicate with one another; you've already seen how the window itself can communicate with views within it. With that, you can move on to actually storing and retrieving data.

Working with Documents: High-level Approach

The Cocoa NSDocument class (File's Owner in this case) knows a great deal about how to save and restore itself. In fact, its default behavior does almost everything. All that you need to do is provide the data to be saved or accept the data that has been retrieved from disk. If you click the File's Owner icon in the nib file and open the AppleScript pane of the Info window, you'll see two handlers that are ready for you to implement, as shown in Figure 19.12.

FIGURE 19.12

Implement handlers for documents.

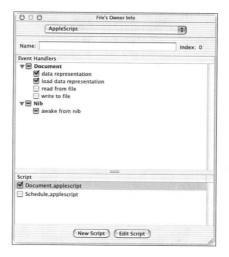

These handlers are called at the appropriate times. Cocoa itself manages tasks such as asking the user for a filename, warning if a file with that name already exists, and so forth.

These routines rely on an internal Cocoa data type, NSData, to actually read and write the data. Cocoa and AppleScript Studio very efficiently move data in and out of the NSData object with very little work on your part. However, NSData is an internal Cocoa data type, which makes it unreadable to other applications. If you need to write data that will be readable by other applications, use the low-level handlers in the following section.

Storing Data to Disk

The first handler, data representation, is invoked when the document needs data representation to be stored; the second, load data representation, is invoked when the data has been retrieved and you need to do something with it.

Here is a typical handler to provide the data from a table view to be stored. You've already seen this code in other contexts.

Because the handler is invoked with a parameter (theObject) that identifies the object invoking it (the document in this case), you can use it as always to locate a window to work with. When you've got the window, you can get the data source attached to your table view.

19

At that point, you extract the data from the data source. You package up that data into a list (which could contain additional information—current sort column, for example), and return that list as the result of the handler. That's all you do. If you provide a list, AppleScript and Cocoa will do the rest.

```
on data representation theObject of type ofType
  set theWindow to window 1 of theObject
  set theDataSource to data source of table view "dataTable" ¬
    of scroll view "dataScrollView" of theWindow
  set thePairs to contents of every data cell of every data row  ¬
    of theDataSource

  set theData to {pairs:thePairs}

  return theData
end data representation
```

Retrieving Data from Disk

The complementary handler is equally simple. It starts with the same two lines to locate the window and the data source. Then, the append line shown previously occurs. The only difference is that the previous handler returns the data itself; this one returns true if it is successful and false otherwise.

```
on load data representation theObject of type ofType with data theData
  set theWindow to window 1 of theObject
  set theDataSource to data source of table view "dataTable" ¬
    of scroll view "dataScrollView" of theWindow

  append the theDataSource with (pairs of theData)

  return true
end load data representation
```

There's an unused parameter in both of these handlers: ofType. If your data can be stored in several formats, you can use this parameter to specify which handler is used.

Working with Files: Low-level Approach

The code in this section lets you get involved with the actual files that are being read and written. Instead of reading and writing NSData objects, you can read and write any information you want in any format you want; text, for example, springs to mind. If you read and write a standard format of data, it can often be read by other applications.

If you need that type of control, here's what you do: Instead of overriding the data representation and load data representation handlers, override the read from file and write to file handlers.

Storing Data to a File

This handler is called just when data is about to be written. The whole user interface—selecting a filename and folder—has already been completed, and it's just a matter of writing out the data.

In most cases, if you're using this format, you want to make your data exchangeable with other applications. You frequently want to use a standard text format. You can obtain data from your application's interface elements by piecing it together from various locations (such as several text fields); or, you can obtain it from a text view that contains all of the data. However you obtain the data, you need to make certain that it is in the format you want.

Here is the handler you need. The second line is the line you modify depending on your needs. The other code can remain as is in most cases.

```
on write to file theObject path name pathname of type ofType
  --set myData to whatever data you are storing
  set theFile to open for access (pathname as POSIX file) with write permission
  write theData to theFile as string
  close access theFile
  return true
end write to file
```

That second line of code can be a complex AppleScript data structure, text, or anything else that makes sense for your application. If you're using an AppleScript data structure, it can only be read easily by other AppleScript Studio applications, so the high-level routines described in the previous section usually make the most sense. Remember that these routines are most often used when you are writing data to be read by other applications and vice versa.

Retrieving Data from a File

The complementary code reads in the data and places it in the appropriate interface elements. Here is the handler:

```
on read from file theObject path name pathname of type ofType
  set theFile to open for access (pathname as POSIX file)
  set myData to read theFile as string
  close access theFile
  --set interface elements to myData
  r=return true
end read from file
```

19

Summary

Data sources are powerful data management tools that implement a form of the model-view-controller paradigm. They separate the data storage (model) from the view of the information (such as that provided in the table and outline views in AppleScript Studio).

This hour has shown you how to work with documents and data sources to develop powerful AppleScript Studio applications. At this point, you're ready to write applications with AppleScript Studio that are just as full of features as applications written using traditional programming languages such as C (and its derivatives) and Java.

Now it's time to move on to the final part of this book. You'll find even more advanced features of AppleScript, and you'll see how it is integrated with other scripting and automation techniques on Mac OS X.

Q&A

Q Can I use a data storage object as a database?

A A definitive yes and no. Yes, the data storage object manages data like a database. However, one of the main differences is that the contents of a data storage object are read into memory all at once and written out all together. A database management system normally reads and writes the amount of data needed at one time. A data storage object is usually fine for storage tasks such as your address book or appointment calendar; it's not usually big enough for a corporate contact database with tens of thousands of entries.

Q Is there a performance impact for using advanced tools such as data sources and outline views?

A Yes. However, this code is used so much throughout Mac OS X that it has been highly optimized. (Apple relies on these technologies in many of its own applications.) Also, remember that almost all interactive applications spend a very large amount of their time waiting for user input.

Q Because the data representation handlers use the standard NSData type, does that mean that I can automatically read and write the data from table and outline views in other applications?

A No. Remember that you need to create the table or outline view and its columns *before* appending the data from the file. Nothing prevents you from storing that information in a file (the same one or another one), using it to constitute the table or outline view, and then populating it. But there is no automatic reload for the data source, its views, and its data.

Workshop

The workshop contains quiz questions and activities to help you solidify your knowledge of the material in this hour. Try to answer all of the questions before looking at the quiz answers that follow.

Quiz

1. What's the difference between using the data representation handlers and the read/write handlers?
2. What's the difference between a data row and a data item?
3. Does it matter which way I draw a connection?

Quiz Answers

1. Data representation handlers read and write NSData objects that can be read by other Cocoa applications. The read/write file handlers can handle text that can be read by applications written using other development environments.

2. A data row appears in a table view and can contain a cell for each column in the table. A data item appears in an outline view and contains a data row as well as a data item. The recursive data item allows you to create the outline.

3. Yes. You draw the connection from the object that sends a message/makes a request/calls a routine to the object that receives the messages/fulfills the request/performs the routine.

Activities

19

The AppleScript Studio examples of table and outline views show you how to edit and delete rows from those views. Implement editing and deleting for your sample applications.

Implement searching for a table or outline view. You'll need to gather the data on which to search—that's similar to gathering the data to enter in a new row. Then, you'll need to loop through all of the rows to find the data. (Hint: See the Mail Search tutorial in "Building Applications with AppleScript Studio," which is part of the AppleScript Studio documentation that you access from the AppleScript Studio Help command of Project Builder's Help menu.

PART IV

Advanced Scripting

Hour

20 Advanced AppleScript Syntax

21 Creating AppleScripts to Control Multiple Applications

22 Using AppleScript Across a Network

23 Beyond AppleScript: Using Services

24 Beyond AppleScript: Shell Scripts, Perl, and Other Scripting Languages

HOUR **20**

Advanced AppleScript Syntax

After having looked at AppleScript Studio, it's back to AppleScript itself for more features. This part of the book looks at more sophisticated uses of AppleScript. Most of the examples are presented as simple scripts that you can enter into Script Editor. However, in practice, you will frequently want to incorporate the ideas in this part of the book into AppleScript Studio applications.

In This Hour

- Script Objects—These bring industrial-strength programming concepts to AppleScript.
- GUI Scripting—A new feature of AppleScript, GUI scripting lets you script the interface of otherwise unscriptable applications.

Script Objects

Given enough trial and error, just about anyone can write computer code. You keep at it, over and over, getting rid of one error after another until finally it runs. But that's not good enough.

Writing successful code means writing code that can be read and understood by people. If your code can't be read and understood, it can't be maintained or modified; it can't be evaluated and assessed. It's a dead end.

This section examines script objects—a powerful and important part of AppleScript that is particularly germane to the issue of writing clean, understandable, and valuable code.

Before starting out on script objects, it's important to note that the techniques in this section become increasingly valuable as your code size increases. What you can get away with in a few lines can become a disaster in thousands of lines of code. For the sake of clarity, the examples in this section are brief. You might think that the slight added complexity that script objects bring to them isn't worth it. Have no fear: When your scripts grow and grow (as all scripts do), you'll need this slight amount of added complexity because, in a strange way, the added complexity makes your code structure simpler. Here's how it happens.

What Is a Script Object?

A *script object* is an element of a script that is identified by name. Like a subroutine, it starts with a keyword followed by an identifier, and it ends with end.

Here's the basic structure:

```
script AnyNameYouWant
-- statements here
end script
```

Within the script object, you can place the same types of elements you place within a script file:

- Properties have names and values.
- Subroutines and handlers respond to specific events and are called as needed.
- AppleScript code not located within a subroutine or handler is executed sequentially (subject to the modifications made by if and repeat statements).

You can execute a script with a run statement:

```
run AnyNameYouWant
```

You can assign a script to a variable and then run it:

```
set x to AnyNameYouWant
run x
```

You can access properties of a script using standard AppleScript syntax:

```
script AnyNameYouWant
property myLabel: "This is a label"
end script

get myLabel of AnyNameYouWant
```

If a script contains a subroutine block, you can execute it:

```
script AnyNameYouWant
  on ShowLabel()
    return "This is a label from a subroutine"
  end ShowLabel
end script

tell AnyNameYouWant
  ShowLabel()
end tell
```

Why would you want to do this? There are two general reasons:

- You can use a script object to store data in its properties. Used this way, script objects function much as instances do in object-oriented programming languages.

- You can declare hierarchies of script objects in which some script objects inherit properties and functionality from parent objects. This, too, is standard object-oriented programming.

Each of these is described in the sections that follow.

Script Objects as Instances

A script object that contains one or more properties stores data for those properties in itself. If you create a copy of a script object, that copy stores its own data for those properties in itself (that is, in the copy). If you create 10 copies of a single script object, you wind up with 10 sets of the properties.

First of all, you need to know how to make a copy of a script object. You just use the copy command:

```
copy AnyNameYouWant to myCopy
```

At this point you can run AnyNameYouWant or you can run myCopy: They are separate script objects. (Note that if you use the set command, you do not create a copy.)

20

Here's a small script object that can be used to contain a news item. It has two properties: a headline and text.

```
script NewsItem
  property headline : ""
  property itemText : ""
end script
```

You can create two copies of this script object and set their data separately:

```
copy NewsItem to firstItem
set headline of firstItem to "Weather"
set itemText of firstItem to "Cooler with showers"

copy NewsItem to secondItem
set headline of secondItem to "Meetings"
set itemText of secondItem to "Zoning Board--7 PM"
```

This is a small data structure that you can use in your scripts. In addition to storing data, you can retrieve it:

```
get headline of firstItem
get headline of secondItem
```

And now, you can write a piece of code that works within a repeat loop. First, set up a list of your items:

```
set allItems to {firstItem, secondItem}
```

Then you can use a repeat statement to loop through each item in the list and get its headline:

```
repeat with anyItem in allItems
  tell anyItem
    get headline
  end tell
end repeat
```

You certainly could collect news items in other ways; you could create a list of records each one of which contains a headline and the item's text. Iterating through that list and accessing each item's records isn't difficult. Here's how you could do that:

```
set allItems to {{headline:"Weather", NewsItem:"Cooler"}, ¬
  {headline:"Meetings", NewsItem:"Zoning--7PM"}}

repeat with anyItem in allItems
  get headline of anyItem
end repeat
```

The question naturally arises: Why do it with a script object? And the answer is revealed as soon as you hide the data. That apparent contradiction is explained next.

In the script objects you've seen here, properties have been declared in the script objects and referenced from outside those objects. You can reference properties from within script objects using subroutines. Instead of writing

```
tell anyItem
  get headline
end tell
```

You can create a subroutine that gets the headline and returns it:

```
script NewsItem
  property headline : "Sample headline"
  property itemText : ""
  on getHeadline()
    return headline
  end getHeadline
end script

tell NewsItem
  set myHeadline to getHeadline()
end tell
```

Using this structure, the data stored in the property is not accessed directly: It is accessed through the subroutine (called an *accessor*). This is one of the core principles of object-oriented code—the separation of data storage from its access. By using accessors such as this, you can manipulate the stored data as you retrieve it.

For example, perhaps your news item contains a URL in addition to a headline and item text. Although the samples shown here have hard coded the data, in real life, you may be allowing users to enter data. Despite warnings in dialogs, you might find that they enter URLs in a variety of ways:

```
http://www.yoursite.com
yoursite.com
www.yoursite.com
```

If you can control the data entry process, you can clean up the URLs. Here's a small script that puts http:// at the beginning of a URL if it's not there:

```
display dialog "Enter URL" default answer ""
set theURL to text returned of the result

if (count of theURL)   7 then
  if get text 1 through 7 of theURL = "http://" then
  else
    set theURL to "http://" & theURL
  end if
else
 set theURL to "http://" & theURL
end if
```

If you're retrieving information from a database, from a syndicated news feed, or from any other source that you don't control, you might not know what the data looks like. You can clean it up with an accessor. Here's the cleanup code placed inside the accessor inside the script object:

```
script NewsItem
  property headline : ""
  property itemText : ""
  property theURL : ""
  on getURL()
    if (count of theURL)   7 then
      if get text 1 through 7 of theURL = "http://" then
        return theURL
      else
        return "http://" & theURL
      end if
    end if
  end getURL
end script

tell NewsItem
  set myURL to getURL()
end tell
```

Although AppleScript will let you access the properties from outside the script object, you can enforce on yourself the limitation of only using accessors. By doing so, you can incorporate this kind of code. (Note that the cleanup code leaves the property data itself untouched. That's often a good and even necessary choice if you're living in a world of shared data.)

Accessors can work in two directions. They're often placed in subroutines that start with get or set depending on what they're doing. Here's the same script object with an additional accessor added to set the URL. When you run this script, you can experiment with various URLs to see that you will always get back a URL that starts with http://. (You can add other edits if you want. Note that this manipulation is not fail-safe; it's used only for purposes of an example.)

```
script NewsItem
  property headline : ""
  property itemText : ""
  property theURL : ""
  on getURL()
    if (count of theURL)   7 then
      if get text 1 through 7 of theURL = "http://" then
        return theURL
      end if
    end if
```

```
      return "http://" & theURL
    end getURL

    on setURL(theIncomingData)
      set theURL to theIncomingData
    end setURL
end script

display dialog "Enter URL" default answer ""
set myURL to the text returned of the result

tell NewsItem to setURL(myURL)

tell NewsItem
  display dialog getURL()
end tell
```

In this section, you've seen how to use script objects as instances to encapsulate data. You've seen how to make multiple copies of script objects and how to use accessors to hide the raw data in a script object's properties. The examples shown here are basic, but they illustrate the point.

However, the major power that is released with script objects only becomes apparent when you look at inheritance, the subject of the next section.

Inherited Script Objects

Script objects can form a hierarchy of inheritance just as objects in object-oriented programming languages do. The rules are the same. If one script object descends from another, it starts by having all of the properties, subroutines, and code of the parent object.

Any script object can be the base of such a hierarchy. To create another script object that is based on the first, you use the parent property. Here is a script object that's similar to those used previously in this hour. For the sake of simplicity, it has only one property.

```
script NewsItem
  property theItem : ""
  on getItem()
    return theItem
  end getItem
  on setItem(someData)
    set theItem to someData
  end setItem
end script
```

20

This script object can have a descendant. When an object has a descendant, it is said to be *overridden*. Here's the basic override of the NewsItem script object:

```
script DescendantNewsItem
  property parent: NewsItem
end script
```

You can access properties and subroutines of the parent script object from the descendant:

```
tell DescendantNewsItem to setItem("my text")
tell DescendantNewsItem to getItem()
```

The subroutines in NewsItem are executed when you tell DescendantNewsItem to run them, and they access the property from NewsItem.

The power of this structure lies in the fact that you can override any of the handlers in the basic script object. For example, you can create a WebNewsItem that sets its data prefixed with http:// as shown here:

```
script WebNewsItem
  property parent : NewsItem
  on setItem (someData)
    set my theItem to "http://" & someData
  end setItem ok jf
end script
```

The setItem handler in the descendant is run instead of the setItem handler in the parent. The getItem handler in the parent is run because there is no override in the descendant.

Note that the handler in the descendant references the property theItem in the parent. In order to do so, it must prefix the reference with my:

```
set my theItem to "http://" & someData
```

If you don't do this, AppleScript will assume that you are referencing a local variable.

You can override script objects repeatedly: WebNewsItem overrides NewsItem, and you could create ImportantWebNewsItem to override WebNewsItem. A single script object can have multiple descendants, but a script object can have only one parent.

Working with inherited objects can make your code easier to write, understand, and maintain. For example, you can create a base object with properties and subroutines that handle a very simple case. You then can override it for a variety of specific cases. The structure of the basic object and its descendants remains the same in each case, but you will need to implement some of the subroutines differently in the different descendants.

It is common for the base object to have some default functionality (and in some cases, none at all). It can serve as a template with subroutines that are empty. As you develop your AppleScript application, you can implement those subroutines in one or more descendants as the need arises.

In the examples shown here, the overridden subroutine replaces the subroutine in the parent script object. This is a common case, but it is not the only one. You can use the continue statement to execute the parent script object's subroutine from the descendant. The following example demonstrates that use as well as a different approach to overriding script objects.

This is a script to retrieve the company or organization for which a person works. Note that this example is a simplification. It does not handle the case of two people with the same last name.

First, a dialog is used to get the name to look up:

```
display dialog "Enter person to look for" default answer ""
set theName to text returned of the result
set theLastName to last word of theName
```

Next, a script object is created to do the lookup in FileMaker. If any error is encountered, a default string is returned.

```
script FMLookup
  on getData(theLastName)
    tell application "FileMaker Pro"
      open "JFDeskDisk:Users:jfeiler:Documents:Contact Management.fp5"
      try
        tell database 1 of document 1
          return cellValue of cell "Company" of (every record where cell ¬
            "Last Name" = theLastName)
        end tell
      on error
        return "No data available"
      end try
    end tell
  end getData
end script
```

Finally, the script object's getData subroutine is called and the result is displayed in a dialog:

```
tell FMLookup
  set found to getData(theLastName)
  display dialog found
end tell
```

20

You can write a different script object to do the lookup using Address Book. Here's what that code looks like:

```
script ABLookup
  on getData(theLastName)
    tell application "Address Book"
      set theOrganization to organization of every person whose ¬
        last name = theLastName
    end tell
    if theOrganization = {} then
      return "No data available"
    else
      return theOrganization
    end if
  end getData
end script
```

Not everyone will be using the example Contact Management database that's distributed with FileMaker. It would be nice to be able to use the FileMaker database if it's there and Address Book otherwise. In fact, it would be even nicer to try FileMaker, and, if that fails, try Address Book, and then, if that fails, do something else (such as provide an error message).

You can do this with `if` statements and `try` blocks, but you can do it more easily by using inheritance. You start from the most general case—the case in which neither Address Book nor FileMaker is available. Here's the basic script object:

```
script DefaultLookup
  on getData(theLastName)
    return "No data available."
  end getData
end script
```

You next move on to the somewhat more general case in which Address Book is used. Because it's installed as part of Mac OS X, it's quite possible that people will be using it. This script overrides `DefaultLookup` and uses Address Book. It's the same code that you've seen previously, but there are two changes.

At the beginning, the parent property is set to indicate that it's a descendant of `DefaultLookup`. Then, instead of returning the string "No data available" if nothing is retrieved from Address Book, this script object uses the `continue` statement to pass control to its ancestor. If you call the `getData` subroutine in `ABLookup` and it fails, the `continue` statement will call `getData` in the parent. And, as you saw in the previous code, that code returns the error string.

```
script ABLookup
  property parent : DefaultLookup
  on getData(theLastName)
```

```
    tell application "Address Book"
      set theOrganization to organization of every person whose ¬
        last name = theLastName
    end tell
    if theOrganization = {} then
      continue getData(theLastName)
    else
      return theOrganization
    end if
  end getData
end script
```

You can proceed on to a descendant of ABLookup—FMLookup, which does the lookup in FileMaker if possible. Again, the code is almost the same as what you've seen before, but the parent property is set, and a continue statement calls the getData subroutine of the parent if necessary.

```
script FMLookup
  property parent : ABLookup
  on getData(theLastName)
    tell application "FileMaker Pro"
      open "JFDeskDisk:Users:jfeiler:Documents:Contact Management.fp5"
      try
        tell database 1 of document 1
          return cellValue of cell "Company" of ¬
            (every record where cell "Last Name" = theLastName)
        end tell
      on error
        continue getData(theLastName)
      end try
    end tell
  end getData
end script
```

As noted previously, this code is simplified for the purpose of the example. One real-world complication is that it does not handle the case in which FileMaker is not available at all. It does handle the case in which the file cannot be opened or there is no appropriate data; to compile, however, FileMaker must be available.

20

Design Considerations

The use of script objects can make complex applications very easy to write and understand. To gain the fullest benefit from them, consider this basic point. Make script objects as self-contained and independent as possible. Although each object may need to know about the properties and subroutines of its parents, it is generally a good idea not to allow any other external information to influence an object. If you do this, you can safely modify an individual script object without causing problems elsewhere in your application.

Sometimes the easiest way to do this is to lay out what you know about the different types of circumstances you'll need to deal with. When you design your script, you'll come to understand that you need an object with certain types of data and certain types of functionality to accomplish your goal. The trick is to be able to look at a variety of such objects and see the underlying commonality to them. When you see that, you'll be able to construct an object hierarchy from that underlying commonality to a variety of specific behaviors.

Fortunately, this type of analytical skill is one of the things that people do best. In fact, it's hard to avoid looking for the patterns in life.

GUI Scripting

Introduced in beta version in late 2002, the new version of System Events allows you to script the interface of most non-Classic applications on Mac OS X. This feature has long been requested by people, and it is implemented in a clever way.

 System Events is installed for you automatically as part of the installation or upgrade of Mac OS X. You don't need to install it separately unless you are specifically installing a modification to it from Apple.

It's important to note that the implementation of GUI scripting is different from AppleScript's implementation within applications. Scriptable applications have dictionaries, and they allow you to write code that manipulates the application and its data. With GUI scripting, you don't script the application; rather, you script System Events, which can interact with the interface elements on the display. The application itself receives apparent mouse clicks and keystrokes that are generated by System Events and AppleScript. From the application's side, it is impossible to know that these apparent mouse clicks and keystrokes have been generated in any but the usual way.

Because GUI scripting relies on the interface, it has a degree of fragility that you must recognize. When you tell an application to carry out an AppleScript command, it will do so. When you tell System Events to select a menu command, you specify it by name, and, if the name changes, or if the command's location in the menu bar changes, the script can break.

Notwithstanding this limitation, GUI scripting can be incredibly important in allowing you to script those missing links—applications that don't have AppleScript dictionaries.

In order to start with GUI scripting, you need to set up access for assistive devices in the Universal Access pane of System Preferences. This option is a check box at the bottom of the pane as shown in Figure 20.1.

FIGURE 20.1

Enable access for assistive devices.

This will allow a stream of information about what's under the mouse to flow through System Events. You can demonstrate this by turning on the option and then running the sample application, UI Element Inspector. As you move the mouse, you'll see a report of what's underneath it. Output from UI Element Inspector is shown in Figure 20.2. As you can see, the pointer is over the window title, "UI Element Inspector"; that is reported as AXValue.

You can download the application and its source code from `http://www.apple.com/applescript/GUI/UI-Inspector.sit` to see how it works.

The most frequently used GUI scripting code is the code to select a menu item in an application that is not otherwise scriptable. Here is Apple's sample code.

First, you activate the application itself:

```
tell application app_name
   activate
end tell
```

20

FIGURE 20.2

Use UI Element Inspector to see what's under the mouse.

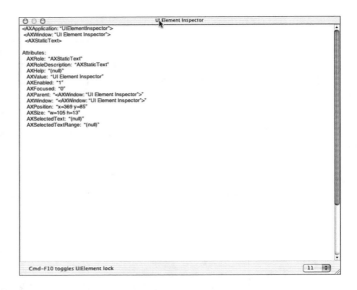

Then you use System Events to communicate with the application's menu bar. Note that you're telling System Events, not the application, to initiate the task.

```
tell application "System Events"
  with timeout of 300 seconds -- 5 minutes
    tell process app_name
      tell menu bar 1
        click menu item menu_item of menu menu_name
      end tell
    end tell
  end timeout
end tell
```

The process for selecting a submenu item is comparable:

```
tell menu bar 1 -- menu bar
  tell menu menu_name -- menu
    tell menu item menu_item -- menu item
      tell menu 1 -- sub-menu
        click menu item submenu_item -- sub-menu item
      end tell
    end tell
  end tell
end tell
```

Summary

You've seen how to use the power of object-oriented programming with script objects. Because they help you structure your code into reusable and self-contained segments, they help you manage large AppleScript projects that otherwise would be a tangle of lengthy and intertwined procedures.

The new GUI scripting feature of AppleScript has also been introduced here. It uses the System Events application and the assistive devices option of Universal Access to let you manipulate interface elements with AppleScript.

Q&A

Q How large does an application have to be before you get benefits from using script objects?

A Just about anything more than a few lines of AppleScript code benefits from script objects. Scripts have a way of morphing into new scripts, and having a good architectural basis makes this easier. In addition, it's good programming style, and you'll gain more experience by using script objects on small projects.

Q Where does the `continue` command go?

A You can use the command in any subroutine of a script object that overrides a similarly named subroutine in an ancestor. Typically, the `continue` command is the first or last executable in the overridden subroutine. Placing it in the middle of the code often leads to bugs. (This applies to any object-oriented language.)

Q When do you have to worry about GUI scripts breaking?

A Because they directly manipulate the interface, any time the interface changes you need to retest your GUI scripts. Typically, changes to the interface of an application take place with new versions or upgrades. Menu commands are sometimes renamed, and they sometimes move. Also, if you are identifying fields within windows by number (as in text field 1), modifications to the windows may cause fields to be renumbered. Finally, remember that some programs modify their interface as they run. The Window menu, for example, is built dynamically. Some applications create windows and data entry fields on the fly.

20

Workshop

The workshop contains quiz questions and activities to help you solidify your knowledge of the material in this hour. Try to answer all of the questions before looking at the quiz answers that follow.

Quiz

1. Does AppleScript support multiple inheritance?
2. How do you indicate that a script object is used as a basis for inheritance?
3. If you are using multiple instances of a script object to store data, how do you create them?

Quiz Answers

1. No.
2. You use the `parent` property to indicate that a script object has a parent. You do nothing in the parent to indicate that it has descendants.
3. Use the `copy` command.

Activities

You know a lot more about object-oriented programming and inheritance than you might think. Open a dictionary such as the System Events dictionary and look at the classes. You'll see an inheritance structure with classes such as check box inheriting from UI element.

Create an AppleScript Studio application and open its resource file with Interface Builder. Normally you work with the Instances tab of the nib window. Click the Classes tab, and examine the hierarchy of the classes you're working with. (Use the buttons at the left of the toolbar in the window to change the display.)

Modify the menu selection script in this chapter to allow a user to enter the name of a menu and the command to execute. That utility can be used to manipulate any application.

Hour **21**

Creating AppleScripts to Control Multiple Applications

Until now, the scripts discussed have worked with single applications. This hour shows you how to move data from one application to another and how to create multiple-application workflows.

This hour presents four scripts, each of which does the same thing in a different way. The task is to extract names and phone numbers from a data source, and then to create a document that contains that information and that can be printed. Two of the scripts extract the data from Address Book (the application that comes with Mac OS X); the other two extract the data from the Contact template that comes with FileMaker Pro. In two cases, the output is sent to Text Edit; in the other two, InDesign is used to present the output.

The point of this procedure is to demonstrate not just how you can move data from one application to another, but how you can write scripts using handlers that can be replaced as your needs and supporting applications change.

In This Hour

- Basic Script Design—Here's the overview of the scripts that will be used throughout this hour.
- Extracting Data from Address Book and Placing It in Text Edit—This is the simplest script, and because both Address Book and Text Edit are part of the normal Mac OS X installation, you should be able to do this yourself.
- Extracting Data from FileMaker and Placing It in Text Edit—This script uses FileMaker as a data source rather than Address Book. You can use it as a template for other databases.
- Extracting Data from Address Book and Placing It in InDesign—This variation on the first script uses InDesign, Adobe's page-layout application, to format the data.
- Extracting Data from FileMaker and Placing It in InDesign—To complete the set, this script combines FileMaker with InDesign.
- Creating Dynamic Pages with InDesign—Finally, this script shows yet another way of working with InDesign. Instead of flowing data into page after page, text frames are created dynamically to receive the data.

Basic Script Design

The script that serves as the basis of this hour is very simple. It contains three subroutines, `getData`, `createDocument`, and `fillDocument`, that are called in its first four lines:

```
set myPeople to getData()
set howMany to count of item 1 of myPeople
set theDocument to createDocument(howMany)
fillDocument(howMany, myPeople, theDocument)
```

This design is used to show how a single script can be modified to use various applications for its processing. It is not presented as an optimized solution: In real life, you can make many changes that will make it run faster.

getData

This subroutine retrieves a list of three lists. The first list consists of names; the second consists of labels for a phone number (such as Work, Home, or Fax); and the third consists of the matching phone numbers.

How this information is retrieved doesn't matter to the script: It's internal to this subroutine in good, structured programming style. This subroutine changes depending on the data source; it differs for the FileMaker and Address Book samples. It is not impacted by whether the output goes to InDesign or Text Edit.

> This type of processing can be memory intensive: You will need to store all of the data in memory at one time before you print out the first page of data. If your particular work flow contains a large number of large data elements (pictures, for instance), this strategy may not work. Instead, you may want a structure that retrieves the *n*th set of data and returns it rather than returning a list of all data at once.

createDocument

The next subroutine creates a document and prepares it to receive the data. In the case of Text Edit, it's just a matter of creating the document. In the case of InDesign, the document is created and a table is placed in it to receive the data. The document is returned from the subroutine for further use.

No data is handled in this subroutine; the only data-related item is the number of rows of data that will be passed in. Although the calculation is not performed in the samples in this hour, you could use this information to determine the number of pages to create in a document.

Although the previous subroutine was dependent on the data source, this one is only dependent on where the data will go. It is the same for scripts that retrieve data from FileMaker and Address Book, but it differs in the InDesign and Text Edit samples.

fillDocument

The final subroutine places the data into the document that was returned from `createDocument`. It is independent of the data source, but it differs between the InDesign and Text Edit samples.

Although it handles data, that data is stored in AppleScript data structures that are created in `getData`. After those data structures have been created, there is no difference in the data.

21

Extracting Data from Address Book and Placing It in Text Edit

Here is the full implementation of the script. The basic four lines described in the previous section are unchanged. All that matters is the three subroutines.

getData

This subroutine collects the data. It is assembled into three lists (theNames, theLabels, and theNumbers). Address Book properly returns missing values where necessary; as a result, you can be assured that the three lists are the same length. (If it simply omitted data values for missing data, the lists might be of unequal length and the data returned would be unusable.)

This is the only subroutine that manipulates data. You might want to modify it so that in the case of a missing phone number, an e-mail address is inserted. When the data leaves here in a list of three lists (the return statement), it is ready to be placed in a document.

```
on getData()
 tell application "Address Book"
  set theNames to name of every person
  set theLabels to label of phone 1 of every person
  set theNumbers to value of phone 1 of every person
 end tell
 return {theNames, theLabels, theNumbers}
end getData
```

createDocument

You've seen before how to create a document with Text Edit; that's all you do here:

```
on createDocument(numberOfRows)
 tell application "TextEdit"
  set myDocument to make new document at front
 end tell
 return myDocument
end createDocument
```

fillDocument

The final subroutine extracts the data from the lists and creates a single long text string to be placed in the document. Note that this is the place in which the missing values are checked.

```
on fillDocument(theCounter, thePeople, theDocument)
 set theNames to item 1 of thePeople
 set theLabels to item 2 of thePeople
```

```
set theNumbers to item 3 of thePeople
set this_text to ""
repeat with rowNumber from 1 to theCounter
 set this_text to (this_text & return & item rowNumber of theNames as string)
 if item rowNumber of theNumbers ≠ missing value then
  if theLabels = missing value then
   set this_text to (this_text & ¬
     ": " & (item rowNumber of theNumbers as string))
  else
   set this_text to (this_text & ¬
     ": " & (item rowNumber of theLabels as string) & ¬
     " " & (item rowNumber of theNumbers as string))
  end if
 end if
end repeat
tell application "TextEdit"
 set the text of theDocument to this_text
end tell
end fillDocument
```

The code as written here assumes that there will be a name for each data record (no phone-number-only records); it assumes also that there may or may not be a phone number, and that the list of theLabels in its entirety may not exist. The reason for this checking is that some data sources may not label phone numbers. (In the template used for FileMaker, the phone numbers are labeled Phone 1 and Phone 2, which is not useful at all for a printed list.)

When you write well-structured code in AppleScript or any programming language, it's important to delineate the boundaries between program units and the degree to which those units know about one another. In this case, the assumptions described here are relevant to the getData and fillDocument subroutines regardless of the data manager or document application that will be used. Some of the considerations, such as the issue of theLabels, are raised by specific applications or databases, but they are best addressed in a general manner as is the case here. What you want to avoid is a line of code such as this one:

```
if theDataSource is "FileMaker"
```

Placing that line of code in the fillDocument subroutine would require that it have an awareness of the peculiarities of data sources. Before long, you might wind up with tests in fillDocument for data flowing from FileMaker, Excel, Address Book, OpenBase, and more.

21

You might consider using a try block as in the following code. That way, you can avoid the if statements.

```
try
 set this_text to (this_text & return & item rowNumber of theNames as string)
 set this_text to (this_text & ¬
    ": " & (item rowNumber of theLabels as string) & ¬
    " " & (item rowNumber of theNumbers as string))
 on error -- just continue
end try
```

The problem with this simplification is that if an error is encountered early in the code, the entry will be skipped entirely, even if some data could be displayed. That, indeed, will be the case in the FileMaker example shown next.

Extracting Data from FileMaker and Placing It in Text Edit

By modularizing the subroutines, it is possible to use FileMaker as a data source by changing only the getData subroutine.

getData

The following subroutine retrieves the data from the FileMaker Contact Management template that ships with FileMaker. You can create a database from that template, enter data, and then run this script.

As mentioned previously, the Contact Management template doesn't provide labels for phone numbers. As a result, the list theLabels is meaningless. The choice here is to set that variable to a missing value. That works because the fillDocument subroutine checks for a missing value in the list itself as described in the previous section.

An alternative method would be to set the value of each element of theLabels to a missing value or to a constant string such as Phone Number. This would take more processing time, and it would require more memory because you would need to populate the entire list with a constant value for each element.

```
on getData()
 tell application "FileMaker Pro"
  open "JFDeskDisk:Users:jfeiler:Documents:Contact Management.fp5"
  tell database 1 of document 1
   tell layout 1
    set theNames to get field "Last Name"
    set theLabels to missing value
    set theNumbers to get field "Phone 1"
   end tell
  end tell
 end tell
```

```
    return {theNames, theLabels, theNumbers}
end getData
```

You will note that this subroutine uses a different method for retrieving data than was the case in Hour 12, "Scripting Mac OS X Applications from Third Parties." There, you saw how to search a FileMaker database and how to set an individual data field. Here, you're retrieving all of the data in the found set from a field in a layout.

createDocument

This is the same code as shown in the previous example.

fillDocument

This is the same code as shown in the previous example.

Extracting Data from Address Book and Placing It in InDesign

This script and the following one demonstrate the use of InDesign to display data from Address Book (this example) or FileMaker (the following example). Similar scripts can be used with QuarkXPress, another widely used page-layout application that is scriptable on Mac OS X.

Page-layout programs let you position elements where you want as opposed to word processing documents, which simply flow text from beginning to end. It is true that you can set margins, page breaks, columns, and the like, but within those constraints, text and graphics flow through the document with relatively little control on your part.

A full discussion of page-layout applications is beyond the scope of this book. Suffice it to say that in addition to concepts familiar from word processing (documents and pages, for example), there are frames that can contain elements such as text or graphics. You can link text frames together so that text flows from one to another. (Newspapers and magazines demonstrate this; two stories on the front page can be continued—each in its own text frame—on interior pages.)

Here is the full script for presenting Address Book data in InDesign.

getData

This is the same code used in the first example:

```
on getData()
 tell application "Address Book"
```

21

```
  set theNames to name of every person
  set theLabels to label of phone 1 of every person
  set theNumbers to value of phone 1 of every person
 end tell
 return {theNames, theLabels, theNumbers}
end getData
```

createDocument

In this subroutine, there's much more work to do than in the subroutine for Text Edit. The subroutine itself falls into three sections:

- The first section of the subroutine sets preferences to create a 10-page document. This is an arbitrary length. (If you are modifying this script for your own purposes, you can use the parameter numberOfRows to compute the number of pages that you actually will need.)

- The second section of the subroutine creates the document and, for each page, creates a text frame. Note that these text frames are explicitly linked to one another in the code. There are other ways of doing this; you could, for example, use an InDesign master page with text frames on it. In yet another approach, you could place additional elements on the pages. (That approach is provided in the final example in this chapter.)

- Finally, the subroutine creates a table that will flow across all of the linked text frames. As usual, the document that was created is returned.

```
on createDocument(numberOfRows)
 tell application "InDesign 2.0.1"
  set myDocPrefs to document preferences
  tell myDocPrefs
   set pages per document to 10
   set myPageHeight to page height
   set myPageWidth to page width
   set pages per spread to 1
  end tell

  set myDocument to make document
  set myMarginPreferences to margin preferences
  set lastFrame to missing value -- no previous one to start
  repeat with pageNumber from 1 to 10
   tell page pageNumber of myDocument
    set myMarginPreferences to margin preferences
    set myX1 to margin left of myMarginPreferences
    set myY1 to margin top of myMarginPreferences
    set myX2 to myPageWidth - (margin right of myMarginPreferences)
    set myY2 to myPageHeight - (margin bottom of myMarginPreferences)
    set myTextFrame to make text frame with properties ¬
     {geometric bounds:{myY1, myX1, myY2, myX2}, contents:" "}
```

```
      end tell
      if lastFrame ≠ missing value then set next text frame of lastFrame ¬
        to myTextFrame
      set lastFrame to myTextFrame
    end repeat

    tell text style range 1 of parent story of ¬
      text frame 1 of page 1 of myDocument
      set myTable to make table with properties ¬
        {row count:numberOfRows, column count:2} at end
    end tell
  end tell
  return myDocument
end createDocument
```

fillDocument

This subroutine is basically the same as those you've seen before. The biggest difference is that in the previous examples, a text string was created in AppleScript, and only at the end of the subroutine was Text Edit asked to set the document's text to that text string. Here, you need to communicate with InDesign from the beginning. The rather lengthy `tell` statement identifies the table that was created at the end of `createDocument`. After that, the same `repeat` loop with embedded `if` statements is used to set the appropriate cells of the table to name and, if available, label and phone number.

```
on fillDocument(theCounter, thePeople, theDocument)
  set theNames to item 1 of thePeople
  set theLabels to item 2 of thePeople
  set theNumbers to item 3 of thePeople
  tell application "InDesign 2.0.1"
    tell table 1 of text style range 1 of parent story of ¬
      text frame 1 of page 1 of theDocument
      repeat with rowNumber from 1 to theCounter
        set text of cell rowNumber of column 1 to item rowNumber of ¬
          theNames as string
        if item rowNumber of theNumbers ≠ missing value then
          if theLabels = missing value then
            set text of cell rowNumber of column 2 to (item rowNumber of¬
              theNumbers as string)
          else
            set text of cell rowNumber of column 2 to (item rowNumber of ¬
              theLabels as string) & " " & (item rowNumber of ¬
              theNumbers as string)
          end if
        end if
      end repeat
    end tell
  end tell
end fillDocument
```

21

Extracting Data from FileMaker and Placing It in InDesign

You have already seen all of the code needed for this variation of the script.

getData

This is the code that was shown in the second example in this hour. It is only repeated here for your convenience. As you can see, this structured, modularized approach lets you easily modify your workflow solutions as your needs change.

```
on getData()
 tell application "FileMaker Pro"
  open "JFDeskDisk:Users:jfeiler:Documents:Contact Management.fp5"
  tell database 1 of document 1
   tell layout 1
    set theNames to get field "Last Name"
    set theLabels to missing value
    set theNumbers to get field "Phone 1"
   end tell
  end tell
 end tell
 return {theNames, theLabels, theNumbers}
end getData
```

createDocument

Use the code from the previous example.

fillDocument

Use the code from the previous example.

Creating Dynamic Pages with InDesign

In each of the four examples shown in this hour, you have seen how to flow text into a document from page to page (or text frame to text frame with InDesign). This final example shows you how to create and lay out individual pages with InDesign. You can use this as a starting point to create catalogs and brochures that contain not just text but also graphics. The code here is simple—one set of data per page; however, you can use it to create pages with multiple data sets.

As with all the scripts in this hour, it starts with the same four lines. They are repeated here for your convenience:

```
set myPeople to getData()
set howMany to count of item 1 of myPeople
set theDocument to createDocument(howMany)
fillDocument(howMany, myPeople, theDocument)
```

getData

You can use either version of getData to collect the information you need. Here is the Address Book code as shown previously in the first and third examples:

```
on getData()
 tell application "Address Book"
  set theNames to name of every person
  set theLabels to label of phone 1 of every person
  set theNumbers to value of phone 1 of every person
 end tell
 return {theNames, theLabels, theNumbers}
end getData
```

createDocument

This code is based on createDocument in the previous example. The chief difference is that only one page is created in the document, and no text frames or tables are created. The fillDocument subroutine will do all the formatting.

```
on createDocument(numberOfRows)
 tell application "InDesign 2.0.1"
  set myDocPrefs to document preferences
  tell myDocPrefs
   set pages per document to 1
   set myPageHeight to page height
   set myPageWidth to page width
   set pages per spread to 1
  end tell
  set myDocument to make document
 end tell
 return myDocument
end createDocument
```

fillDocument

Whereas the fillDocument subroutine in the previous example added data to the table that flows through the text frames, this version lays out an individual page. There are three sections to the subroutine:

- First of all, within the repeat loop, a page is added to the document.
- Next, a text frame is created and data (the appropriate element of theNames) is placed in it.

21

- Finally, the same tests are applied for missing values, and, if necessary, another text frame is created and filled with data.

```
on fillDocument(theCounter, thePeople, myDocument)
 set theNames to item 1 of thePeople
 set theLabels to item 2 of thePeople
 set theNumbers to item 3 of thePeople
 tell application "InDesign 2.0.1"
  repeat with rowNumber from 1 to theCounter
   tell document preferences of active document
    set pages per document to ((pages per document) as number) + 1
   end tell

   tell page rowNumber of myDocument
    set myTextFrame to make text frame with properties ¬
    {geometric bounds:{"6p0", "6p0", "18p0", "18p0"}} --, text:"test"}
    set the text of myTextFrame to item rowNumber of theNames as string

    if item rowNumber of theNumbers   missing value then
     set myTextFrame to make text frame with properties ¬
     {geometric bounds:{"18p0", "18p0", "36p0", "36p0"}}
     if theLabels = missing value then
      set the text of myTextFrame to ¬
      (item rowNumber of theNumbers as string)
     else
      set the text of myTextFrame to ¬
      (item rowNumber of theLabels as string) &¬
      " " & (item rowNumber of theNumbers as string)
     end if
    end if
   end tell
  end repeat
 end tell
end fillDocument
```

The possibilities for expanding this code are truly limitless. You can examine the data on a record-by-record basis and construct rules for its display. If your data is varied, those rules can interact in many different ways, and, with no additional effort on your part, you can wind up with a document in which each page is different. (You may need to tweak the rules—or the resultant document—so that those differences are seen in a positive manner and not as the result of random layout choices.)

Summary

The structure of the scripts in this hour has been constant: All data is retrieved, and then it is placed in documents. This is fine, particularly for small projects. In other cases, you may want to construct a different architecture, one in which instead of a getData subroutine you have a `getDataForRecordNumber (n)` subroutine. As you examine data in the `fillDocument` subroutine, you can choose not just how to display it (one record might have several images, while another might have none), but also whether or not to retrieve additional relevant data. The rules that you create in this way will let you execute the resultant script over and over with appropriate and different results.

This is a powerful way of integrating your applications. But there's more. The next hour shows you how to expand these possibilities by integrating applications across a network—both a local area network and the Internet itself.

Q&A

Q **What are some of the considerations for when to flow data into a document or table as opposed to when to place it in frames or other specific elements?**

A If you're working on a document in which pagination matters, you may want to work with frames. In a document where the page breaks don't matter so much (perhaps a Web page), a continuous flow may be easier.

Q **Is it better to extract all the data and then format it, or to do it item by item?**

A This depends on the data and what you're doing with it. For a fairly limited amount of data, extracting it as a first step is fine. For large amounts of data (either many records or substantial data within a single record), you may not have sufficient memory or even disk space to do it other than item by item.

Q **If my multiple-application script doesn't work, what's the best way of troubleshooting it?**

A Try using Script Editor to work on each application's code separately. If you're retrieving data from an application, replace the retrieval code with hard-coded data that you set in the script and watch what happens.

Workshop

The workshop contains quiz questions and activities to help you solidify your knowledge of the material in this hour. Try to answer all of the questions before looking at the quiz answers that follow.

Quiz

1. Can `try` blocks always substitute for `if` statements?
2. Why don't you need a `repeat` block to get every name in your Address Book?

21

Quiz Answers

1. No, because you may need to check for specific sequences of conditions with `if` statements. A `try` block can identify different errors, but the sequence won't be identified.

2. AppleScript can use the `get every` clause to do that in a single operation.

Activities

Perhaps you don't have InDesign or FileMaker, but you should have Address Book and Text Edit installed as part of Mac OS X. Based on the scripts in this hour, try the following:

- Create a document with all of the addresses in your Address Book.
- Create a document with a list of all the names of people without addresses.

Write a script to send an e-mail message to the first person in your Address Book for whom you have an e-mail address but no street address. (This can be modified to send an e-mail message to all such people, but you must be careful not to spam all your friends!)

Hour **22**

Using AppleScript Across a Network

In this hour, you'll find a variety of ways to use AppleScript on networks—local area networks as well as the Internet. You'll see how to issue AppleScript commands across a network, how to use AppleScript on a Web server to handle CGI requests such as parsing forms, and how to use AppleScript to access the new Web services technology that is sweeping the Web.

In This Hour

- Mounting Remote Disks—This is the simplest networking task for AppleScript.
- How AppleScript Works Across a Network—Here is the basic terminology you need to know.
- What You Need to Do on the Client Mac—Set up your Mac to initiate AppleScript commands to a remote computer.

- What You Need to Do on the Server Mac—These are the steps to take to allow a Mac to handle AppleScript requests from other computers.
- Using AppleScript to Process CGI Requests—Use AppleScript to parse HTML forms.
- Using Web Services—One of the most important new features of the Web, Web services allow you to interact in an automated way with remote sites.
- Using Web Services with Script Editor—This is the simple way of programming Web services.
- Using Web Services with AppleScript Studio—You can use the Soap Talk example to access Web services.

Mounting Remote Disks

The simplest way of using AppleScript across a network is to access documents on remote disks. To do so, you need to connect to the remote server. You can do that manually outside your script, or you can automate it with AppleScript.

 The URLs and disk names used in this section are examples. You'll need to substitute your own IP addresses, disk, and usernames.

Mounting afp Volumes

There are two syntaxes for mounting remote disks. The first uses the Apple File Protocol (afp) schema in a URL as in this example:

```
mount volume "afp://192.168.0.5:548/"
```

You may be prompted for a user ID and password to access the remote server. Then, you'll see a dialog in which you can choose the volume to mount, as shown in Figure 22.1.

You can specify the volume to mount in the AppleScript command by placing its name at the end of the URL as shown here:

```
mount volume "afp://192.168.0.5:548/jfvdt"
```

You can provide the user ID and, optionally, the password, at the beginning of the URL using this syntax:

```
mount volume "jfeiler@afp://192.168.0.5 /"
mount volume "jfeiler:passwd@afp://192.168.0.5 /"
```

FIGURE 22.1

Choose the volume to use.

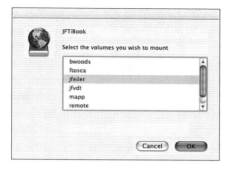

Using the Server Name

The second form uses a natural-language syntax to describe the volume to mount:

```
mount volume "jfvdt" on server "JFTiBook" as ¬
    user name "jfeiler" with password "passwd"
```

Ejecting Disks

When you are finished working with the disk, you can eject it using the AppleScript command shown here:

```
tell application "Finder" to eject disk "jfvdt"
```

How AppleScript Works Across a Network

In addition to mounting remote disks and accessing their files, you can also communicate with running applications over the network. AppleScript on a network can work exactly the same way it does on a single computer. Apple events are sent back and forth across a TCP/IP network just as they are on a single computer. (Old-style AppleTalk networks are no longer supported; only TCP/IP networking is now supported on the Macintosh.) For developers, this is handled in the Program-to-Program Communications (PPC) toolbox .

In addition to standard AppleScript and Apple events, you can use AppleScript to use XML-RPC and SOAP applications across a network or the Internet. These are discussed in the second half of this hour. The first half is devoted to traditional AppleScript.

The terminology used in this chapter reflects the terminology generally used in network environments:

- The *client* initiates an action.
- The *server* responds to the client's request, handles it, and returns data to the client.

This structure was easy to understand in the old days when servers were mainframe computers and clients were dumb terminals or teletypes. Today, though, a specific computer can be a client and a server in various environments almost at the same time. (Peer-to-peer networking is an example of a situation in which clients are servers and servers are clients.) In addition to being client and server, a single computer can simultaneously be a client to one computer and a server for a separate computer. Nonetheless, for a specific transaction, it is usually easy to determine which computer is the client (originator) and which the server (responder). In the sense of a transaction, it is quite possible for a computer running Mac OS X Server to be a client.

The script runs on the computer from which you start it. That's where the processing takes place, and it's that computer's memory that's used. If a `tell` block addresses an application on another computer, an Apple event is sent to that application on the other computer. The request is carried out there, and the result is returned to the computer on which the script is running.

What You Need to Do on the Client Mac

To use AppleScript across a network, all you have to do is to specify the computer on which an application you want to use is running. Instead of writing

```
tell application "TextEdit"
```

you write this:

```
tell application "TextEdit" of machine "eppc://jfeiler@192.168.0.5"
```

The URL with the `eppc` prefix specifies a computer, a username, and an optional password. The username precedes the computer and is separated from it by a @. If you provide a password, it follows the username, and is separated from it by a : as shown here:

```
tell application "TextEdit" of ¬
    machine "eppc://jfeiler:secretpassword@192.168.0.5"
```

The computer can be specified in the typical dot-delimited IP address shown previously, or it can be a domain name as shown here:

```
tell application "TextEdit" of machine "eppc://jfeiler@www.yourcompany.com"
```

You don't need to supply the username and password; if one or both are missing, you'll be prompted to enter them, as shown in Figure 22.2. (If you don't enter a username, the name that you use to log in will be entered automatically; you can always change it in the dialog.)

FIGURE 22.2

Provide a username and password.

When you check the syntax in your script—either with the Script Editor Check Syntax button or by running the script—AppleScript needs to connect to the application's dictionary. If you haven't provided the username and password, that's when you will first be asked for it.

If the application isn't running or if the connection cannot be made to the remote computer, you'll see a dialog like the one shown in Figure 22.3 indicating that it can't connect to the dictionary.

FIGURE 22.3

The application must be running on the server computer in order to access its dictionary.

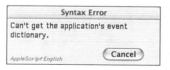

Another dialog you may see is shown in Figure 22.4. It appears when the remote application unexpectedly quits.

FIGURE 22.4

The application must be running on the server computer in order to access its dictionary.

What You Need to Do on the Server Mac

On the server side, you need to allow remote connections in general, and you need to set up a user account and password for people to access your computer.

Mac OS X Server is a version of Mac OS X that is designed for running
servers that offer services including file sharing, Web hosting, mail, and
more. You can use it to set up file sharing, but for relatively small groups,
you can use the standard Mac OS X software. That is the software that is
described in this section.

Allowing Remote Connections for File Sharing

To allow people to connect for file sharing, use the Sharing pane in System Preferences
as shown in Figure 22.5. (This process is the same for people who will be connecting via
AppleScript as well as for people who will be connecting using the Finder's Connect To
Server command in the Go menu.)

FIGURE 22.5

*Turn Personal File
Sharing on.*

The afp address is shown at the bottom of the window when you select Personal File
Sharing. That's the address that you use in your AppleScript mount volume statement.

Remember that your network address may be dynamic and may change
from time to time. Your network administrator can tell you if this is the
case. If so, you are safer mounting remote disks by name. Also note that if
the network address shown here begins with 169, there is probably something wrong with your network connection. (169 is a default address that is
set automatically when an actual address cannot be located.)

Allowing Remote Connections for Apple Events

Just as you have to allow access for file sharing, you will need to turn on Remote Apple Events, as shown in Figure 22.6. (This is the same window you use to turn other sharing features on and off with the other check boxes.)

FIGURE 22.6

Turn on Remote Apple Events.

Setting Up User Accounts for Remote Access

Use the Accounts pane in System Preferences to set up accounts for users to access your computer.

Security Issues

As soon as you allow people to access your computer over a network, you need to be aware of security concerns. Not only are you allowing them access to your files, but if you turn on Remote Apple Events, they can direct applications on your computer to obey their bidding.

AppleScript runs over a TCP/IP network; that can be a local intranet or it can be the Internet itself. Apple events are sent using port 3031; Apple File Protocol uses port 548. You can use the Firewall tab in System Preferences to allow access to these ports. (If you enable Personal File Sharing or Remote Apple Events, this is done automatically.) Figure 22.7 shows the Firewall tab.

If your computer is behind a firewall (that is, if you have a firewall on a router or network switch in addition to the firewall you can set with System

Preferences), you can turn off access to those ports from outside your local area network. In that way, people on your network can use Personal File Sharing and Remote Apple Events, but people from outside will not be able to get through the firewall.

Security is becoming a matter of increasing concern. Automated tools (often called *sniffers*) roam the Internet looking for unprotected computers that they can compromise. Setting up appropriate security is not necessary because you distrust your friends and colleagues with whom you work; rather, it's a necessary response to the possible intrusion from these automated tools about which you know nothing.

FIGURE 22.7

You need to allow access to the appropriate ports for Personal Web Sharing and Remote Apple Events to work.

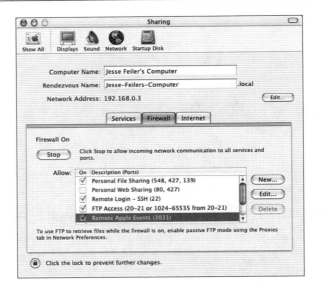

Using AppleScript to Process CGI Requests

The previous sections of this hour showed you how to use AppleScript across a network in much the same way that you use it on a single computer. Now, it's time to add more features and complexity.

When you fill in a form on a Web page, it is generally processed by a CGI program. CGI—Common Gateway Interface—is a specification for small programs that can be called by a Web server to handle such needs. People often write CGI programs in Perl or in Java, but there is really no limit on the languages you can use. If the Web server can execute the program, and if the data is passed properly, there are no problems.

If you are running Mac OS X Server, you are using Apache as the Web server, and it is automatically configured to handle AppleScript plug-ins. All you need is to write your own AppleScript CGI handler. Fortunately, most of the work is done for you. There's a CGI script on Apple's Web site at Essential Subroutines in the AppleScript Guidebook located at `http://www.apple.com/applescript/guidebook/sbrt/index.html`. This section shows you how to modify that script for your own purposes.

Creating the HTML

There are two parts to this process: creating the form with HTML and then modifying the CGI handler to deal with the data. Figure 22.8 shows a typical HTML form.

FIGURE 22.8

Use a form to allow users to enter data onto a Web page.

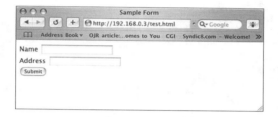

Here is the HTML code for that Web page:

```
<!DOCTYPE HTML PUBLIC "-//W3C//DTD HTML 4.01 Transitional//EN">
<html>
  <head>
    <title>Sample Form</title>
    <meta http-equiv="Content-Type" content="text/html; charset=iso-8859-1">
  </head>
  <body>
    <FORM ACTION="testcgi" METHOD="POST">
      Name <input type="text" name="namefield"><BR>
      Address <input type="text" name="addressfield"><br>
      <INPUT TYPE="submit" VALUE="Submit">
    </FORM>
  </BODY>
</HTML>
```

There are two points you need to notice here:

- The `action` of the form is the name of the script to be executed on the Web server. It must match the name of your AppleScript file. In many cases, the script will need to be in another directory from the Web page—it may be called CGI-bin.

- The names of the data entry fields (`namefield` and `addressfield`) must match the names used in your script.

Modifying the Script from Apple

Although there are a number of subroutines in the script, the main one—the one you need to modify—is shown here:

```
on handle CGI request this_request ¬
  searching for search_string ¬
  with posted data post_arguments ¬
  using access method GET_or_POST ¬
  from address this_client ¬
  from user user_name ¬
  using password user_password ¬
  with user info user_information ¬
  from server server_application ¬
  via port server_IP_port ¬
  executing by this_script_path ¬
  of content type MIME_type ¬
  referred by referring_page ¬
  from browser client_browser ¬
  of action type action_type ¬
  from client IP address client_address ¬
  with connection ID server_connection

    set the form_contents to my process_arguments(post_arguments)
    -- returns a list of form items and their values
    -- {{"FORMITEM1", "FORMITEM1VALUE"}, {"FORMITEM2", "FORMITEM2VALUE"},etc.}

    -- ACTIONS WITH PROCESSED FORM DATA GO HERE
    -- this example returns the form items and their values
    set the body_content to ""
    repeat with i from 1 to the count of the form_contents
      copy item i of the form_contents to {form_item, item_value}
      set the body_content to ¬
        the body_content & form_item & ": " & item_value & "<BR>" & return
    end repeat

    -- return HTML to the user
    return http_header & HTML_opening & body_content & HTML_closing
end handle CGI request
```

The first executable line of the subroutine calls another subroutine to parse the input from the user:

```
set the form_contents to my process_arguments(post_arguments)
```

After that, as the comments in the script show, do whatever you want with the data. The default action in the script is to create a Web page displaying the data that was sent, but you probably want to do something different. You might want to store the data you've received in a database. In other cases, you might want to send an e-mail with an authorization code to the user. Here is how you would do that.

First, parse the data received from the user:

```
set the form_contents to my process_arguments(post_arguments)
```

Next, create a Web page to be returned to the user indicating that an e-mail message is on its way:

```
set the body_content to "Thank you, "
copy item 1 of the form_contents to {form_item, the_name}
set the body_content to ¬
  the body_content & the_name & ¬
    ". The password will be sent to your address.<BR>" ¬
    & return

return http_header & HTML_opening & body_content & HTML_closing
```

Finally, use the code you've seen previously to create and send an e-mail message:

```
copy item 2 of the form_contents to {form_item, the_address}
tell application "Mail"
  set theSubject to "Access Code"
  set theBody to "The access code is SECRET."
  set theSender to "yourname@yourplace.com"
  set newMessage to make new outgoing message with properties ¬
    {subject:theSubject, content:theBody, sender:theSender, visible:true}
  tell newMessage
    make new to recipient at end of to recipients with properties ¬
      {name:the_name, address:the_address}
  end tell
  send newMessage
end tell
```

You can do just about anything you want in a CGI script. The only thing you need to remember is that the script is run by the Web server itself using its own level of security. Typically, that is a different level of security than for people who are actually logged into the computer. Also, if it is making database calls, it needs to be allowed access to the database because it—the Web server—not the remote user is the actual database client.

Using Web Services

When you write CGI scripts using AppleScript, people across the network can launch scripts from Web pages without knowing that they're written in AppleScript (or in any other language). More or less, the reverse situation applies to Web services: These can be written in a variety of languages, and you can access them through AppleScript on a client computer.

The Web started as an interactive point-and-click way of viewing data and following hyperlinks. It has evolved into the backbone of operations for many organizations and processes. Web services allow commands and instructions—not mouse clicks—to be sent to sites that respond appropriately.

Web services are built on several sets of standards. Extensible Markup Language (XML) is used for data input; XML-RPC and SOAP protocols are used to actually transmit, execute, and return data from commands. In both cases, a *method name* is used to identify what work the service should do; a set of *parameters* is passed providing the data to be used. When all is done, a *result* is returned.

> Web services are growing in popularity. Some sites such as Google and Amazon offer Web services interfaces so that you can access their information from scripts and programs. Other sites offer Web services either as demonstrations or as part of their normal operations. You can find many listed at http://www.xmethods.net.
>
> In addition, Web services interfaces to Web sites are often being added to existing applications. Some people thought that Web services would suddenly appear everywhere and change the nature of the Web, but that's not how things happen today. Web services are here, they are real, and their use is growing, but experts have predicted that it may be a good 5 or 10 years before they are used to their full advantage.

XML-RPC

This protocol uses XML to encode messages, and HTTP to transport them over the Internet. This transport is the familiar HTTP POST request used for forms. Parameters are sent in the request in a predefined order.

There are two parts to use in executing an XML-RPC call from AppleScript:

- A `tell` block identifies the server that will handle the request.
- Use the `call xmlrpc` AppleScript statement to pass in the name of the method to be invoked and the parameters (by order) that need to be passed.

In part because XML-RPC relies on the order of parameters (not their names), many people today are using the SOAP protocol, which is more flexible and powerful.

SOAP

As with XML-RPC, there are two parts to a SOAP call: the `tell` block and the `call SOAP` AppleScript statement. You can find many examples of SOAP Web services at http://www.xmethods.net. Clicking on a listed service will show you the summary seen in Figure 22.9.

FIGURE 22.9

Review Web services at http://www.xmethods.net.

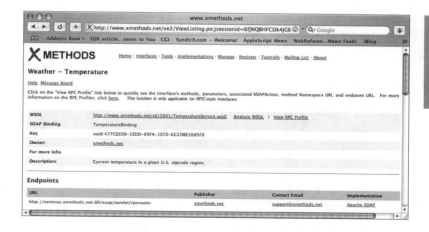

If you click the View RPC Profile link in the upper right of the window shown in Figure 22.9, you'll see the operations or methods contained in the method as shown in Figure 22.10.

FIGURE 22.10

Use the parameters shown in the RPC profile.

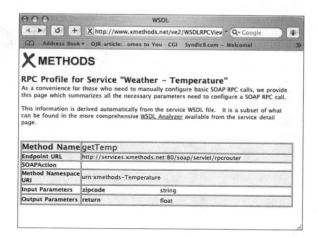

The SOAP call goes within a `tell` block that is addressed to an application on a remote computer. The application name and remote computer address are provided in the Endpoint URL entry on the first line of the table in Figure 22.10. The application is the last part of the Endpoint URL; the address is the previous part. Thus, for the entry shown in Figure 22.10

```
http://services.xmethods.net:80/soap/servlet/rpcrouter
```

the application is rpcrouter and the address is http://services.xmethods.net:80/soap/
servlet. Thus, the tell statement is

tell application "rpcrouter" of "http://services.xmethods.net:80/soap/servlet"

Alternatively, you can write

tell application "http://services.xmethods.net:80/soap/servlet/rpcrouter"

The call SOAP statement takes four parameters. Their names and descriptions are provided here:

- **Method name**—This is the method name shown at the top of the table in Figure
  22.10. A single interface may have several methods, each with its own set of argu-
  ments.
- **Method namespace**—This is the Method Namespace URI from Figure 22.10.
- **Parameters**—These are shown in the Input Parameters section of the table in
  Figure 22.10.
- **Action**—This is the SOAPAction shown in the table in Figure 22.10. It is often
  blank, as is the case here.

Rather than constructing the call each time, many of the AppleScript samples use a subroutine to make the call and handle basic error checking. Here is the subroutine as provided in the Current Temperature by ZIP Code script:

```
on SOAP_call(SOAP_Endpoint_URL, SOAP_app, method_name, method_namespace_URI, ¬
  method_parameters, SOAP_action)
  try
    using terms from application "http://www.apple.com/ "
      tell application SOAP_Endpoint_URL
        set this_result to call soap ¬
          {method name:method_name ¬
            , method namespace uri:method_namespace_URI ¬
            , parameters:method_parameters ¬
            , SOAPAction:SOAP_action}
      end tell
    end using terms from
    return {true, this_result}
  on error error_message number error_number
    if the error_number is -916 then ¬
      set the error_message to ¬
        "The script was unable to establish a connection to the Internet."
    return {false, error_message}
  end try
end SOAP_call
```

To call it using the parameters shown in Figure 22.10, you would write

```
copy my SOAP_call("http://services.xmethods.net:80/soap/servlet", "rpcrouter", ¬
  "getTemp", "urn:xmethods-Temperature", {zipcode:"95014"}, "")
  to {call_indicator, call_result}
```

You can handle the results with this code:

```
if the call_indicator is false then
  beep
  display dialog "An error occurred." & return & return ¬
    & call_result buttons {"Cancel"} default button 1
else
  display dialog call_result
end if
```

Using Web Services with Script Editor

The Current Temperature by ZIP Code script is set up to call the getTemp method described here. You can modify the script so that it can access any SOAP service. The following script is built on Current Temperature by ZIP Code, and it allows you to enter each of the variables needed for the call.

This script accepts one pair of label/value parameters for the call. That's correct for getTemp, which requires only a ZIP Code. If you need more than one pair, you'll need to modify the script.

```
display dialog "SOAP Endpoint?" default answer ""
set SOAP_Endpoint_URL to text returned of the result

display dialog "SOAP Application?" default answer ""
set SOAP_app to text returned of the result

display dialog "Method name?" default answer ""
set method_name to text returned of the result

display dialog "Method namespace URI?" default answer ""
set method_namespace_URI to text returned of the result

display dialog "SOAP action?" default answer ""
set SOAP_action to text returned of the result

display dialog "label" default answer ""
set the_label to text returned of the result as text
display dialog "value" default answer ""
set this_text to text returned of the result as text
```

```
set the method_parameters to {the_label:this_text}

copy my SOAP_call ¬
  (SOAP_Endpoint_URL, SOAP_app, method_name, method_namespace_URI, ¬
  method_parameters, SOAP_action) to {call_indicator, call_result}
if the call_indicator is false then
  beep
  display dialog "An error occurred." & return & return & call_¬
    result buttons {"Cancel"} default button 1
else
  display dialog call_result
end if

on SOAP_call(SOAP_Endpoint_URL, SOAP_app, method_name, method_namespace_URI, ¬
  method_parameters, SOAP_action)
  try
    using terms from application "http://www.apple.com/placebo"
      tell application SOAP_app of machine SOAP_Endpoint_URL
        set this_result to call soap ¬
          {method name:method_name ¬
            , method namespace uri:method_namespace_URI ¬
            , parameters:method_parameters ¬
            , SOAPAction:SOAP_action}
      end tell
    end using terms from
    return {true, this_result}
  on error error_message number error_number
    if the error_number is -916 then ¬
      set the error_message to ¬
        "The script was unable to establish a connection to the Internet."
    return {false, error_message}
  end try
end SOAP_call
```

Using Web Services with AppleScript Studio

The Soap Talk example in AppleScript Studio does precisely what the preceding script does: It lets you enter all the parameters for a SOAP call. The Soap Talk application is shown running in Figure 22.11. The same call described in the previous section is set up in the window.

As you saw in Part III, "Working with AppleScript Studio," one of the big advantages of using AppleScript Studio is that you can get a number of different user inputs in a single dialog. This is certainly easier than the sequence of dialogs used in the Script Editor example.

FIGURE 22.11

Use Soap Talk to execute a SOAP command.

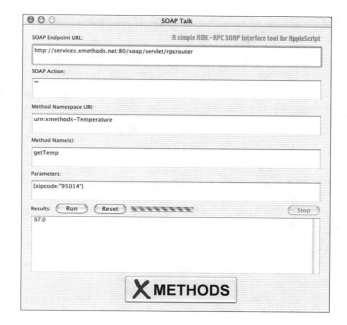

Summary

This hour has shown you how to use AppleScript beyond your own computer—from mounting a remote volume, to running scripts on another Macintosh, and then to using Web services. You can use AppleScript as the glue to tie together applications and computers in any way that you want.

There are other tools you can use to accomplish these tasks; some work with AppleScript itself, others are complementary to it. The final two hours of this book move beyond AppleScript itself to examine some of those technologies that are available to you on Mac OS X.

Q&A

Q How much do I need to worry about Web services being compatible with the Mac?

A Well-behaved Web services that are written according to the industry standards are platform neutral. This is one of the reasons they are so popular.

Q When is it safe to put a password into AppleScript code that connects to a server?

A Although it's never really safe to do this, if you need to allow someone to run a script to connect to a remote computer and you don't want to tell them the password, you can embed it in an AppleScript that is compiled as run-only. This is not extremely secure, but it is safer than giving out the password.

Q Can you turn on file sharing on another computer?

A Normally you have to turn file sharing on from the computer whose files you want to share. It is possible to do this if you have enabled ssh; you can then use the command line in Terminal from another computer to turn on file sharing.

Workshop

The workshop contains quiz questions and activities to help you solidify your knowledge of the material in this hour. Try to answer all of the questions before looking at the quiz answers that follow.

Quiz

1. What do you have to do in the HTML on a Web page to have AppleScript used to parse a form?
2. Why do you have to worry about security for a CGI-parsing script?
3. What happens if you try to connect to an application on a remote computer and the application is not running?

Quiz Answers

1. Place the name of the script in the form's ACTION parameter.
2. CGI programs run under the Web server's ID and frequently have more privileges than individual users.
3. AppleScript will attempt to make the connection, but, unlike the case on your own computer, it will not attempt to launch the application.

Activities

Explore the Web services available from http://www.xmethods.net and experiment with them using Script Editor and Soap Talk.

Using the principles described in the previous hour, create a Text Edit document that reports the results of a Web services call.

HOUR 23

Beyond AppleScript: Using Services

The architecture of Mac OS X allows small tasks and processes to run together and communicate with one another. One of the most interesting features of this architecture is services. You can mix and match the functionality of applications in ways that the application designers never thought of. This hour provides you with an introduction to services, and it shows you how you can use AppleScript Studio to make them usable on your applications. Note that Web services (described in the preceding hour) can be accessed by Mac OS X services; however, Web services and Mac OS X services are completely separate concepts.

In This Hour

- A Services Overview—Here are the basics of what's involved.
- How Services Work—There's a little terminology you'll need to know.

- Enabling Services with AppleScript Studio—This is what you should do with all of your AppleScript Studio applications so that services can be used with them.
- Why Use Services with AppleScript Studio?—Remember that you can't anticipate what users will be able to do with your application, so it's a good idea to make them services ready.
- Services from Script Editor—Script Editor can provide a number of services to other applications.

A Services Overview

Services in Mac OS X provide a means for you to use the functionality of an application without launching it directly. Here is an example of the use of services.

An AppleScript Studio application is developed to use the Web service described in the previous hour to get the temperature for a given ZIP Code. (The code will be provided later in this hour.) Figure 23.1 shows the initial window.

FIGURE 23.1

Enter a ZIP Code to find the temperature.

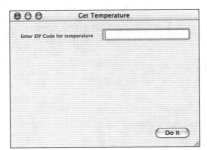

When you enter a ZIP Code and click the button, the Web service is invoked, displaying the results shown in Figure 23.2.

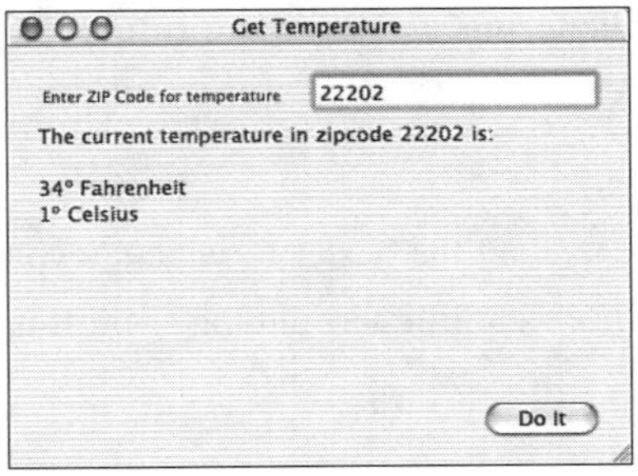

FIGURE 23.2

Web services provide the result.

The process is the same as that shown in the previous hour, although the interface is more attractive. At this point, however, you can use built-in services to go further. If you select the result, you can email it using the Send Selection command in the Mail item of the Services menu as shown in Figure 23.3.

FIGURE 23.3

Use the Mail service to send selected text.

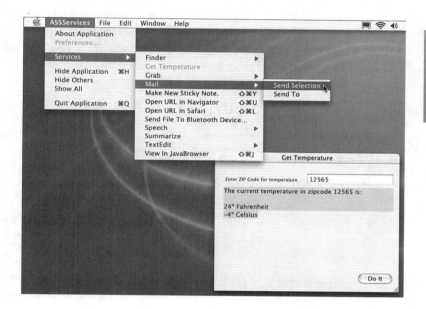

23

Mail is automatically opened, the text is inserted in a new message, and you are ready to address it as shown in Figure 23.4.

FIGURE 23.4

The message is ready to send.

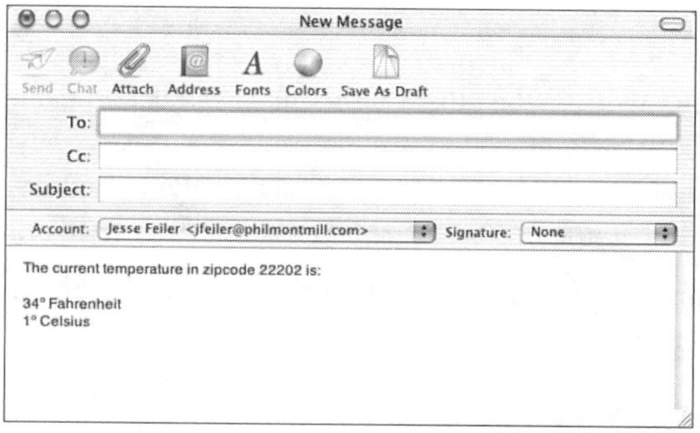

If you are developing an AppleScript workflow, you can incorporate the email message into your script. But for all the power of automated workflows, they are not the answer to everything. There are many cases in which you want to script a certain amount of the process, and then let the user take over. In those cases, services can be invaluable.

Even more important, when you create an AppleScript Studio application, you can use services to add all sorts of functionality to your application just by enabling them. There's little you have to do; the next section will show you what's necessary. Then you'll see more about other types of services that you can use.

How Services Work

Services rely on selections and standard data types for their functionality. There are three types of services: processors, providers, and combinations.

Processor Services

In the example shown here, you select the text to be sent as a first step. The application lets the system know that text has been selected, and the Services menu then enables those services that can act on text. If you had selected an image, different services would be enabled.

In addition to the Mail service, Send Content To, other standard services that are enabled for selected text include Make New Sticky Note, Start Speaking Text, and other services that apply to text.

These are all examples of *processor services*: They take data from an application and act on it.

Provider Services

Provider services work in the other direction: They take no data from the application, but rather provide it to the application. Like processor services, they rely on data types: If you have selected an interface element that can contain graphics, for example, provider services that provide graphics are enabled.

A common graphic provider is Grab: It takes a screen shot of the screen, and then places it in the interface element you have selected.

Combination Services

Combination services both process and provide data. Spell-checkers, encryption, and data conversion services all fall into this category.

Under the Hood

There are two keys to making services work. The application providing the service needs to register its service, and the application using the service needs to register its data.

An application that wants to provide services needs to register that fact with the operating system when it is launched. It does so by specifying the data types that it can receive (for a processor service) and the data types it can send (for a provider service). It also indicates the code to be invoked when a user requests the service as well as the command to appear in the Services menu.

> This information is specified in the application Info.plist. Implementing services involves writing code—but often that is code that's already present in the application. The DemoAssistant example in Developer Tools, as installed on your hard disk (/Developer/Examples/AppKit/DemoAssistant), provides a step-by-step guide to implementing services.

The application using the service needs to provide the operating system with information about the type of data that is selected or that can be pasted into the selected interface element. If the data type selected matches a data type that a service uses, that service is enabled in the Services menu.

Neither the service nor the application knows about the other: Each simply reports and recognizes data types. Because there are so many standard data types (text, Rich text, JPEG and TIFF images, and so forth), it is possible for services and applications to meet on common ground in many cases.

It's important to note that applications built using the Cocoa framework—and that includes all AppleScript Studio applications—automatically can use services. The notification of data types selected or that can be pasted into selected interface elements is done automatically. Thus, you're well on your way to extending your AppleScript Studio application with services.

Enabling Services with AppleScript Studio

The same Web services code that was used in the previous hour to get the temperature for a ZIP Code is used here. In the previous hour, it was used in Script Editor; now, it's used in AppleScript Studio. In the example provided here, the result of the temperature Web service is placed in a field that is selectable. If it's selectable, it can be used with a service—such as emailing the result.

You've seen in Part III, "Working with AppleScript Studio," how to add interface elements to an AppleScript Studio window; you've also seen how to create on clicked handlers that can access text fields by referring to the window of the object that was clicked. Using those techniques, you can create an on clicked handler that retrieves data from a text field named entryField and places it in another field called resultField:

```
-- SET THE DEFAULT VALUES
property SOAP_Endpoint_URL : "http://services.xmethods.net:80/soap/servlet"
property SOAP_app : "rpcrouter"
property method_name : "getTemp"
property method_namespace_URI : "urn:xmethods-Temperature"
property SOAP_action : ""

on clicked theObject
  tell window of theObject
    set this_text to the contents of text field "entryField"

    -- CREATE THE PARAMETER RECORD
    set the method_parameters to {zipcode:this_text}

    -- CALL THE SOAP SUB-ROUTINE
    copy my SOAP_call ¬
      (SOAP_Endpoint_URL, SOAP_app, method_name, method_namespace_
    URI, method_parameters, SOAP_action) to {call_indicator, call_result}
    if the call_indicator is false then
      beep
      display dialog "An error occurred." & ¬
        return & return & call_result buttons ¬
        {"Cancel"} default button 1
    else
      -- CONVERT THE RESPONSE TO FAHRENHEIT AND CELSIUS
      set this_temp to the call_result as number
      if this_temp is -999 then
        display dialog "No temperature information is available for zipcode " &
        this_text & "." buttons {"OK"} default button 1
      else
        set temp_F to this_temp as degrees Fahrenheit
        set temp_C to (round ((temp_F as degrees Celsius) as number)) as string
        set temp_F to (round (temp_F as number)) as string
        set contents of text field "resultField" to
          "The current temperature in zipcode " & this_text & " is: " & ¬
          return & return & ¬
          temp_F & "degrees Fahrenheit" & return & temp_C & "degrees Celsius"
      end if
    end if
  end tell
end clicked
```

That's almost all you need to do, but there's one more step. In order to make the result selectable and thus eligible for use by a service, you need to select the result text field and edit its attributes to make it selectable as shown in Figure 23.5. (The Selectable attribute is in the box of Options at the lower left.)

FIGURE 23.5

Make the result field selectable.

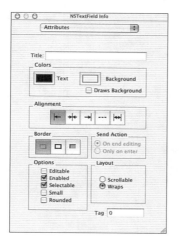

23

The reason this step is necessary is that the result field is not a data entry field: It's a text field used only to display results. By default, it is not selectable. By default, text entry fields are editable and selectable.

You can use a provider service to get data for your AppleScript Studio application. One way of doing this is to use one of the graphics services—such as the screen shot service, Grab—to insert graphics into your application.

If you create an AppleScript Studio application with a text view, you can choose to allow graphics in it as shown in Figure 23.6 where the Graphics Allowed check box for a text field is selected.

After you've done that, you can use the Grab service to create a screen shot that is automatically placed in your text as shown in Figure 23.7. Note that this is not a case of using Grab to create a screen shot and then pasting it in: You simply use the Grab services menu, and Grab together with Cocoa and the operating system do the rest.

FIGURE 23.6
Allow graphics in text views to enable graphics services.

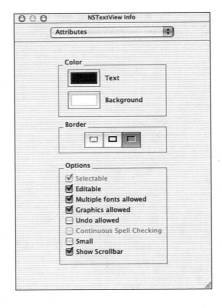

FIGURE 23.7
Insert graphics in text views.

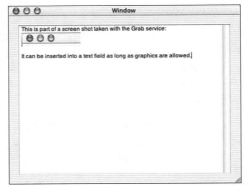

The text view interface element is in the Cocoa palette in the Data section (not the Views section where you find text fields). The element includes a scroller to handle the text.

Why Use Services with AppleScript Studio?

One of the keys to developing effective and productive solutions on Mac OS X is combining all of the tools and software that you already have in a way that is convenient and logical to you. Like AppleScript itself, services let you use parts of applications in ways that make sense to you.

It's not always possible to make everything fit together absolutely perfectly; that's one reason why AppleScript Studio and the Cocoa framework are so powerful. You can use them to create data flows and syntheses that do fit together well.

23

Services from Script Editor

Three services from Script Editor are available in any services-aware application when text is selected. They are described in the following sections.

Make New AppleScript

If you select text and choose the Make New AppleScript command from the Script Editor Services submenu, the selected text will be pasted into a new script editing window in Script Editor. The text need not be a complete script; it need not even be correct. When it is in Script Editor, you can check the syntax, modify it, save it, and do whatever you want with it.

Get Result of AppleScript

Select some text in a text field and choose Get Result of AppleScript from the Script Editor submenu in the Services menu. The text will be interpreted as AppleScript and run by Script Editor, and the selected text will be replaced by the result.

You can use this to quickly perform calculations: If you select 14*7 and choose Get Result of AppleScript, it will be replaced by 98 (the result of the calculation). You can select several lines of AppleScript code. For example, you can type and then select the following in Text Edit (or in any text field):

```
tell application "Finder"
get the selection as string
end tell
```

After you choose Get Result of AppleScript, that text will be replaced with something like

```
"JFDeskDisk:Users:jfeiler:Documents:Projects:Current Projects:TYAS:Book:¬
  Chapter23:23FIG06.pcx"
```

(The actual result will depend on what you have selected.)

Run As AppleScript

The Run As AppleScript command on the Services menu runs the selected text. Unlike Get Result of AppleScript, the text you have selected is not modified by the script (unless the script specifically does so).

Summary

In this hour, you've seen how to integrate Mac OS X services with AppleScript and AppleScript Studio. You've also seen how to use the Services menu to bring Script Editor into any text editing field of a services-aware application.

What more is there to learn about AppleScript and scripting in general on Mac OS X? In the final hour, you'll learn a bit about the non-AppleScript scripting languages that are distributed as part of Mac OS X.

Q&A

Q Why are Mac OS X services so important?

A For users, they provide the ability to use pieces of application software without using the entire program. (See the section on writing and running AppleScript code in any text field of a services-aware application.) For developers, services can drastically reduce the cost of bringing software to market. Only the specific functionality in which the developer and user are interested needs to be packaged. This opens opportunities for many smaller developers as well as for large developers who want to develop and distribute small and inexpensive pieces of software.

Q How do Mac OS X services fit in with other new technologies?

A The idea of packaging functionality for use by others has been around for a long time. It's something that users want and something in which many developers are interested. Other technologies today that address this type of functionality include Web services and Java applets that can easily be shared.

Workshop

The workshop contains quiz questions and activities to help you solidify your knowledge of the material in this hour. Try to answer all of the questions before looking at the quiz answers that follow.

Quiz

1. What do you have to do to a field in a window in Interface Builder to make it usable by services?

2. What is the difference between the Get Result of AppleScript and Run As AppleScript services from Script Editor?

Quiz Answers

1. Make it selectable or editable.

2. Get Result of AppleScript replaces the selected text with the result; Run As AppleScript runs the scripts but leaves the selected text alone.

Activities

Use the Services menu to create a Mail message for someone in your Address Book.

23

Hour **24**

Beyond AppleScript: Shell Scripts, Perl, and Other Scripting Languages

This hour provides an introduction to other scripting languages on Mac OS X as well as Terminal, the application you use to execute shell commands and scripts.

In This Hour

- Using Terminal—Here's a quick introduction to using the command line in Terminal.
- Running AppleScript from Terminal—Here's how to type in command-line AppleScript commands and run them from Terminal.

- Running AppleScript As Commands from Applications—You've seen how to run Terminal from AppleScript; now here's how to reverse the process and run AppleScript via the command line.
- Automatically Running Scripts—Here's how to install scripts to be run at specific times automatically.
- Other Scripting Languages—More scripting languages are available on Mac OS X; here's a brief summary of the other scripting languages you'll find.

Using Terminal

In Hour 11, "Scripting Mac OS X Applications from Apple, " you saw how to script Terminal, the Mac OS X command-line application. This hour goes into Terminal and commands in more detail, showing you how to use AppleScript and other scripting languages to accomplish your goals.

Although this chapter provides information about Terminal and scripting, it cannot cover the full scope of UNIX scripting available with Mac OS X. Other resources for Terminal and scripting include online help from Terminal, Apple's support pages (including the Mac OS X discussion), as well as books on Darwin and UNIX.

In this section, you'll find the basics of Terminal along with a very few commands—but they're the basic commands that you'll need to manipulate script files.

Terminal is one of the applications installed in the Utilities folder inside the Applications folder as part of Mac OS X.

When you launch Terminal, a window like that shown in Figure 24.1 opens.

The window can be customized, so yours may look different, but this is a standard configuration. Within the window, you'll see the date and time of your last login. If you don't recall having logged in at that time, don't worry; the login may have occurred when you restarted your computer. (In Figure 24.1, the login referenced as coming from the console was, in fact, such a login.)

The commands you type in are interpreted by a *shell*, which parses them and then converts them to instructions to the operating system. A variety of shells are provided with

Mac OS X; by default, you use the `tcsh` shell. (Others are `psh`, `bash`, and the like.) The name of the shell appears in the window's title bar.

FIGURE 24.1

Use Terminal to execute commands.

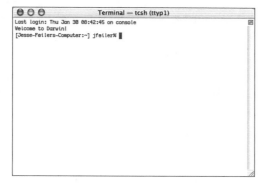

When Terminal is ready for input, it displays a *prompt* in square brackets. You can customize the prompt if you want; by default, it's the *sharename* set in the Sharing pane of System Preferences. (The sharename with the addition .local is your Rendezvous name.)

What Commands Are Available?

The command line in Terminal lets you execute a variety of commands. The Darwin core of Mac OS X includes UNIX, and many UNIX commands are usable. These commands let you manipulate the computer and its environment: You can work with files, set up users, and even connect to other computers, all from the command line.

Some of these commands are simple—copying or renaming a file, for example. Other commands invoke processes that can be quite complex.

What they all have in common is the absence of a graphical user interface. When you use the Finder to work with files, you point and click at the files you want to use. When you're using the command line, you need to describe the files by name. Similarly, when you use a text editor with a graphical user interface, you can select a word to copy, spell check, or delete; when you're using a command-line-based editor, you need to identify the word by location because the mouse doesn't come into play. (You can use the mouse in limited ways to copy and paste material to and from the command line as well as to drag files and folders to it, but Terminal converts those mouse actions to text that is displayed on the command line.)

In addition to standard UNIX commands, Apple has added a number of Darwin commands to access features of Mac OS X. For example, you can run Software Update from

24

the command line. This is a perfect example of a process that doesn't require the graphical user interface, and thus can be run easily from the command line.

There are many reasons for using the command line to run applications. By automating tasks, AppleScript lets you run tasks overnight or at other times when your computer would otherwise be idle. Command-line tasks are particularly amenable to being run automatically in this way because by definition they don't need user involvement.

Command-line tasks can be run not only from Terminal but also from within applications. You'll see later in this hour how to execute an AppleScript command from within a Carbon or Cocoa application that otherwise knows nothing about AppleScript.

Using the Command Line

Next, you'll see a welcome prompt: Darwin, the core of Mac OS X, is what you're running. You're not in the world of Aqua and graphical user interfaces here. What this window is displaying is what you would see on a teletype or dumb terminal; these were the primary input/output devices for user interaction with computers in the days before graphical user interfaces. The text in the window scrolls up as it is displayed; you can use the scroll bar to look back (just as you could look back at the roll of paper coming out the back of a teletype), but only the current line of the display is active.

You can copy text from previous lines and paste it into the current line at the insertion point—in this case, the black rectangle.

The Format of Commands

Individual commands generally consist of a single word. Some commands, such as `date`, can be executed without any additional entries. Most commands take one or more parameters, and many allow one or more options.

Parameters are entered in a required order because they are not named.

Options are usually identified by letters, and they are prefixed with a dash. Here is the output from the command `date`, which displays the current date:

```
Fri Jan 31 14:32:21 EST 2003
```

Using the option to display the date in universal time (command `date -u`), the output is

```
Fri Jan 31 19:32:24 GMT 2003
```

Syntax for commands is provided online in Terminal using *man pages*, which share a common format. You can access a man page for any command by typing

```
man date
```

where "date" is the name of the command in which you are interested.

Each man page includes a synopsis of the command showing the command, its options, and its parameters. Parameters are underlined, and they are described in the text that follows. You substitute a value for the underlined parameter; the other elements of the synopsis are typed as is. Optional elements of the command are shown in square brackets. Thus, for the synopsis

```
time [-lp] utility
```

the following are all legal versions:

```
time myutility
time -l myutility
time -p myutility
time -lp myutility
```

(The parameter utility is replaced by an actual name of a utility—in this case, `myutility`.)

Finally, note that capitalization matters on the command line: `-m` is not the same as `-M`.

Using Files for Input, Output, and Errors

All commands can have access to three files: STDIN, STDOUT, and STDERR. Those files provide input, accept output, and receive error messages (if any). By default, those files all use the Terminal: Output that goes to the STDOUT file is displayed for you to see, and input read from STDIN is read from what you type in.

The reason for specifying these three files is so that you can replace the interactive Terminal window with actual files. You do so by *redirecting* input and output.

To redirect output to a file rather than the Terminal window, you use the > character followed by the name of a file to which you want output to go. The `date` command, shown previously, displays the current date and time in the Terminal window. To send it to a file called mydate, use the following syntax:

```
date >mydate
```

This will create a file called mydate and place the output in it. If you want to append output to an existing file, use >>. Thus, the command

```
date >>mydate
```

will add another line to the existing mydate file (if any). If there is no mydate file, one will be created.

24

> In Hour 11, you saw how to use piping to send the output from one com-
> mand into another command. This is done without your having to create
> intermediate files yourself.

Using Files for Commands

In addition to typing a single command at a time, you can create text files with multiple commands. Normally one command is placed on each line, but you can place several on a line (either in a file or in Terminal) if you separate the commands with semicolons (;).

It's awkward to use a single line to edit a text file, and so a number of full-screen editors are available in Terminal. These include vi, emacs, pico, and many others. Each one presents a full screen's worth of text, and you can use command keys to move from one line to another to do your editing.

Another way of editing a text file is to use Text Edit. If you use the Make Plain Text command from the Format menu, the file will consist only of text and can be read by Terminal. If you save such a file with a suffix .command, it will be opened automatically and run by Terminal if you double-click it.

Lines in a file that begin with # are comments. The first line indicates the shell that should be used to interpret the commands in the file:

```
#! /bin/tcsh
```

Working with Files in Terminal

The prompt in Terminal includes the current working directory. You can access files in this directory by simply typing their name. To access files in another directory, you need to include path information such as

```
/users/jfeiler/Documents/sampletext.command
```

You can change from one directory to another by using the cd command: Simply type in the name of the new directory following cd, and you'll see it in the prompt.

With Mac OS X and Terminal, there's an easy way to avoid typing lengthy filenames. Simply drag a file or folder onto the command line in Terminal, and its full name will be placed on the line. Thus, to change the directory to your Pictures folder, drag the Pictures folder into Terminal as shown in Figure 24.2.

FIGURE 24.2

Drag folders into Terminal to get their path names.

When you release the mouse button on the drag, the path name will be placed in the command line, as shown in Figure 24.3.

FIGURE 24.3

A path name appears when you release the dragged folder in Terminal.

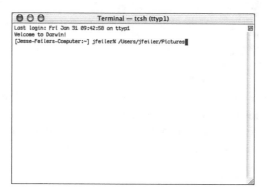

To change your directory to the Pictures folder, type cd (note the space following the command), drag the Pictures folder into Terminal, and then press Return to execute the command. As you can see in the prompt in Figure 24.4, that will change your directory.

Listing a Directory and Displaying a File

Among the many commands you can use in Terminal, there are two that you may frequently use as you work with scripts. In order to list the contents of the current directory, use the ls command. It has a variety of options, but the simple command itself provides a quick listing of the names of the files in the directory as shown in Figure 24.5.

FIGURE 24.4

Change your directory with the cd *command and the dragging of a folder.*

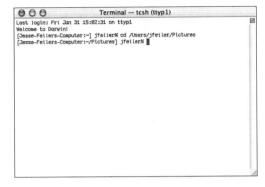

FIGURE 24.5

Use ls *to list a directory's files.*

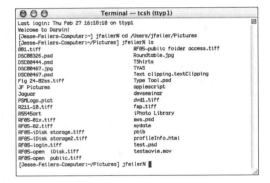

To quickly list the contents of a text file, you can use the cat command. This is appropriate for relatively brief files, such as files created as output from commands. If you used the previous example of placing output from the date command into a file called mydate, Figure 24.6 demonstrates what the cat mydate command will show:

FIGURE 24.6

Use cat *to display a text file.*

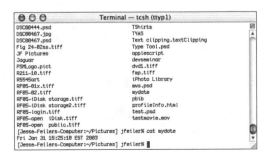

Changing Permissions

There's another command you may need to use when you work with scripts and Terminal. You can set permissions for files using the Info window in the Finder. You can set those permissions to Read Only, Read & Write, or No Access. You can set those permissions for the owner of the file, for the group that has access to the file, and for everyone else. That's fine for the Finder, but there's another permission that comes into play with Terminal.

In addition to read and write permissions, a file can be executable or not. Scripts need to be executable in order to run. In order to set a file's permission to executable, you need to use the chmod command. (This situation arises most often if you use Text Edit to create a script file; by default, Text Edit files are not executable.)

To set a file as being readable, writable, and executable by everyone (user, group, and others), use this syntax:

```
chmod ugo=+rwx thefilename
```

Often, all you care about is making the file executable for yourself, so you can simply set all permissions with

```
chmod +wrx thefilename
```

> For more on permissions and the command line in general, see Jesse Feiler's *Mac OS X Jaguar: The Complete Reference*.

Using sudo

There's one last tip for working with Terminal. There are some commands that are *privileged*—most users can't execute them. You can log in as a privileged user to execute them, but the simplest way is to prefix the command with sudo. You will be asked for an administrator password, and then the command can be executed. This is the way in which you can remove directories that you don't own, for example.

Running AppleScript from Terminal

Hour 11 showed you how to script Terminal and run a command such as date from AppleScript. Here's the sample script again:

24

```
tell application "Terminal"
  do script "date"
end tell
```

Now that you've seen a bit more about how Terminal works, it's time to look at the complementary process: using Terminal to run AppleScript commands.

Among the commands that Apple has added to standard UNIX commands are two specifically geared to AppleScript:

- `osacompile` is used to compile a script.
- `osascript` is used to execute AppleScript commands.

You'll see how to use them in this section.

The temperature Web service used as an example in Hour 22, "Using AppleScript Across a Network," is used again here. In Hour 22, you saw how to call it from an interactive script as well as from the SOAPTalk example in AppleScript Studio. Here the parameters are used in a noninteractive and very simple SOAP call from AppleScript:

```
tell application "http://services.xmethods.net:80/soap/servlet/rpcrouter"
  call soap {method name:"getTemp", parameters:{zipcode:"12565"}, ¬
    method namespace uri:"urn:xmethods-Temperature", SOAPAction:""}
end tell
```

You'll see how to run this script from Terminal using the commands themselves as well as from an AppleScript file. There are a number of reasons for doing this. You may want to incorporate a script into a saved set of shell commands that you are executing. In other cases—such as the Web services script shown here—the AppleScript code may be simpler than code written in other languages or scripts. Additionally, you may want to use the scheduling features of the command line or the interface to the C programming languages as described in the following sections.

Running a Script from Terminal

The first step is to create the script as you would normally do in Script Editor. Figure 24.7 shows the script entered and run as a test.

In Terminal, execute the script using the `osascript` command followed by the name of the file. As you can see in Figure 24.8, the simplest way to do this is to type `osascript` (remember to follow the command with a space) and drag the file from the Finder into Terminal. The full filename will be entered automatically for you. This frees you from worrying about the path, special escape characters for embedded blanks in the name, and the like.

FIGURE 24.7
Use Script Editor to enter and test the script.

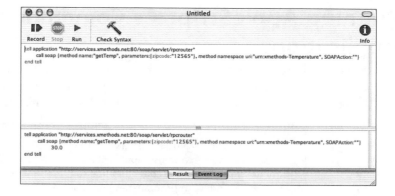

FIGURE 24.8
Execute the script in Terminal.

24

Running AppleScript Commands from Terminal

You can execute this simple script's commands from Terminal using the osascript command. To execute it in this way, you'll need to make a few minor typographical changes.

The osascript command is described fully on its man page. The basics are simple:

- Each line of AppleScript code starts with -e and is enclosed in single quotes.

- The osascript command may execute several lines of AppleScript code. At the end of each line, use the continuation character for the command line (\) so that all of the AppleScript lines are interpreted as a single osascript statement.

Here's the same script shown previously prepared for execution in Terminal:

```
osascript \
-e 'tell application "http://services.xmethods.net:80/soap/servlet/rpcrouter"' \
-e 'call soap {method name:"getTemp", parameters:{zipcode:"12565"},
  method namespace uri:"urn:xmethods-Temperature", SOAPAction:""}' \
-e 'end tell'
```

Note that the third line of code shown here is presented on two lines for readability. It must be entered on a single line in Terminal. Note, too, that before the line continuation characters on each line (\), there is a blank space.

Running AppleScript As Commands from Applications

You can run AppleScript as commands from applications written in C or its derivatives (C++ and Objective-C on Mac OS X). This means that they can be run from Cocoa and Carbon applications along with any other command-line commands.

> You can use the NSAppleScript class in the Cocoa framework to compile and run scripts. You can also use Apple events in Carbon to achieve the functionality of scripts. Using the command-line call can be simpler if you are just starting to work with programming on Mac OS X.

You accomplish this by using the C system function. Simply place the entire osascript command with its script commands or its filename within the parentheses of the system function, and it will be executed.

You can write a very basic Cocoa application to execute any AppleScript code in this way. If you want to capture the output from the command, you can use the popen function, which opens a pipe for a command and writes to it. Figure 24.9 shows such an application in action.

FIGURE 24.9

Run AppleScript from within a Cocoa application.

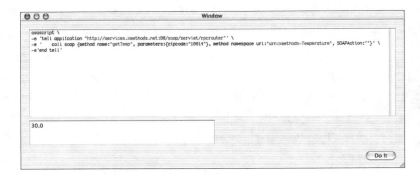

The following is the Objective-C code that is used to implement the Do It button. The two text fields in the window are called inputField and outputField. (Note that inputField is a text view that can accommodate numerous lines of text; outputField is a simple text field with only one line.)

```
- (IBAction)doIt:(id)sender
{
  FILE *tempFile;
  NSMutableString *outputStream;
  char buff [1000];
  tempFile = popen ([[inputField string]cString], "r");
  fgets (buff, 1000, tempFile);
  outputStream = [NSString stringWithCString:buff];
  [outputField setStringValue:outputStream];
  pclose (tempFile);
}
```

The full code for this project is available on this book's Web site, http://www.samspublishing.com, in the Hour 24 folder.

24

Automatically Running Scripts

One of the powerful features of the Mac OS X UNIX core is that it can carry on tasks automatically. Commands such as at and batch let you schedule jobs on a one-shot basis. You can use cron and periodic for routine scheduling.

cron

A UNIX *daemon* (a process that runs in the background) called cron wakes up—generally once a minute—to check to see if there are jobs waiting to be run. You schedule jobs using the crontab command, which stores them in a table. Although this is not particularly complex, many people prefer to use the periodic command, discussed next, to handle their scheduling of repeated tasks. The crontab in Mac OS X is shown in Figure 24.10; it manages the scheduling of periodic tasks.

FIGURE 24.10
The Mac OS X crontab.

```
●●●                    crontab
# /etc/crontab
SHELL=/bin/sh
PATH=/etc:/bin:/sbin:/usr/bin:/usr/sbin
HOME=/var/log
#
#minute hour   mday   month   wday   who    command
#
#*/5     *      *      *       *      root   /usr/libexec/atrun
#
# Run daily/weekly/monthly jobs.
15      3      *      *       *      root   periodic daily
30      4      *      *       6      root   periodic weekly
30      5      1      *       *      root   periodic monthly
```

After some introductory commands and some comments (the lines beginning with #), three tasks are specified at the end of the file.

The third line from the bottom specifies a daily task. It is run at 15 minutes past the third hour (3:15 a.m.). It is run on every day of the month (mday), every month, and every weekday (wday). It is run by the root user, and the command that is run is periodic daily.

The second line from the bottom specifies a weekly task—periodic weekly. It is run at 4:30 a.m. on the sixth day of the week (Saturday).

The final line runs periodic monthly at 5:30 a.m. on the first day of the month. All of this is set up for you, so you don't have to change anything: You just have to arrange your scripts so that they are executed by the periodic command.

> This scheduling that is set by default in Mac OS X relies on your computer being on overnight. If you do not leave your computer on overnight (or if it is asleep), the periodic jobs will not run. In many cases, this isn't a problem. However, if you are running with very little free disk space, you may find that problem exacerbated. Leaving the computer on overnight may help clear up peculiar behavior. You don't have to do it all the time; one night will allow the daily log cleanup tasks to run. If you leave it on from Friday night to Saturday morning, you'll hit the weekly tasks; likewise, leave it on overnight on the last day of a month to let the monthly tasks run.

periodic

The periodic command executes the scripts in specified directories when it runs as specified in the crontab file. The directories are named daily, weekly, and monthly; they reside in the etc directory, which is one of the UNIX directories you normally do not see. If you want to add scripts to the periodic command, you simply add them to the appropriate directory and everything will work. Those scripts can include standard UNIX shell commands—and, as you have seen, they can also include AppleScript commands.

The only problem you have is how to make those directories visible. You can use the command line in Terminal to navigate to those directories just as you would in any UNIX system. However, if you're used to the Macintosh, it's probably easier to use the Finder to manipulate these files—just as you do for the files you normally see.

To make the directories visible, you must take three steps.

First, use the Finder's Find command from the File menu to open the window shown in Figure 24.11.

FIGURE 24.11
Open the Find window.

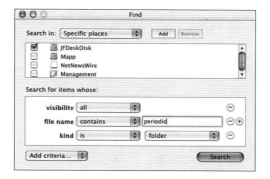

Set Visibility to All, and enter `periodic` for the filename. If you want to make the search more efficient, use the Add Criteria button in the lower left of the window to narrow it to folders. When you click Search, the Finder will look for the folder.

The results are shown in the window you see in Figure 24.12.

FIGURE 24.12

Find returns a list of folders and files.

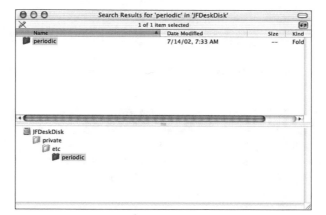

When you click on a file or folder in the upper pane of the window, you'll see its location on disk in the lower pane. If more than one periodic folder is shown, click each in turn until you see the hierarchy shown in Figure 24.12.

When you have identified the correct periodic folder, double-click it in the Search Results window. It will be opened in a standard Finder window as shown in Figure 24.13.

FIGURE **24.13**
Folders that are normally invisible can be opened from the Search Results window.

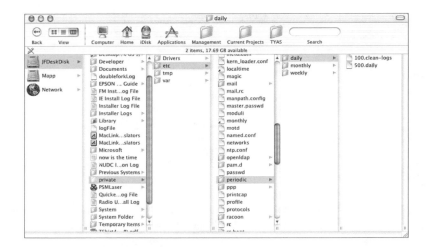

You can see the scripts that are scheduled to be run in each periodic cycle. If you want to add others, simply drag them to the appropriate folder.

> Upgrades to the operating system may modify the standard periodic files. For that reason, it's generally a good idea to add new files if you want to modify the standard files rather than modifying the existing files.

Other Scripting Languages

Other scripting languages are installed for you on Mac OS X. Among them are Perl, Ruby, and Python. You can write scripts in these languages and run them from the command line in Terminal. You also can place them in your Scripts folder so that they appear in the Script menu from where you can run them.

Perl

Perl is one of the most popular scripting languages. It's available on many platforms, and it has become a mainstay of many system administrators and Webmasters. One of its great strengths is its powerful text manipulation features. You can use it to find, match, or replace text. It is often used to parse verbose logs and to format them into readable output.

Perl has been used extensively on Web sites for handling forms; it's also commonly used for parsing e-mail messages.

Ruby

Ruby is an object-oriented scripting language. It incorporates strict object-oriented structure and provides a number of powerful and useful features such as automatic memory collection.

Python

Python is another object-oriented scripting language. Among its features are a particularly easy-to-use C-language extension mechanism.

Summary

24

From simple tasks through complex scripts and the sophistication of AppleScript Studio, you've seen how to use AppleScript to automate your work, integrate applications, and use the power of Web services. In this hour, you've also seen how to use AppleScript and the command line in Terminal to execute commands in the UNIX shell.

There's more to learn about AppleScript, but at this point, the best way to learn it is to use it. You've seen the basics, and you've seen an overview of what you can do with the technology. Explore it and find out how you can use it to customize your environment.

Remember that the AppleScript Web site remains an important resource for information and links to various AppleScript pages on the Web. Visit it often to see what's new. It's also worthwhile to keep up with Apple's new technologies: the iLife applications (iDVD, iPhoto, iMovie, and iTunes) as well as applications such as Address Book, iSync, and Backup use AppleScript and the other technologies described in this book. As new features are added, they are often available through scripts as well as the traditional point-and-click interface.

Keep your eyes open for automation opportunities. This means looking for repetitive tasks as well as for patterns in the work that you do that might not immediately appear to be repetitions. How can you redefine tasks so that they are, indeed, repeatable and automatable? Answering this question will make you not just a power user, but a power architect of sophisticated solutions.

Q&A

Q What are the biggest pitfalls in using AppleScript?

A The biggest pitfalls are not specific to AppleScript; they're common to many programming and scripting languages. In my experience, they include the following:

- Incompleteness—If you're going to automate a task, make sure you understand it, including the exceptions that can occur.
- Lack of error handling—Use `try` blocks and test for unexpected results.
- Thinking small—You may be writing a one-shot script, but give it the same attention you'd give to a mission-critical task.
- Lack of documentation—You're not going to remember what you were thinking of when you look at that script next year. Use comments.

Q Do I have to worry about AppleScript being discontinued by Apple?

A It's now an integral part of Mac OS X, and it's supported throughout the operating system and in the developer products. It's here to stay.

Q What do I do if I need to script an application that's not scriptable?

A Investigate the UI Elements scripting plug-in. Check to see if another scripting language such as Visual Basic is supported and if you can access it either via AppleScript or through the UI Elements.

Workshop

The workshop contains quiz questions and activities to help you solidify your knowledge of the material in this hour. Try to answer all of the questions before looking at the quiz answers that follow.

Quiz

1. How do you see invisible files in the Finder?
2. How do you put multiple commands on a single line in Terminal?
3. How do you execute privileged commands in Terminal?
4. How do you get output from a command-line command in an application?

Quiz Answers

1. Use the Find command in the Finder's File menu and set Visibility to All.
2. Separate them with semicolons.

3. Use `sudo`.

4. Use the `popen` function to create a pipe that receives the command's output; then display the contents of the string.

Activities

Return to the very first activity in Hour 1, "Introducing AppleScript," of this book: "What types of actions and processes would you like to script?" Which of those tasks can you now script? What other opportunities have you found for scripting? If there are tasks that you haven't figured out how to script, can you figure out how to get around the problems?

24

PART V
Appendixes

A   Constants and Predefined Variables

B   Operators

C   Third-party Script Editors

APPENDIX **A**

Constants and Predefined Variables

This appendix lists constants and predefined variables in AppleScript. You cannot use them as names of your own variables. Some have specific meanings and values—such as bold; others—such as current application—have specific meanings but changeable values, as seen in Table A.1.

TABLE A.1   Constants in AppleScript

Name	Comments
current application	Set using the parent property.
false	
true	
all caps	
all lowercase	
bold	

continues

TABLE A.1   continued

Name	Comments
condensed	
expanded	
hidden	
italic	
outline	
plain	
shadow	
small caps	
strikethrough	
subscript	
superscript	
underline	
weekday	Property of a date in the sense of day of the week, not weekday as opposed to weekend. Use as in `get weekday of (current date)`. Possible values: Monday, Mon; Tuesday, Tue; Wednesday, Wed; Thursday, Thu; Friday, Fri; Saturday, Sat; Sunday, Sun.
month	Property of a date. Use as in `get month of (current date)`. January, Jan; February, Feb; March, Mar; April, Apr; May, May; June, Jun; July, Jul; August, Aug; September, Sep; October, Oct; November, Nov; December, Dec.
minutes	As in `(10 * minutes)` for 10 minutes.
hours	As in `(4 * hours)` for 4 hours.
days	As in `(3 * days)` for 3 days.
weeks	As in `(10 * weeks)` for 10 weeks.
ask	For use in the saving clause of the `close` command, as in `saving ask` to put up a Save dialog.
no	As in `saving no` for no Save dialog.
yes	As in `saving yes` for automatically saving on close.

The constants listed in Table A.2 are used in `ignoring` and `considering` statements. The default setting is indicated for each.

TABLE A.2 Constants Used in `ignoring` and `considering` Statements

application responses	Wait for responses, handle errors and results. (`considering`)
case	Differentiate between upper and lowercase. (`ignoring`)
diacriticals	Differentiate between characters with diacriticals. (`considering`)
expansion	Treat character pairs such as OE as equivalent to special characters such as œ. (`considering`)
hyphens	In comparing strings, hyphens matter. (`considering`)
punctuation	In comparing strings, punctuation matters. (`considering`)
white space	In comparing strings, spaces, tabs, and returns matter. (`considering`)

Predefined variables differ from constants in that you can set their values. Normally it's not a good idea to do so, but there are cases in which you might want to do so temporarily. The predefined variables are shown in Table A.3.

TABLE A.3 Predefined Variables in AppleScript

Name	Comments
return	The Return character.
space	The Space character.
tab	The Tab character.
version	Current version of AppleScript.
pi	Real. The value pi (roughly 3.14159).
result	Value of the most recently evaluated command or expression. May be undefined.
missing value	No data for something. Not the same as undefined.
me	Current script.
anything	Anything (rarely used).

A

APPENDIX B

Operators

AppleScript operators are listed in this appendix. They include standard arithmetic operators as well as the logical operators that programmers are used to. In addition, some AppleScript-specific operators for manipulating lists, records, dates, and strings are provided.

Within categories, operators are divided by the types of operands to which they apply. Remember that expressions in parentheses are evaluated first. Thus, the multiplication operator that works on two numbers can work on the following expression:

```
4 * (year of (current date))
```

If the year of the current date is 2003, that expression is evaluated first, and the result of the multiplication is 8012 (4 * 2003).

Arithmetic Operators

Operators that work on two numbers:

*	Standard multiplication.
+	Addition.
-	Subtraction.
÷, /	Division.
^	Exponentiation.
div	Integer division: The integer part of the result is returned. It is not rounded.
mod	Integer division: The remainder part of the result is returned as an integer.

Operators that work on a date and a number:

+	Add days, weeks, hours, or minutes to a date. You can use the predefined constants days, weeks, minutes, hours, as in (current date) + (2 * weeks).
-	Subtract days, weeks, hours, or minutes.

Operator that works on two dates:

-	Returns the number of minutes between two dates. Convert to other units with the predefined constants. For example, the number of weeks between two dates is *(date1 - date2)/weeks*.

Boolean Operators

Operators that work on two Booleans:

and	true if both terms are true.
or	true if either term is true.

Operators that work on one Boolean:

not	true if the Boolean is false; false if it is true.

Containment Operators

Operators that work on lists, records, and strings:

starts with, begins with	A list or string begins with a value, list, or string, as in "Hello" begins with "He" or {1, 2, 3} starts with {1, 2}. (Note that these operators cannot be used with records.)

`ends with`	A list or string ends with a value, list, or string. (Note that these operators cannot be used with records.)
`contains`	The specified value, list, or string appears anywhere within the list or string. The elements you search for must appear in the same order in the list or string. Thus, `{1, 2, 3} contains {1, 3}` is false, whereas `{1, 2, 3} contains {1, 2}` is true.
`does not/doesn't contain`	The reverse of `contains`.
`is in, is contained by`	The order of the `contains` operator's operands is reversed, as in "He" is in "Hello" rather than "Hello" contains "He." This may make for more readable code.
`is not in, is not contained by`	The reverse of `is in` or `is contained by`.

Equality Operators

Operators that work on two expressions:

`=, equal(s), equal to,` `is, is equal to`	The two expressions evaluate to the same value.

`≠, does not/doesn't equal, is not,`
`is not equal (to), isn't,`
`isn't equal (to)`
	The two expressions do not evaluate to the same value.

`&`	Concatenation. If the two expressions are strings, the result is a single string; otherwise, the result is a list containing the expressions as its items.
`as`	Returns an expression as a specified class. Most often used to convert to the `string` class, as in `(current date) as string`.
`a reference to`	A reference to an expression or value rather than to the value itself. Many AppleScript commands require references rather than values as parameters.

B

Comparison Operators

Operators that work on two strings, integers, reals, or dates:

`<, comes before, is less than,`
`is not/ isn't greater than`
`or equal (to), less than`
	Less than comparison. Note that for strings, character-by-character comparisons are performed. Thus, `"two " < "two"` is false (note the space at the end of the first operator). Use Script Editor to experiment if you will be comparing strings in any manner other than equality.

`>, comes after, (is) greater than,` `is not/isn't less than or equal (to)`	Greater than comparison.

`≤, <=, does not/doesn't come after,`
`is less than or equal (to),`
`is not/isn't greater than,`
`less than or equal (to)`
	Less than or equal comparison.

`≥, >=, does not/doesn't come before,`
`(is) greater than or equal (to),`
`is not/isn't less than`
	Greater than or equal comparison.

APPENDIX C

Third-party Script Editors

You can use third-party AppleScript software that helps you develop and debug your scripts. You don't need to use it; you can use Script Editor (installed in the AppleScript folder when you install Mac OS X), or you can use AppleScript Studio (part of Apple's Developer Tools and described in Part III, "Working with AppleScript Studio," of this book).

Whether you choose scripts or development tools, the fact that you have a choice makes your life easier. Apple provides the basic AppleScript technology, and you can use it in whatever way you want.

Three major AppleScript applications from third parties let you write scripts, debug them, and analyze the applications for which you're writing scripts. Each of these excellent products comes with a modest fee. If you prefer, you can use Script Editor from Apple (discussed in Hour 8, "Introducing Script Editor") and UI Examiner (discussed in Hour 20, "Advanced AppleScript Syntax"). Both of them are free, but neither offers the range of features provided in the three products described in this section:

- Smile
- Script Debugger
- PreFab UI Browser

Smile

Smile (`http://www.satimage.fr/software/en/softx.html#smile`) is a script development environment that goes far beyond Apple's Script Editor. If you're going to be writing lengthy or complex scripts, you should check out Smile. (Scripts are scripts, so scripts that you write in Smile are editable in Script Editor and vice versa.)

You can set preferences in Smile to control the formatting of specific semantic elements as shown in Figure C.1.

FIGURE C.1

Set semantic formatting in Smile.

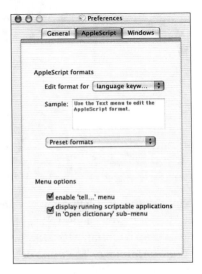

The editing window of Smile works much the way editing windows in integrated development environments (IDEs) do: It is sensitive not just to the text that's entered but also to its semantics. In Smile, for example, the individual handlers in your script are accessible from a pop-up button in the top of the window as shown in Figure C.2.

FIGURE C.2

Smile index handlers in your scripts.

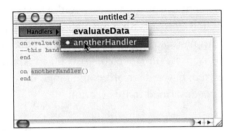

Finally, you'll be able to use the palette of dialog elements shown in Figure C.3 to build complex dialogs. You can't do this with Script Editor, but you can do this (and more) with AppleScript Studio, which is described in Part III of this book.

FIGURE C.3

Build complex dialogs.

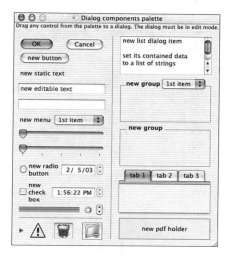

The Scripts menu within Smile provides a variety of scripts that help you manipulate scripts and dialogs. With Object eXpert, shown in Figure C.4, you can identify and change properties for objects in dialogs.

FIGURE C.4

Object eXpert lets you manipulate dialog objects.

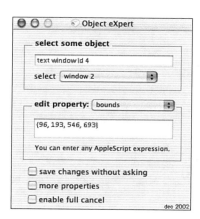

Script Debugger

Script Debugger (`http://latenightsw.com/sd3.0/index.html`) is much more than just a debugger. Its script editing window, shown in Figure C.5, is similar to the Script Editor window that lets you write and run code. However, it provides tabs at the top to let you monitor the progress of a script as you write and run it.

FIGURE C.5

Script Debugger's script window lets you write and run scripts.

Script Debugger also provides a wide range of preferences for the editing of scripts in the Preferences window shown in Figure C.6.

FIGURE C.6

Set preferences for displaying, editing, and debugging in Script Debugger.

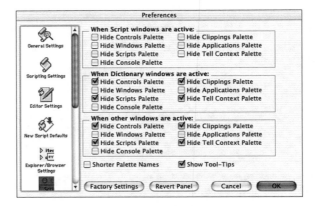

As you write a script with a `tell` block addressing a specific application, the AppleScript semantic elements for that application are displayed, as shown in Figure C.7.

Figure C.7

View the semantic elements in Script Debugger.

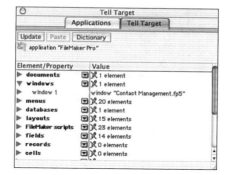

Clicking the Dictionary button will take you to a window that displays the relevant dictionary. (There's more about AppleScript dictionaries in Part II, "Writing Scripts with Script Editor.") For now, it's worth noting that in Script Debugger you can look at a dictionary not only in text form but in an object model form that will be familiar to object-oriented programmers. The Object Model display is shown in Figure C.8.

Figure C.8

Examine an object model with Script Debugger.

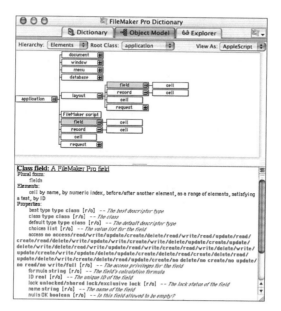

The same information can be viewed in the Explorer tab, which presents it in an expandable list format, as shown in Figure C.9.

FIGURE C.9

Examine the object model in an expandable list.

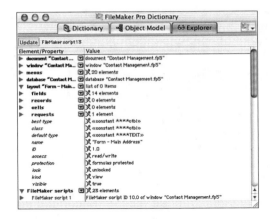

The Scripts window, shown in Figure C.10, has scripts you can run to manipulate your script as you write it. It also has clippings of standard chunks of AppleScript syntax that you can drag into your script as you're writing it.

FIGURE C.10

Use the Scripts window as you develop scripts.

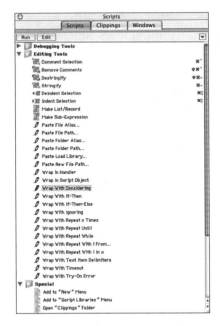

PreFab UI Browser

Like Script Debugger, PreFab UI Browser (http://www.prefab.com/uibrowser/) promises a limited set of functionality in its name and then goes far beyond that promise in its implementation. It, too, helps you write scripts. In this product, you'll find a helpful suite of tools to help you work with the new GUI scripting that's described further in Hour 20.

With an application running, you can use UI Browser to examine its interface elements. Figure C.11 shows the initial window that displays the interface elements.

FIGURE C.11
Interface elements are shown in the UI Browser window.

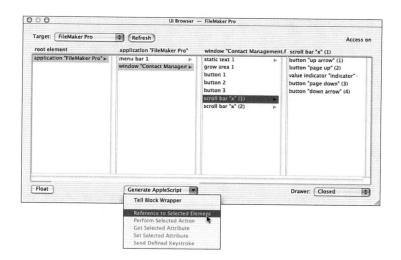

The pop-up menu just to the left of the center of the window at the bottom lets you generate AppleScript code for a selected element. You can choose to create a `tell` block or a reference to the object. An automatically generated reference to the selected interface object is shown in Figure C.12.

FIGURE C.12
UI Browser can automatically generate AppleScript code snippets.

C

As shown in Figure C.13, you can use the Drawer pop-up menu in the lower right of the window to examine features of a selected interface element. Here you see the list of actions available. Other choices are shown in the pop-up menu.

FIGURE **C.13**
Examine the actions for a selected element.

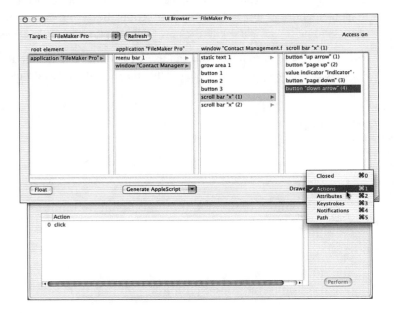

If you select an action, you can then use the Generate AppleScript pop-up menu again to generate code to start that action. Choose Perform Selected Action from that pop-up menu, and UI Browser will automatically generate the code as shown in Figure C.14.

FIGURE C.14
Automatically generate code for actions.

In addition to actions, you can choose to see attributes of a selected element, as shown in Figure C.15. The pop-up menu in the lower right is set to Attributes, and they are displayed in the drawer at the bottom. If you select one, you can use the Generate AppleScript pop-up menu as shown to produce code to get that attribute. In this case, the automatically generated code is

```
get title of button "page down"  of scroll bar "x"  of window ¬
   "Contact Management.fp5"
 of application process "FileMaker Pro"
```

You can copy it into a script or modify it in any way that you want.

FIGURE C.15

View attributes of selected elements.

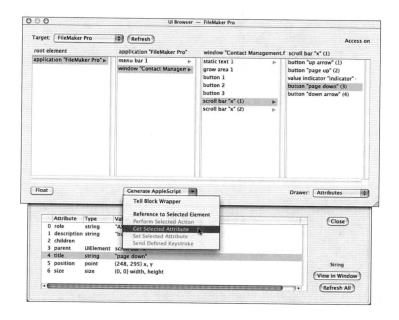

Finally, if you select the Path command in the pop-up menu, UI Browser generates the code to use for a series of nested tell blocks or other commands that need to drill down to a selected object as shown in Figure C.16. One way to use this automatically generated code would be in the following nested tell blocks:

```
tell application "FileMaker Pro"
  tell window "Contact Management.fp5" (1)
    tell scroll bar "x" (1)
      tell button "page down" (3)
        --do something
      end tell
    end tell
  end tell
end tell
```

FIGURE C.16

Automatically generate an object's path.

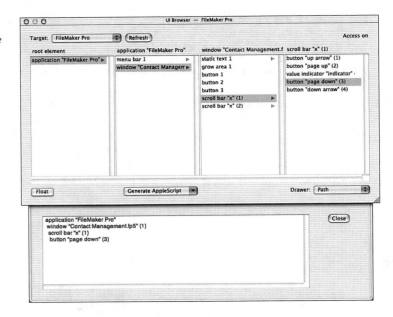

GLOSSARY

-- The comment character that causes all further characters on that line to be ignored in AppleScript.

(* and *) Delimiters for multiline comments.

~ The path from the root of a hard disk to an individual user's home directory.

¬ The Script Editor continuation character for multiple line statements.

Apple Developer Connection (ADC) Apple's resource for developers. Various forms of membership (including free online) are available through the site at `http://developer.apple.com`.

Apple events The underlying technology that supports AppleScript.

AppleScript Studio The set of development tools from Apple including Cocoa, Project Builder, and Interface Builder.

C++ An object-oriented extension to the C language. It is the native language of the Carbon framework on Mac OS X.

Carbon The C++ libraries and framework for Mac OS 9 and Mac OS X.

Cocoa The object-oriented framework and application development environment on Mac OS X derived from NeXTStep. It is the basis of AppleScript Studio.

command line   The text-based entry of commands directly to the Darwin core of Mac OS X. Accessed through Terminal.

handler   A subroutine called in response to an AppleScript-defined message, such as `on run`.

Interface Builder   The graphical user interface application that lets you build interfaces for AppleScript Studio, Carbon, Cocoa, and other programming languages on Mac OS X.

item   An individual value in a list. Accessed by number or relative position (first/last) for lists.

list   An ordered list of items.

Objective-C   An object-oriented extension to the C language. It is the native language of Cocoa.

object oriented   A programming methodology in which data and functionality are packaged within structured objects.

Open Scripting Architecture (OSA)   The basic architecture for creating scriptable applications and for writing scripting components to implement scripting languages, of which AppleScript is one implementation.

Perl   A scripting language that can be used on the command line.

Project Builder   The application-development application from Apple on Mac OS X.

Python   A scripting language that can be used on the command line.

record   An unordered list of named properties.

Ruby   A scripting language that can be used on the command line.

Script Menu   The menu that appears at the right-hand side of the menu bar and that contains the scripts located in the `/Library/Scripts` and `~/Library/Scripts` folders.

scriptable   An application that contains an AppleScript dictionary and that can be scripted by directing `tell` commands to it.

Scripts menu   A menu within an application that contains one or more scripts for that application's use.

services   The ability of one application to access functionality from another application using the clipboard as a data transfer mechanism.

subroutine   A collection of AppleScript statements that are invoked either in response to a handler request or a user-defined call using on.

suite   A collection of classes and commands defined for a specific purpose. Suites can be defined for individual applications or for common purposes (as in the Standard suite and Text suite).

target   The application or object within an application to which a tell block's commands are sent.

tell statement/tell block   A set of commands addressed to an application or object within an application (the target).

Terminal   The application that lets you access the command line.

INDEX

SYMBOLS

& operators, 369
¬ (continuation character), 34, 72, 86

A

accessing
    files through Terminal, 346
    Menus palette, 193
    remote servers, 312
accessors, 285-286
acgi dispatcher utility script, 56
action handlers, 211
add actions (folder action scripts), 36

adding
    Address Book entries to dialogs, 152
    commands to menus, 193
    data rows to data sources, 264-265
    icons to dialogs, 149
    interface elements to Interface Builder (AppleScript Studio), 172-173
    menus, 193
    tab views
        AppleScript Studio applications, 253
        windows, 203
Address Book
    data, extracting to inDesign, 303-305
    data, extracting to Text Edit, 300-301

    entries, adding to dialogs, 152
    scripting applications, 127-128
Adobe Studio Exchange Web site, 25
afp (Apple File Protocol) syntax, mounting remote disks, 312-313
aliases, 22
album information scripts (iTunes collection scripts), 45
Ambrosia Software Web site, 248
America Online scripting applications, 136
append command, 267
AppKit framework (Cocoa application framework), 161
Apple events, 13-14

AppleScript
  application commands,
    running as, 352-353
  Applications, 9-10
  CGI handlers, writing,
    319-321
  commands, 96, 349-351
  document templates,
    268-272
  files, 166
  Mac OS X v10.2
    upgrades, 20-23
  networking
    clients, 313-315
    file sharing remote
      connections, 316
    Remote Apple Events
      remote connections,
      317
    servers, 313-315
    tell blocks, 314
    user account remote
      access, 317-318
  string constants, 100
  Web sites, 25, 30
**AppleScript Central Web
site, 52**
AppleScript Info blog, 52-54
**AppleScript Sourcebook
Web site, 54**
**AppleScript Studio, 159,
371**
  AppleScript pane (Info
    window), 209, 272
    data representation
      hand-
      lers, 273-274
    load data representa-
      tion handlers,
      273-274
    tab view names, 204

applications
  adding images,
    249-252
  adding text views, 253
  button controls, 249,
    252-254
  debugging, 232-238
  designing, 242-247
  error catching, try
    blocks, 247
  help tags, 248
  providing documenta-
    tion, screen shots,
    248
Cocoa application frame-
  work, 161-163
Container View suite,
  190-191
Control View suite, 188
data sources
  append command, 267
  building, 263
  data cells, 262
  data columns, 262-264
  data items, 263
  data rows, 263
  data rows, adding,
    264-265
  data rows, entering
    data, 265-266
  entering bulk data
    additions, 267
  extracting data, 267
downloading, 160
graphics services, 335
Help Viewer, 254-255
Interface Builder, 161
  adding images to
    applications, 251
  adding interface
    elements, 172-173
  building handlers,
    174-176

buttons, setting
  attributes, 174
clicked handlers, 186
designing table views,
  168-169
help tags, 248
implementing handlers,
  176-177
Info window, 167-172,
  184-186, 208-209,
  213, 216, 252-254,
  269-274
interface elements,
  index numbers, 186
multiple data fields,
  244
naming text fields, 173
navigating, 167
nib files, 167, 183
opening, 167
opening palettes, 183
palette window, 167
SimpleApp Project,
  183
Stepper control,
  244-245
Views palette, 215-218
More Complex App
  Project, 201-207
Project Builder, 161
  adding images to
    applications, 249
  AppleScript files, 166
  AppleScript Studio
    Help, 188
  AppleScript Studio
    Terminology
    Reference, 188-189
  application files, 166
  building project files,
    165
  clicked handlers, 187

debugging AppleScript Studio applications, 233

dragging/dropping project files, 166

locating projects, 164

nib files, 166

Preferences, 222

Targets tab, 223-231

templates, 164, 168

window layout, 165

Project Builder Debugger (Project Builder), 234-238

provider services, 335

Savable Table View Project, 262

Script Editor continuation character, 260

services, 330-337

SimpleApp Project, 182

building windows, 183-184

configuring Interface Builder, 183

enabling menus, 197-198

identifying window elements, 184

implementing menu commands, 194-195

menu commands, capturing error messages, 196

menu commands, factoring applications, 195-196

naming text fields, 184-186

setting text field attributes, 184

testing, 187

writing handlers, 186-187

syntax, 188, 193

class commands, 192

class events, 192

elements, 190-191

object properties, 189

TableView Project, 162-163

Web services, 326

AppleScript Studio Help (Project Builder), 188

AppleScript Studio Terminology Reference (Project Builder), 188-189

AppleScript Web site, 25

AppleScript-defined variables, 99-100

applets, 21

AppleWorks scripting applications, 137-138, 142

application class, 113-114

AppleWorks, 137

elements, viewing definitions, 123-124

locating, 123

application commands, 96

application files (AppleScript Studio), 166

Application menu (Script Editor), 84

application servers, 32

applications

Apple event support, 13-14

AppleScript Studio applications

adding images, 249-252

adding text views, 253

button controls, 249, 252-254

debugging, 232-238

designing, 242-247

error catching, try blocks, 247

help tags, 248

providing documentation, screen shots, 248

building

AppleScript document templates, 268-272

Project Builder (AppleScript Studio), 164

commanding, tell blocks, 94-95

commands, running AppleScript, 352-353

date and time settings, 244-245

extensions, Info.plist (Targets tab), 227-228

factoring, menu commands, 195-196

icons, Info.plist (Targets tab), 226

run-only applications, 21

scripting, reading dictionaries, 122-124

scripting applications

address book, 127-128

America Online, 136

AppleWorks, 137-138, 142

Disk Copy, 130

DVD Player, 129

FileMaker, 138-140

Help Viewer, 125

Image Captures, 130-131

Internet Connect, 129

Internet Explorer, 141

mail, 126-127

Microsoft Office, 140-141

Netscape, 141

Photoshop, 142-143

PowerPoint (Microsoft Office), 141

Print Center, 129

Retrospect, 143-144

Terminal, 130-131

TextEdit, 128-129

Word (Microsoft Office), 140

services, registering, 333

signatures, Info.plist (Targets tab), 227-228

suites, 14

tell blocks, 25

types, Info.plist (Targets tab), 227-228

Aqua Human Interface Guidelines, 152-153

arithmetic operators, 368

artist information scripts (iTunes collection scripts), 45

as operators, 369

assigning scripts to variables, 283

Attach Folder Action (folder action scripts), 37

Attributes pane (Info window), 204, 252-254

automated scripts, running, 11, 353-356

automating tasks, 11

B

backups, Retrospect scripting applications, 143

blocks, 15

handlers

folder actions, 16

idle handlers, 65, 75

open handlers, 64

quit handlers, 65

return statements, 74

run handlers, 63-64

subroutines, 63

infinite loops, 66

parameters, 61-62

recursive processing, 65

syntax, 60

tell blocks, 16, 25

try blocks, 77-78

blogs, 52-54

boolean operators, 368

bounds changed handlers, 212

breakpoints, 235, 238

Build Phases settings (Targets tab), 230-231

Build Phases window (Targets tab), 231

build styles (Targets tab), 231

building

applications

AppleScript document templates, 268-272

Project Builder (AppleScript Studio), 164

data columns (data sources), 263

data sources, 263

dynamic pages in inDesign, 307-308

handlers, 174-176

HTML forms, 319

on clicked handlers, 334

Project Builder (AppleScript Studio) project files, 165

scripts, 86

folder action scripts, 37

multiple application scripts, 298-306

syntax, 12-15

SimpleApp Project windows, 183-184

spreadsheets, AppleWorks, 138

text documents, AppleWorks, 137

Web services, 322-325

buttons

AppleScript Studio application design, 249, 252-254

default buttons, 149

Interface Builder (AppleScript Studio) buttons, setting attributes, 174

menu buttons, enabling/disabling, 246-247

naming, 149

C

capturing error messages, menu commands, 196

cat command (Terminal), 348

catalogs, AppleScript applications, 9

cd command (Terminal), 347

CDs
    AppleScript applications, 10
    event scripts, 12

cell value handlers, 262

CGI (Common Gateway Interfaces), writing handlers, 319-321

changing file permissions in Terminal, 349

chmod command (Terminal), 349

classes
    application class, 113-114
        AppleWorks, 137
        locating, 123
        viewing elements, 123-124
    clipping class, 117
    commands, 192
    Container and Folders suite (Finder) classes, 116
    container class, 116
    events, 192
    Files suite (Finder) classes, 117
    Finder Items suite classes, 113-116
    Internet location file class, 117
    item class, 116
    NSDocument class, 269, 272
    package class, 117
    person class, 128
    script syntax, 15
    suites, 15, 89

clauses, 72-73

clicked handlers, 186-187, 194, 210

clients, networking, 313-315

clipboard, copying/pasting UNIX data, 138

clipping class, 117

close command, 111

close subfolder actions (folder action scripts), 36

Cocoa application framework (AppleScript Studio), 161-163

Color Picker, 214

Color Well, 214

ColorSync scripts, 37

column views (Interface Builder), 170

combination services, 332

combo boxes, 207-210

commands, 188
    append command, 267
    AppleScript commands, 96, 349-351
    application commands, 96, 352-353
    cat command (Terminal), 348
    cd command (Terminal), 347
    chmod command (Terminal), 349
    class commands, 192
    close command, 111
    count command, 112
    cron command (UNIX), 353-354
    Darwin commands, 343
    date command, 130-132
    delete command, 112
    designing, 246-247

direct objects, 96

display dialog command, 148

do script command (Photoshop), 142

Finder Items suite commands, 115

Get Result of AppleScript command (Script Editor services), 337

ls command (Terminal), 347

make command, 112, 129

Make New AppleScript command (Script Editor services), 337

menu commands
    capturing error messages, 196
    enabling/disabling, 246-247
    factoring applications, 195-196
    implementing, 194-195

menus
    adding to, 193
    enabling, 197-198

naming, 193

open command, 111, 142

osacompile command, 350

osascript command, 350-351

periodic command (UNIX), 353-356

privileged commands (Terminal), 349

Retrospect make command (Retrospect), 144

Retrospect reply command (Retrospect), 143

Retrospect status command (Retrospect), 143-144

reveal command, 115

Run as AppleScript command (Script Editor services), 338

script syntax, 15

scripting addition commands, 96

search command (Help Viewer), 255

show command, FileMaker scripting applications, 139

Standard Suite (Finder) commands, 111-113, 129

suites, 15, 88-89

Terminal commands, 344-349

UNIX commands, 130-132, 343, 350-356

update command, 115

user-defined commands, 96-97

comments, creating scripts, 86

comparison operators, 370

compiling scripts, 21

compound conditional statements, 72

conditional statements, 71

compound conditional statements, 72

else clauses, 72-73

simple conditional statements, 72

try blocks, 77-78

writing, 73-74

connecting

sliders, 213

steppers to data entry fields, 244-245

Connections pane (Info window), 208-209, 213, 271

considering statements, constants, 364-365

constants, 16, 363

AppleScript string constants, 100

considering statements, 364-365

ignoring statements, 364-365

Container and Folders suite (Finder), 116

container class, 116

Container View suite (AppleScript Studio), tab views, 190-191, 202

attributes, setting, 204

controlling with pop-up tabs, 205-207

identifiers, 204

labels, 204

names, 204

Sliders tab, 213

tabless tab views, 203

windows, adding to, 203

containment operators, 368-369

control statements, 13, 101

Control View suite (AppleScript Studio), 188

controlling

tab views, 205-207

tabless tab views, 203

Controls menu (Script Editor), 86

copying

script objects, 283

data to clipboard, 138

count command, 112

Create DVD from Folders script (iDVD collection scripts), 43

createDocument subroutine

inDesign, building dynamic pages, 307

multiple application scripts, building, 299

Address Book to InDesign scripts, 304

Address Book to Text Edit scripts, 300

FileMaker to inDesign scripts, 306

FileMaker to Text Edit scripts, 303

cron command (UNIX), 353-354

Cronathon utility script, 56

Currency formatters, 216

Current Date & Time scripts (Info scripts), 31

Custom Class pane (Info window), 269

customizing

Finder toolbar, 22

Project Builder, 222

D

Darwin commands, 343

data cells (data sources), 262

data columns (data sources), 262-264

data entry errors, preventing

entry field labels, 246

formatters, 243

multiple data fields,
244-245

proper data entry field
examples, 243-244

**data entry fields, connecting
to steppers, 244-245**

**data fields, multiple data
fields, 244**

**data representation
handlers, 273-274**

data rows

data sources, 263

data sources, adding to,
264-265

entering data, 265-266

table views, 261

data sources

append command, 267

building, 263

bulk data additions,
entering, 267

data, extracting, 267

data cells, 262

data columns, 262-264

data items, 263

data rows, 263

adding to data sources,
264-265

entering data, 265-266

date command, 130-131

Date formatters, 216

**dates and times, setting in
applications, 244-245**

**debugging AppleScript
Studio applications,
232-238**

declaring variables, 70

**default buttons, specifying,
149**

delete command, 112

designing

AppleScript Studio
applications, 242

adding images,
249-252

adding text views, 253

button controls, 249,
252-254

command design,
246-247

error catching, try
blocks, 247

help tags, 248

menu design, 246-247

preventing data entry
errors, 243-246

providing documenta-
tion, screen shots,
248

column views (Interface
Builder), 170

commands, 246-247

menus, 246-247

script objects, 291

table views (Interface
Builder), 168

AppleScript table view
settings, 171-172

configuring control
settings, 169

setting attributes, 170

dialogs

Address Book entries,
adding, 152

buttons, naming, 149

display dialog command,
148

icons, adding, 149

information, displaying,
148-149

sizing, 148

user input, receiving,
150-151

dictionaries

address book dictionaries,
127-128

classes, 188

commands, 188

iCal, 122-124

opening, 88

reading, 122-124

suites, 88-90

**direct objects, commands,
96**

**directories, listing/switching
in Terminal, 346-347**

**Disk Copy scripting
applications, 130**

**display comment actions
(folder action scripts), 36**

**display dialog command,
148**

displaying

information in dialogs,
148-149

text file contents in
Terminal, 348

**Document Types, Info.plist
(Targets tab), 228-230**

Document.nib files, 269

**do script command
(Photoshop), 142**

downloading

AppleScript Studio, 160

iDVD collection scripts,
42

iPhoto collection scripts,
40

iTunes collection scripts,
44

QuickTime collection
scripts, 46

toolbar scripts, 46

**drag-and-drop handlers,
212**

dragging/dropping Project Builder (AppleScript Studio) project files, 166

droplets, 21

dummy handlers, 174, 187, 194

DVD Player scripting applications, 129

DVDs
  AppleScript applications, 10
  event scripts, 12

E

Edit Folder Action (folder action scripts), 37

Edit menu (Script Editor), syntax, 85

editing
  handlers, 212
  text files (Terminal), 346

ejecting remote disks, 313

elements, 114-115
  definitions, viewing, 123-124
  interface objects, 190-191
  script object elements, 282-283

else clauses (conditional statements), 72-73

else if statements, 73

email scripts, 33-34

email.cgi utility script, 56

EMBED Tag Wizard script (QuickTime collection scripts), 46

enabling
  folder action scripts, 36
  menu buttons, 246-247

menu commands, 246-247

menus, 197-198

services in AppleScript Studio, 333-335

equality operators, 369

error messages
  capturing, menu commands, 196
  hiding, FileMaker scripting applications, 139
  syntax error messages, 86-87

error statements, 77

Event Log window (Script Editor), opening, 90

events, 192

Example Scripts script (iDVD collection scripts), 44

executing script objects, 282

exit statements, 74

expressions, 101

extensions, Info.plist (Targets tab), 227-228

extracting data from data sources, 267

F

factoring applications, menu commands, 195-196

fields
  data entry fields, connecting to steppers, 244-245
  multiple data fields, 244
  text fields, 208-210

File menu (Script Editor), 84-85

FileMaker
  data, extracting
    inDesign, 306
    Text Edit, 302-303
  scripting applications, 138-140

file sharing, 316

File's Owner icon (nib files), 269

files
  accessing, Terminal, 346
  AppleScript files, 166
  application files (AppleScript Studio), 166
  data, retrieving/storing, 275
  event scripts, 12
  multiple script files, handlers, 179
  nib files, 166
    Document.nib, 269
    File's Owner icon, 269
    Interface Builder (AppleScript Studio), 167
    Mainmenu.nib, 269
    SimpleApp Project, 183
    viewing in outline view, 270
  Project Builder (AppleScript Studio) project files
    building, 165
    dragging/dropping, 166
  script files, 20-21
  STDERR files, 345
  STDIN files, 345
  STDOUT files, 345

Files suite (Finder), 117

fillDocument subroutine
inDesign, building dynamic pages, 307-308
multiple application scripts, building, 299
Address Book to InDesign scripts, 305
Address Book to Text Edit scripts, 300-301
FileMaker to inDesign scripts, 306
FileMaker to Text Edit scripts, 303

Finder
Container and Folders suite, container class, 116
Files suite, 117
Finder Basics suite, 114-115
Finder Items suite, 113-116
Legacy suite, 117
scripting, 108-109
scripts, 31
Standard suite, 110-112
toolbar, 22-24
Window Classes suite, 117

Finder Basics suite, 114-115
Finder Items suite, 113-116
Finder window, 22
firewalls, user account remote access, 317
folder actions, 16
Font Sampler scripts (Info scripts), 31
FontSync scripts, 37
Formatter pane (Info window), 216

formatters, 215, 218
Currency formatters, 216
data entry errors, preventing, 243
Date formatters, 216

formatting, Terminal commands, 344-345
Foundation framework (Cocoa application framework), 161
frameworks
AppKit framework (Cocoa application framework), 161
Apple event support, 14
Foundation framework (Cocoa application framework), 161

G

getData subroutine
inDesign, building dynamic pages, 307
multiple application scripts, building, 298
Address Book to InDesign scripts, 303-304
Address Book to Text Edit scripts, 300
FileMaker to inDesign scripts, 306
FileMaker to Text Edit scripts, 302-303

Get Result of AppleScript command (Script Editor services), 337
global variables, 98

Grab service, 332, 335
graphics, 332, 335
GUI Scripting, 292-293

H

handlers, 103, 246-247.
See also **subroutines**
action handlers, 211
bounds changed handlers, 212
building, 174-176
cell value handlers, 262
CGI handlers, writing, 319-321
clicked handlers, 186-187, 194, 210
data representation handlers, 273-274
drag-and-drop handlers, 212
dummy handlers, 174, 187, 194
editing handlers, 212
folder actions, 16
idle handlers, 65, 75
implementing, 176-177, 210
interface elements, 169, 176-178
key handlers, 212
load data representation handlers, 273-274
mouse handlers, 212
multiple script files, 179
nib handlers, 211
on clicked handlers, building, 334

open handlers, 64
quit handlers, 65
return statements, 74
run handlers, 63-64
script objects, 282
tab view handlers,
212-213
table view, 178
try blocks, 77-78
view handlers, 212
help tags, 248
Help Viewer (AppleScript
Studio)
opening, 254
search command, 255
scripting, 29, 125
hiding error messages,
FileMaker scripting
applications, 139
HTML (Hypertext Markup
Language), 32, 319
http (HyperText Transfer
Protocol), 32

I

iCal dictionary, 122-124
Icon Position controls
(Attributes pane), 252
icon view, outlets, 271
icons
dialogs, adding to, 149
File's Owner icon (nib
files), 269
Info.plist (Targets tab),
226
identifying SimpleApp
Project window elements,
184

idle handlers, 65, 75
iDVD collection scripts,
42-44
iDVD Companion script
(iDVD collection scripts),
42-43
if statements, 71-73, 301
ignoring statements,
constants, 364-365
Image Capture Scripting,
47, 130-131
image manipulation scripts
(toolbar scripts), 47
image view objects, 214
implementing
handlers, 176-177, 210
menu commands, 194-195
inDesign
Address Book data
extraction scripts,
303-305
dynamic pages, building,
307-308
FileMaker data extraction
scripts, 306
infinite loops, 66
Info.plist (Targets tab),
226-230
Infomotions, Inc. Web site,
56
Info scripts, 31
inheritance, 109
inherited script objects,
287-291
instances, script objects,
283-287

Interface Builder
(AppleScript Studio), 161,
168
buttons, setting attributes,
174
handlers
building, 174-176
clicked handlers, 186
implementing, 176-177
help tags, 248
images, adding to
applications, 251
Info window, 167-168
AppleScript pane, 209,
272-274
AppleScript table view
settings, 171-172
Attributes pane,
252-254
configuring control set-
tings, 169
Connections pane,
208-209, 213, 271
Custom Class pane,
269
Formatter pane, 216
identifying window
elements, 184
naming columns, 170
naming text fields,
184-186
setting column view
attributes, 170
setting table view
attributes, 170
setting text field
attributes, 184
interface elements
adding, 172-173
index numbers, 186

multiple data fields, 244
navigating, 167
nib files, 167, 183
opening, 167
palette window, 167
palettes, opening, 183
SimpleApp Project, 183
Stepper control, 244-245
table views, designing,
    168-169
text fields, naming, 173
Views palette, formatters,
    215-218
interface elements
handlers, 169, 176-178
    action handlers, 211
    bounds changed
        handlers, 212
    clicked handlers, 210
    drag-and-drop
        handlers, 212
    editing handlers, 212
    key handlers, 212
    mouse handlers, 212
    nib handlers, 211
    tab view handlers,
        212-213
    view handlers, 212
index numbers, 186
Interface Builder
    (AppleScript Studio),
    adding to, 172-173
naming, 169, 210
scripting, 187
Views interface elements,
    183
interface objects, 190-191
**Internet Connect scripting
    applications, 129**
**Internet Explorer scripting
    applications, 141**

**Internet location file class,
    117**
**iPhoto collection scripts,
    40-41**
**iPhoto Librarian utility
    script, 56**
item class, 116
**iTunes collection scripts,
    44-45**

K – L

key handlers, 212

Legacy suite (Finder), 117
**listing Terminal directories,
    347**
**load data representation
    handlers, 273-274**
locating
AppleScript Studio
    projects, 164
application classes, 123
loops, 74-76
ls command (Terminal), 347

M

**Mac OS X, AppleScript
    applications, 9**
Mac OS X c10.2, 20-23
macscripter.net Web site, 55
MacSQL utility script, 56
**mail scripting applications,
    126-127**

mail scripts, 33-34
Mainmenu.nib files, 269
make command, 112, 129
**Make New AppleScript
    command (Script Editor
    services), 337**
**man pages, Terminal,
    344-345**
menu bars, 193
menus
adding, 193
Application menu
    (Script Editor), 84
buttons, enabling/
    disabling, 246-247
commands
    capturing error
        messages, 196
    enabling/disabling,
        246-247
    factoring applications,
        195-196
    implementing, 194-195
    naming, 193
Controls menu (Script
    Editor), 86
designing, 246-247
Edit menu (Script Editor),
    85
enabling, 197-198
File menu (Script Editor),
    84-85
naming, 193
pop-up menus
    connecting to text
        fields, 208-210
    controlling tab views,
        205-207
Script menu, 22-24
submenus, 24
Menus palette, 193

Microsoft Office scripting applications, 140-141
model-view-controller paradigm, 265
modifying
   menu bars, 193
   Script menu, 24
More Complex App Project, 201-207
mounting remote disks, 312-313
mouse handlers, 212
multiple application scripts, building,
   Address Book to inDesign scripts, 303-305
   Address Book to Text Edit scripts, 300-301
   createDocument subroutine, 299-300, 303-306
   FileMaker to inDesign scripts, 306
   FileMaker to Text Edit scripts, 302-303
   fillDocument subroutine, 299-301, 305-306
   getData subroutine, 298-306
multiple data fields, 244

N

namespaces, 71
naming
   buttons, 149
   columns in column view (Interface Builder), 170
   commands, 193

interface elements, 169, 210
menus, 193
text fields, 173
variables, 99
natural-language syntax, mounting remote disks, 313
navigating
   Interface Builder (AppleScript Studio), 167
   Terminal command line, 344
   World Wide Web, scripts, 30
navigation scripts, 35
nesting, tell blocks, 95
NetNewsWire, 53-54
Netscape scripting applications, 141
networking
   clients, 313-315
   file sharing remote connections, 316
   Remote Apple Events remote connections, 317
   servers, 313-315
   tell blocks, 314
   user accounts, remote access, 317-318
news aggregators, 53-54
nib files, 166-167, 183, 269-270
nib handlers, 211
NoName Software Web site, 56
NSDocument class, 269, 272
NSDocument objects, 271

O

objects
   commanding, tell blocks, 95
   connections, 208-209
   direct objects, commands, 96
   image view objects, 214
   interface objects, elements, 190-191
   NSDocument objects, 271
   outlets, 209, 271
   properties, 189
   script objects
      assigning scripts to variables, 283
      copying, 283
      descendants, 288
      designing, 291
      elements, 282
      elements, handlers, 282
      elements, properties, 282-283
      elements, subroutines, 282-283
      executing, 282
      inheritance, 287-291
      instances, 283-287
   view objects, 190
on clicked handlers, building, 334
Open Application (Apple events), 13
open command, 111, 142
Open Documents (Apple events), 13
open folder actions (folder action scripts), 36

open handlers, 64

opening

Color Picker, 214

dictionaries, 88

Event Log window
(Script Editor), 90

Help Viewer (AppleScript
Studio), 254

Interface Builder
(AppleScript Studio),
167

palettes (Interface
Builder), 183

Result window (Script
Editor), 90

operators

& operators, 369

arithmetic operators, 368

as operators, 369

boolean operators, 368

comparison operators, 370

containment operators,
368-369

equality operators, 369

osacompile command, 350

osascript command, 350-351

outlets, 209, 271

outline views, 260

data items, 261

data sources

building, 263

data cells, 262

data columns, 262

data columns, building,
263

data columns, sorting,
264

data items, 263

data rows, 263

data rows, adding,
264-265

data rows, entering
data, 265-266

entering bulk data
additions, 267

extracting data, 267

nib files, viewing, 270

P

package class, 117

palettes

Container Views palette,
203

Menus palette, 193

opening, 183

Views palette (Interface
Builder), 215-218

panes

AppleScript pane (Info
window), 204, 209,
272-274

Attributes pane (Info
window), 204, 252-254

Connections pane (Info
window), 208-209, 213,
271

Custom Class pane (Info
window), 269

Formatter pane (Info
window), 216

Universal Access pane
(System Preferences),
293

parameters, 13, 61-62

path names, Terminal, 346

**periodic command (UNIX),
353-356**

Perl, 356

**permissions, changing in
Terminal, 349**

person class, 128

Personal File Sharing, 316

**Photoshop scripting
applications, 142-143**

**Photo Summary script
(iPhoto collection scripts),
40-41**

**Photo to iDVD Background
script (iPhoto collection
scripts), 41**

**point-and-click versus
scripting, 10**

pop-up menus

tab views, controlling,
205-207

text fields, connecting to,
208-210

**PowerPoint (Microsoft
Office) scripting
applications, 141**

predefined variables, 365

Prefab UI Browser, 377-379

**Preferences (Project
Builder), 222**

prepositions, 61-62

preventing data entry errors

entry field labels, 246

formatters, 243

multiple data fields,
244-245

proper data entry field
examples, 243-244

**Print Center scripting
applications, 129**

**Print Documents (Apple
events), 14**

privileged commands
   (Terminal), **349**
processor services, **332**
programming syntax
   constants, 16
   handlers, folder actions,
      16
   interactive commands, 17
   tell blocks, 15-16
   variables, 16-17
progress indicators
   scripts, writing, 192
   starting, 214
Project Builder
   (AppleScript Studio), **161,
   164**
   AppleScript
      files, 166
      studio applications,
         debugging, 233
   AppleScript Studio Help,
      188
   AppleScript Studio
      Terminology Reference,
      188-189
   application files, 166
   clicked handlers, 187
   images, adding to
      applications, 249
   nib files, 166
   Preferences, 222
   Project Builder Debugger,
      234-238
   project files
      building, 165
      dragging/dropping, 166
   projects, locating, 164
   Targets tab, 223
      Build Phases settings,
         230-231
      build styles, 231
      Info.plist, 226-230

   Settings, 225
   Target Summary
      settings, 224
   templates, 164, 168
   window layout, 165
Project Builder Debugger
   (Project Builder), **234-238**
properties, **98, 115, 189,
   282-283**
provider services, **332, 335**
Python, **357**

Q – R

QuickTime collection
   scripts, **46**
Quit (Apple events), **14**
quit handlers, **65**

reading dictionaries, **122-
   124**
real estate, AppleScript
   applications, **9**
receiving user input
   dialogs, 150-151
   speech synthesis, 151
   TextEdit, 152
recursive processing
   (subroutines), **65**
redirecting Terminal
   input/output, **345**
references, **15, 108-109**
registering services in
   applications, **333**
Remote Apple Events, **317**
remote connections
   file sharing, 316
   Remote Apple Events, 317

remote disks
   ejecting, 313
   mounting, 312-313
remote servers, accessing,
   312
Remove Folder Action
   (folder action scripts), **37**
repeat clause format
   (syntax), **128**
repeat forever statements,
   74
repeat until statements,
   75-76
repeat while statements, **75**
repeat with/from/to
   statements, **76**
repeat with/in statements,
   76
repeat x times statements,
   75
repetition statements, **74-76**
result text field (services),
   335
Result window (Script
   Editor), **90**
retrieving data
   disks, 274
   files, 275
Retrospect make command
   (Retrospect), **144**
Retrospect reply command
   (Retrospect), **143**
Retrospect scripting
   applications, **143-144**
Retrospect status command
   (Retrospect), **143-144**
return data (Apple events),
   13
return statements, **74**
reveal command, **115**
RSS readers, NetNewsWire,
   53-54

Ruby, 357
Run as AppleScript command (Script Editor services), 338
run handlers, 63-64
run-only applications, 21
run-only scripts, Script Editor, 85
run statements, script objects, 282
running
  AppleScript commands from Terminal, 349-351
  AppleScript from application commands, 352-353
  scripts
    automated scripts, 11, 353-356
    Script menu, 24
    Terminal, 350
Runtime Labs Web site, 56

S

Savable Table View Project, 262
saving data to disks, 273-274
scope (variables), 71
screen shots, 248
Script Debugger, 374-375
script editing window (Script Editor), 84
Script Editor, 371
  AppleScript studio applications, debugging, 233
  applets, 21
  Application menu, 84

Controls menu, 86
Edit menu, syntax, 85
Event Log window, 90
File menu, 84-85
Result window, 90
run-only scripts, 85
script editing window, 84
script files, 20-21
scripts, 35
  checking syntax, 86
  creating, 86
  dictionaries, 88-90
  launching, 90
  syntax error messages, 86-87
services, 337-338
Web services, 325-326
Script Editor continuation character (AppleScript Studio), 260
script files, 20-21, 179
Script menu, 22-24
script objects
  copying, 283
  descendants, 288
  designing, 291
  elements, 282-283
  executing, 282
  inheritance, 287-291
  instances, 283-287
  variables, assigning scripts to, 283
scripting
  ¬ (continuation character), 72, 86
  additions, 25, 96
  automated scripts, running, 11
  complex tasks, automating, 11

conditional statements, 71
  compound conditional statements, 72
  else clauses, 72-73
  simple conditional statements, 72
  try blocks, 77-78
  writing, 73-74
control statements, 13
event scripts, 12
Finder
  inheritance, 109
  references, 108-109
Help Viewer, 29
interface elements, 187
repetition statements, 74-76
routine tasks, automating, 11
Script Editor, 30
scripting additions, 25
speech recognition, 11
syntactical scripting, 12-13
syntax, 12-13
  checking, 86
  classes, 15
  commands, 15
  Editor menu (Script Editor), 85
  error messages, 86-87
  programming syntax, 15-17
  references, 15
  suites, 14
variables
  declaring, 70
  scope, 71
versus point-and-click, 10

How can we make this index more useful? Email us at indexes@samspublishing.com

Web sites
  Adobe Studio
    Exchange, 25
  AppleScript, 25
  AppleScript Web site,
    30
  World Wide Web, navigat-
    ing, 30
scripts
  ¬ (continuation character),
    34, 86
  Address Book
    data extraction to
      inDesign scripts,
      303-305
    data extraction to Text
      Edit scripts, 300-301
    scripting applications,
      127-128
  album information scripts
    (iTunes collection
    scripts), 45
  AppleScript Studio scripts,
    debugging, 232-238
  America Online scripting
    applications, 136
  AppleWorks scripting
    applications, 137-138,
    142
  artist information scripts
    (iTunes collection
    scripts), 45
  automatically running,
    353-356
  ColorSync scripts, 37
  commands, 96-97
  comments, 86
  compiling, 21
  control statements, 101

Create DVD from Folders
  script (iDVD collection
  scripts), 43
dictionaries, reading,
  122-124
Disk Copy scripting
  applications, 130
DVD Player scripting
  applications, 129
editors
  AppleScript Studio,
    371
  Prefab UI Browser,
    377-379
  Script Debugger,
    374-375
  Script Editor, 371
  Smile, 372-373
  UI Examiner, 371
EMBED Tag Wizard script
  (QuickTime collection
  scripts), 46
Example Scripts script
  (iDVD collection
  scripts), 44
expressions, 101
FileMaker
  data extraction to
    inDesign scripts, 306
  data extraction to Text
    Edit scripts, 302-303
  scripting applications,
    138-140
Finder scripts, 31
folder action scripts, 35-37
FontSync scripts, 37
handlers, 103
Help Viewer scripting
  applications, 125
iDVD collection scripts,
  42-44

iDVD Companion script
  (iDVD collection
  scripts), 42-43
Image Capture Scripting,
  47, 130-131
image manipulation scripts
  (toolbar scripts), 47
Info scripts, 31
inheritance, 109
Internet Connect scripting
  applications, 129
Internet Explorer scripting
  applications, 141
iPhoto collection scripts,
  40-41
iTunes collection scripts,
  44-45
mail scripts, 33-34,
  126-127
Microsoft Office scripting
  applications, 140-141
multiple application
  scripts, building
  Address Book to
    inDesign scripts,
    303-305
  Address Book to Text
    Edit scripts, 300-301
  createDocument sub-
    routine, 299-300,
    303-306
  FileMaker to inDesign
    scripts, 306
  FileMaker to Text Edit
    scripts, 302-303
  fillDocument subrou-
    tine, 299-306
  getData subroutine,
    298-306
navigation scripts, 35

Netscape scripting applications, 141
Perl, 356
Photoshop scripting applications, 142-143
Photo Summary script (iPhoto collection scripts), 40-41
Photo to iDVD Background script (iPhoto collection scripts), 41
PowerPoint (Microsoft Office) scripting applications, 141
Print Center scripting applications, 129
Python, 357
QuickTime collection scripts, 46
readability, 101
references, 108-109
Retrospect scripting applications, 143-144
Ruby, 357
running from Terminal, 350
run-only scripts, 85
Script Editor scripts, 35
Script menu, running from, 24
Set View Options script (toolbar scripts), 47
Show Image File script (iPhoto collection scripts), 41
SMIL script (QuickTime collection scripts), 46
Snapshot script (toolbar scripts), 47

song title scripts (iTunes collection scripts), 45
structures, 102-105
subroutines, 103-104
syntax, dictionaries, 88-90
tell blocks, 94-96, 102
Terminal scripting applications, 130-131
TextEdit scripting applications, 128-129
toolbar scripts, 46-47
utility scripts, 55-56
variables
    AppleScript-defined variables, 99-100
    assigning to, 283
    global variables, 98
    naming, 99
    properties, 98
    user-defined variables, 97-99
Web services, 32-33
Word (Microsoft Office) scripting applications, 140
ScriptWeb Web site, 55
Scruffy Software Web site, 56
search command (Help Viewer), 255
security
    sniffers, 318
    user accounts, remote access, 317-318
servers
    application servers, 32
    networking, 313-315
    remote serversm accessing, 312

services
    AppleScript Studio, 330-337
    applications, registering services, 333
    combination services, 332
    graphic services (AppleScript Studio), 335
    processor services, 332
    provider services, 332, 335
    result text field, 335
    Script Editor services, 337-338
Set View Options script (toolbar scripts), 47
setting
    column view attributes, 170
    Interface Builder (AppleScript Studio) button attributes, 174
    tab view attributes, 204
    table view attributes, 170
    Target Summary settings, 224
Settings (Targets tab), 225
shells, 342
SherlockWeb services, 32
show command, FileMaker scripting applications, 139
Show Image File script (iPhoto collection scripts), 41
ShowTime network, AppleScript applications, 9
signatures, 227-228

SimpleApp Project, 182
  handlers, writing, 186-187
  Interface Builder
    (AppleScript Studio),
    configuring, 183
  menus
    commands, capturing
      error messages, 196
    commands, factoring
      applications, 195-196
    enabling, 197-198
    implementing com-
      mands, 194-195
  testing, 187
  windows, 183-186
**simple conditional
  statements, 72**
single-line tell blocks, 96
**Single Window template
  (Project Builder), 222**
sizing dialogs, 148
sliders, connecting, 213
Sliders tab (tab view), 213
**SMIL (Synchronized
  Multimedia Integration
  Language) script
  (QuickTime collection
  scripts), 46**
Smile, 372-373
**Snapshot script (toolbar
  scripts), 47**
sniffers, 318
**SOAP (Simple Object
  Access Protocol), 32,
  322-325**
**Some Windows template
  (Project Builder), 222**
**song title scripts
  (iTunes collection scripts),
  45**
**sorting data columns (data
  sources), 264**

Speakable Items folder, 11
**specifying default buttons,
  149**
**speech recognition,
  scripting, 11**
speech synthesis, 151
**spreadsheets, creating
  (AppleWorks), 138**
**Standard suite (Finder),
  110-113, 129**
starting
  GUI Scripting, 293
  Personal File Sharing, 316
  progress indicators, 214
  Remote Apple Events, 317
statements
  conditional statements, 71
    compound conditional
      statements, 72
    else clauses, 72-73
    simple conditional
      statements, 72
    try blocks, 77-78
    writing, 73-74
  considering statements,
    constants, 364-365
  else if statements, 73
  error statements, 77
  exit statements, 74
  if statements, 71-73
  ignoring statements,
    constants, 364-365
  repeat forever statements,
    74
  repeat until statements,
    75-76
  repeat while statements,
    75
  repeat with/from/to
    statements, 76
  repeat with/in statements,
    76

  repeat x times statements,
    75
  repetition statements,
    74-76
  return statements, 74
  run statements, script
    objects, 282
STDERR files, 345
STDIN files, 345
STDOUT files, 345
**Stepper control (Interface
  Builder), 244-245**
**steppers, connecting to data
  entry fields, 244-245**
storing data in files, 275
string constants, 100
subroutines, 63, 103-104.
  See also **handlers**
  accessors, 285-286
  createDocument
    subroutine, 299-300,
    303-307
  fillDocument subroutine,
    299-306
  getData subroutine,
    298-307
  infinite loops, 66
  parameters, 61-62
  recursive processing, 65
  script objects, 282-283
suites (dictionaries)
  Address Book suite,
    127-128
  applications, 14
  classes, 15, 89
  commands, 15, 88-89
  Container and Folders
    suite (Finder), 116
  Files suite (Finder), 117
  Finder Basics suite,
    114-115

Finder Items suite, 113-116

Help Viewer suite, 125

Legacy suite (Finder), 117

Print Center suite, 129

script syntax, 14

Standard suite
  commands, 113
    make command, 129

Standard suite (Finder), 110-112

Window Classes suite (Finder), 117

switching Terminal directories, 346-347

syntactical scripting, 12-13

syntax
  afp syntax, mounting remote disks, 312-313
  AppleScript Studio syntax, 188-193
  blocks, 60
  checking, 86
  commands, 96-97
  control statements, 101
  dictionaries
    reading, 122-124
    suites, 88-90
  Edit menu (Script Editor), 85
  error messages, 86-87
  expressions, 101
  handlers, 103
  inheritance, 109
  mail scripts, 34
  natural-language syntax, mounting remote disks, 313
  programming syntax, 15-17

references, 108-109

repeat clause format, 128

scripts
  building, 12-13
  classes, 15
  commands, 15
  readability, 101
  references, 15
  structures, 102-105
  suites, 14
  subroutines, 62, 103-104
  tell blocks, 94-96, 102
  Terminal commands, 344-34
  variables, 97-100

System Events, GUI Scripting, 292-293

System Preferences (Universal Access pane), 293

T

tab view handlers, 212-213

tab views, 202
  attributes, setting, 204
  identifiers, 204
  labels, 204
  names, 204
  pop-up menus, 205-207
  Sliders tab, 213
  tabless tab views, 203
  windows, adding to, 203

table views, 260
  AppleScript table view settings, 171-172
  attributes, setting, 170
  control settings, configuring, 169
  data rows, 261

data sources
  building, 263
  data cells, 262
  data columns, 262
  data columns, building, 263
  data columns, sorting, 264
  data items, 263
  data rows, 263
  data rows, adding, 264-265
  data rows, entering data, 265-266
  entering bulk data additions, 267
  extracting data, 267
  designing, 168-169
  handlers, 178
  updating, 178

tabless tab views, controlling, 203

TableView Project, 162-163

target outlets, 209

targets (Finder window), 22

Targets tab (Project Builder), 223
  Build Phases settings, 230-231
  build styles, 231
  Info.plist, 226-230
  Settings, 225
  Target Summary settings, 224

television menu listings, AppleScript applications, 9

tell blocks, 16, 25, 210, 233
  applications, commanding, 94-95
  nesting, 95
  networking, 314

objects, commanding, 95
script structure, 102
single-line tell blocks, 96
SOAP, 323
templates
AppleScript document
templates, 268-272
Project Builder
(AppleScript Studio)
templates, 164, 168
Single Window template
(Project Builder), 222
Some Windows template
(Project Builder), 222
Terminal, 342
AppleScript commands,
344-351
command line, 344
Darwin commands, 343
directories, 346-347
files
accessing, 346
permissions, changing,
349
input/output, redirecting,
345
man pages, 344-345
multiple commands,
handling, 346
path names, 346
scripting applications,
130-131
scripts, running, 350
STDERR files, 345
STDIN files, 345
STDOUT files, 345
text files
displaying contents,
348
editing, 346
Unix commands, 343

**text documents, creating
(AppleWorks), 137**
Text Edit, 152
Address Book data
extraction scripts,
300-301
FileMaker data extraction
scripts, 302-303
scripting applications,
128-129
text files, editing, 346
text fields
combo boxes,
connecting to, 208-210
naming, 173
pop-up menus,
connecting to, 208-210
text files
contents, displaying in
Terminal, 348
editing in Terminal, 346
text views, 253-254
**times and dates, setting in
applications, 244-245**
toolbars
customizing, 22
removing, 24
scripts, 46-47
**try blocks, 77-78, 196, 247,
301**

U

UI Examiner, 371
**uneditable text views,
253-254**
**Universal Access pane
(System Preferences), 293**

UNIX
clipboard, copying/pasting
data to, 138
commands, 343
cron command,
353-354
date command,
130-131
periodic command,
353-356
update command, 115
**updating table views,
handlers, 178**
**user accounts, remote
access, 317-318**
**user-defined commands,
96-97**
**user-defined variables,
97-99**
**user input, receiving,
150-151**
utility scripts, 55-56

V

variables, 16-17
AppleScript-defined vari-
ables, 99-100
declaring, 70
global variables, 98
naming, 99
predefined variables, 365
properties, 98
scope, 71
scripts, assigning to, 283
user-defined variables,
97-99

view handlers, 212
view objects, 190
viewing
    class commands, 192
    element definitions,
        123-124
    menu bars, 193
views
    icon view, outlets, 271
    outline views, 260-267,
        270
    table views, 260-267
Views interface elements,
    183
Views palette (Interface
    Builder), formatters,
    215-218

W

Web services, 33
    AppleScript Studio, 326
    building
        SOAP, 322, 325
        XML-RPC, 322
    Script Editor, 325-326
    Sherlock, 32
Web sites
    Adobe Studio Exchange,
        25
    Ambrosia Software, 248
    AppleScript, 25, 30
    AppleScript Central, 52
    AppleScript Sourcebook,
        54
    Aqua Human Interface
        Guidelines, 153
    Infomotions, Inc. Web
        site, 56
    macscripter.net, 55

More Complex App
    Project, 201
NoName Software Web
    site, 56
Runtime Labs Web site,
    56
Savable Table View
    Project, 262
Script Debugger, 374
ScriptWeb, 55
Scruffy Software Web site,
    56
SimpleApp Project, 182
Smile, 372
TableView Project,
    162-163
Window Classes suite
    (Finder), 117
windows
    Build Phases window, 231
    Event Log window (Script
        Editor), 90
    Info window (Interface
        Builder), 167-168
        AppleScript pane, 209,
            272-274
        AppleScript table view
            settings, 171-172
        Attributes pane,
            252-254
        configuring control set-
            tings, 169
        Connections pane,
            208-209, 213, 271
        Custom Class pane,
            269
        Formatter pane, 216
        identifying window
            elements, 184
        naming columns, 170
        naming text fields,
            184-186

setting column view
    attributes, 170
setting table view
    attributes, 170
setting text field
    attributes, 184
palette window (Interface
    Builder), 167
Result window (Script
    Editor), 90
script editing window
    (Script Editor), 84
tab views, adding to, 203
Word (Microsoft Office)
    scripting applications, 140
World Wide Web,
    navigation scripts, 30
writing
    CGI handlers, 319-321
    conditional statements,
        73-74
    More Complex App
        Project, 201-207
    progress indicator scripts,
        192
    Savable Table View
        Project, 262
    SimpleApp Project, 182
        building windows,
            183-184
        configuring Interface
            Builder, 183
        enabling menus,
            197-198
        identifying window
            elements, 184
        implementing menu
            commands, 194-195
        menu commands,
            capturing error mes-
            sages, 196

menu commands,
    factoring
    applications, 195-196
naming text fields,
    184-186
setting text field
    attributes, 184
writing handlers,
    186-187

X

XML-RPC (Extensible
  Markup Language-
  Remote Procedure Call),
  322
XML (Extended Markup
  Language), 32
XML-RPC (XML Remote
  Procedure Call), 32

Your Guide
to Computer
Technology